ONE GOAL

Also by John Powers

The Short Season
Yankees (with George Sullivan)

ONE GOAL

A Chronicle of the 1980 U.S. Olympic Hockey Team

John Powers and
Arthur C. Kaminsky

1817

HARPER & ROW, PUBLISHERS, New York
Cambridge, Philadelphia, San Francisco, London
Mexico City, São Paulo, Sydney

Portions of *One Goal* have appeared, in somewhat different form, in the *Boston Globe*.

ONE GOAL. Copyright © 1984 by John Powers and Arthur C. Kaminsky. All rights reserved. Printed in the United States of America. No part of this book may be used or reproduced in any manner whatsoever without written permission except in the case of brief quotations embodied in critical articles and reviews. For information address Harper & Row, Publishers, Inc., 10 East 53rd Street, New York, N.Y. 10022. Published simultaneously in Canada by Fitzhenry & Whiteside Limited, Toronto.

FIRST EDITION

Designer: C. Linda Dingler

Library of Congress Cataloging in Publication Data

Powers, John, 1948–
    One goal.

    1. Hockey—United States. 2. Winter Olympic Games
(13th : 1980 : Lake Placid, N.Y.) I. Kaminsky, Art.
II. Title.
GV848.4.U6P68 1984   796.96'2'0973   83-47540
ISBN 0-06-015200-1

84 85 86 87 88 10 9 8 7 6 5 4 3 2 1

For Anne and Bill, who know why

For A and A, who also know why

CONTENTS

A section of photographs follows page 150.

ACKNOWLEDGMENTS

We want this book to deal not so much with one goal, one game, one February as with American hockey and the people who play it. Thus, our debts extend from Boston's Commonwealth Avenue to Minnesota's Iron Range.

Foremost, we are grateful to Herb Brooks and the members of the 1980 U.S. Olympic hockey team, whose insights and anecdotes filled dozens of tape cassettes. This is truly their book.

We also owe sincere thanks to:

Buz Wyeth and Ed Burlingame, who embraced the idea and nursed the manuscript through several birthing stages.

Roone Arledge, for putting his outstanding commentators, Jim Lampley and Anne Simon, on airplanes constantly, thus providing them with the leisure time to review our manuscript and consequently offer incisive and decisive criticisms of the work in progress. And particularly to Jim for giving us our title.

Craig Patrick, for sharing his unique window on this team and its coach.

Jack Hughes, Ralph Cox and Don Waddell, who were more than generous with their remembrances.

Ken Dryden, who played the game as well as anyone ever has, and brought that same standard of excellence to his incredibly thorough review of our manuscript.

Ed Swift, whose dispatches about the Games, the team and

hockey in Wisconsin and Minnesota for *Sports Illustrated* made for invaluable reading.

Gus Hendrickson, for his reminiscences of John Harrington, Mark Pavelich and Minnesota-Duluth hockey.

Jack Kirrane, who brought back 1960 and Squaw Valley intact.

Bob Johnson, who talked volubly about 1976, Badgermania and his son.

Jack Parker, for his total recall of his Terriers.

Dr. George Nagobads, who knew the Russians by heart.

Chuck Robertson, for explaining Detroit's unique junior hockey program.

The Iron Range Interpretative Center, a mother lode of up-state Minnesota lore.

Dukes Knutson, for turning over his files on UMD hockey.

Don Clark, archivist of college hockey, for his assistance with photos and facts.

Mike Moran, Bob Paul and Don Miller of the USOC, for photos and facts.

Hal Trumble, Bob Fleming and the rest of the AHAUS crew, without them, no team, no victory, no book.

Bob Murray, the man who is crucial to the careers of many of the players and who always applied a valuable and critical eye to the project.

David Harrop, who first inspired the idea for this book many years before Lake Placid.

The *Boston Globe, New York Daily News, Wisconsin State Journal, Capital Times, Minneapolis Star, Minneapolis Tribune, Duluth News Tribune,* and *Duluth Herald* (especially Bruce Bennett) for making their files available.

The U.S. Hockey Hall of Fame, which still keeps the moments alive.

Joanne Bentele, typist and secretary extraordinaire. She labored patiently and mightily over the many versions that preceded the final product.

Elaine LePage, for providing tea and sympathy.

PROLOGUE

The terrifying thing was that they looked so ordinary, so un-threatening. Their equipment was second-rate—creaky skates and dull red uniforms that had a fading, Goodwill-shop look to them.

They were a hockey team without ornament, without personality, without controversy. Nothing about the Russians ever hinted that they could—and would—bury you.

They seemed to prefer it that way, taking refuge in anonymity, turning it to their advantage. When the Soviet National team traveled, they offered the curious a glimpse, a taste, then moved on. The players would step out of the arena in long fur coats, their wet hair slicked back, their faces dead-pan.

There would be time for a quick autograph, perhaps, scrawled in Cyrillic script. An exchange of *znachki,* the lapel pins Russians carry about by the pocketful. The barest of introductions—"What you name? Frank? Me Vladimir."

If you were a Russian *émigré* family living in the area, there might be a picture with one of the team stars, grinning, his arm around your shoulder.

Then it would be, Please, I must go to bus.

It had not always been that way. In 1960, at Squaw Valley, the Russian players roamed freely, bumming cigarettes, exchanging pins, offering to trade sticks. They'd watch *The Untoucha-*

bles, then go around pulling index fingers (Chee-cah-go, boom-boom) on the Americans.

Nikolai Sologubov, their effervescent captain, had been something of a mascot for the U.S. team that year, always popping up, grinning and joking. When the Americans had been catching their breath, down 4–3 to the Czechs with twenty minutes to play in the final game, it had been Sologubov who came by their dressing room and advised them, in pantomime, to take oxygen.

The Americans had already brought down the Russians by one late, dramatic goal. By beating the Czechs, they clinched their first—and only—Olympic gold medal.

There had been less charity from, and contact with, the Russians ever since, the reticence mostly on the Soviet side. They kept to decidedly separate tables, the players moving about in groups of three, the KGB man never far off. They did not come close to losing to the Americans again.

It was 1980 now, and Herb Brooks, who'd been the last player cut from the 1960 U.S. Olympic team, was coaching this one. Their first Olympic game was three days away; for a final tune-up, they would play the Russians—who were now, unquestionably, the finest hockey team in the world.

Brooks had tried to break down the aura, tried to humanize the Russians whenever the U.S. team watched them on film. Boris Mikhailov, their captain, had a long, mournful face and a sloppy, almost silly grin. "Looks like Stan Laurel," Brooks had told his players. "You're worried about Stan Laurel?"

They were terrified of Stan Laurel. The Americans skated onto the mushy ice at New York's Madison Square Garden, saw the red jerseys and the red helmets, watched Mikhailov and his linemates glide out for the face-off—and stood in awe.

Robbie McClanahan, who was passing up his senior year in college to play for the U.S. squad, lined up across from the seasoned international veteran Valery Kharlamov, glanced at the face—so impassive, so unsettling—and rolled his eyes. *What am I doing out here?* McClanahan asked himself.

So the Americans played as if dazed and the Russians gave them a tutorial, hockey pinball by the numbers. Helmut Balderis, one of the Second Wave players the Russians had developed for the eighties, threaded a pass to veteran Aleksandr Maltsev in the slot and goalie Jimmy Craig never had a chance. One-to-nothing, four minutes in.

Then Vladimir Krutov, another Second Waver, cut in from the right and slid the puck deftly beneath Craig. Two-nothing, nine minutes elapsed. Then Krutov again, taking a 100-foot breakaway pass from a defenseman and highballing in alone for a third one five minutes later. Then Kharlamov, barely a minute later, whipping another between Craig's legs. Fifteen minutes, four goals.

Twice the Americans had a man-advantage. Twice, they failed to muster even one shot on goal. The hell with it, they decided in between periods. Let's just go back out and skate.

For the next fifteen minutes, the Olympians matched the Russians bump for bump, stride for stride, idea for idea and held the score. Then the Russians came up the ice the way they did in practice, four quick passes, the puck barely staying on the stick and Vladimir Petrov, one of their certified magicians, flipped a fifth goal past Steve Janaszak, who'd relieved Craig a few minutes earlier.

"The puck never stopped," defenseman Mike Ramsey realized. "I've never seen so many pretty passes." That was the Russian style; baroque demolition was a specialty. "Forget it," decided Mark Johnson, the best American player. "They're in another world."

The Russian hockey world was planned, subsidized and continuous.

Its hockey player was listed as an engineer or a student or an army lieutenant; the occupational label was irrelevant. He had to be listed as something, because unemployment—i.e., parasitism—was a crime against the state. He could not be listed as a hockey player, because professionalism was a crime against Olympus.

The important thing was, he was always available and he was completely subsidized. The state paid him a salary, provided him with an apartment and an automobile, staked him to a month's vacation by the Black Sea and allowed him to spend his certificate rubles in special shops normally open only to foreign tourists or the party elite.

The state had spotted him at age 7 or 8 in one of its sports classes and had tracked his development carefully—testing, analyzing, then testing again.

When found promising, he'd been isolated as early as 10 or 11 and sent to special schools for more intensive training. Weaknesses were shored up, native gifts honed, a respect for team play and the joys of selflessness instilled.

By his late teens, he was playing for an elite team and being groomed for the national select side, the Worlds and the Olympics. Gold medals were rewarded by promotions, fat bonuses and the rare opportunity to be a conspicuous consumer. By the curious Olympic definition of an amateur, it was all entirely legal.

In the Russian world, the same team could be used to play the Dutch National squad or the National Hockey League All-Stars; and it could be kept together year-round, year after year.

American Olympic teams were transitory as May flies, thrown together a few months before the Games and scattered to the wind the moment the Olympic flame was extinguished. Their players were collegians or recent graduates, gathered hastily, if hopefully, from the few disparate hotbeds where hockey flourishes in the United States. The haphazard selection process, critics said, was the team's greatest weakness, with youth, regionalism and the calendar all conspiring against success. But in this world, the world of the Christians, the Johnsons and Brookses, those were the only available elements.

If it all came together for you, you could beat the Russians on their terms, in their world. One time, one night, one goal. Once in a generation.

1

CINCINNATUS RENOUNCED

The Olympic ideal may have been Greek, but for American athletes the role model was Roman, a consul-turned-gentleman-farmer named Cincinnatus.

When the empire was threatened in 458 B.C., the man emerged from his fields, vanquished the Aequi and Volsci, then returned to his fields.

For sixty years, U.S. Olympians were summoned in much the same fashion. They trooped out of anonymity once a quadrennium, bore off their medals, then faded back into obscurity, usually the poorer for it.

It was amateurism according to Avery Brundage, the crusty president of the International Olympic Committee, an American businessman with the ideals of a Monegasque prince. "I've never known of any athlete too poor to compete in the Olympic Games," Brundage maintained, and American athletes, in a perversely ironic sort of way, were living proof.

There were no government subsidies, no cash compensations from the U.S. Olympic Committee for workdays missed. If a man wanted to compete for the United States, he found an understanding boss, put his wife to work, joined the armed forces or took time off from college. Or simply went unemployed for a few months.

The captain of the 1960 U.S. hockey team was a 31-year-old

Massachusetts fireman with a wife and two children who took a four-month unpaid leave for the privilege. After Jack Kirrane helped knock off the Russians and Canadians and found himself an overnight national hero, he went back to Brookline, put his gold medal in a drawer and climbed back on his fire truck.

It was a system that made for rather peculiar rosters—a few collegians, a couple of jobless 23-year-olds, a handful of servicemen, an insurance salesman or civil servant on a leave-of-absence lark. All of them thrown together for a grand adventure.

Ever since 1920, when the United States sent a hockey team to Antwerp for the first Olympic hockey tournament, these forays had a lovely picaresque flavor to them.

The officials rounded up a bunch of Eastern collegians, a fine Lost Generation sampling, put them on an ocean liner and huzzahed them over the horizon. Later, the team manager would write a formal report for the bound volume, a Letter from St. Moritz, and the team would belong to the archives. It went that way until after the Second War.

The Americans would trifle with European sides, winning by twenty or so goals, dissipate a bit in Chamonix or Garmisch-Partenkirchen, lose valiantly to the Canadians and return home bemedaled. In 1920, 1924 and 1932, that meant silver; in 1936, bronze.

Once, in 1933, ten gentleman rakes, most of them Ivy Leaguers just out of college, had managed to win the World title. They left by ocean liner on Christmas Eve, hopscotched from London to Paris to Chamonix to Milan and points between; and left a trail of empty champagne bottles, enraged French waiters and sputtering German hotel keepers.

"They smoke, drink, dance and spend scarcely a night in bed," a Viennese newspaper said of them. "But the minute they get on the ice they are as if transformed, never showing the slightest fatigue."

Only one goal was scored on the "crazy Americans" at the World tournament in Prague. When they defeated the Canadians in overtime for the championship, it was the last shining moment for American hockey for a quarter century.

The players reveled in the literal amateurism of it all, savored the sacrifice, the hardship. Later, in the fifties, when the price of a medal climbed sharply, when the Russians began taking the game seriously, the philosophy grew even more Calvinist. The greater the self-denial, the greater the glory.

The Russians were filling their teams with Army lieutenants and career Ph.D.s. The best Swedish players drove sleek automobiles. The Canadians sent their best amateur club, which had been together all season.

The Americans selected their team much the way they selected their army on the occasion of a world war, by general muster. In mid-November, usually, the word would go forth: All those interested in representing your country turn out at Boston and Minneapolis.

Maybe two-thirds of sixty invitees would eventually turn up, producing a dozen or so serious candidates in each city. They'd come together and play an exhibition game, and maybe eighteen or so would be chosen for the Olympic team.

Given periodic feuds between the U.S. Olympic Committee and the Amateur Hockey Association—the sport's governing body in the United States—fiascoes were known to result.

The worst, a Mack Sennett special, happened in 1948 when both the USOC and the AHA sent teams to St. Moritz. The USOC squad, assured by their officials that they were *the* team, donned white U.S.A. overcoats, marched in the opening ceremonies, then arrived at the rink to find the AHA team in uniform, ready to face off against the Swiss.

Swiss Olympic organizing officials, who knew their financial fate rested almost solely on ice-hockey receipts, hadn't wanted to offend the international federation that recognized the AHA team.

"We got the fancy white Olympic jackets," said Bill Briell, one of the disgusted USOC players. "But the other team got to play."

For most of the tournament, the International Olympic Committee, offended by the whole fracas, refused to recognize the hockey matches as part of the Games. Finally, after the AHA team had placed fourth, the IOC decided that the games would count but the Americans would be disqualified.

The USOC and AHA got together—literally—in 1952 and picked a team by committee that brought home the silver medal from Oslo. Bureaucratic wrangling seemed behind them. But so, it turned out, were the days of casual amateurism. By 1956 the Russians arrived with a decade of quiet preparation behind them and wiped out everybody at Cortina, crunching the Americans by four goals.

The Canadians had always been better. Now the Socialists were too. What happened at Squaw Valley in 1960 was a brilliant aberration, Cincinnatus' Last Stand. The Americans upset Canada and Russia by a goal, rallied to crush Czechoslovakia and win the gold medal for the first—and only—time. The home ice had helped and the goaltending had been magnificent. But the Americans had also been prepared this time, naming Jack Riley coach two years in advance, sending him to Europe to scout the Russians, getting a squad in training at West Point for a full month.

Yet, the team Riley put together could barely beat the best American college varsities on a barnstorming tour, and actually had lost to the Warroad Lakers and Green Bay Bobcats, local midwestern amateur clubs.

Riley needed a scorer, he realized. He'd reserved two spots —for defenseman John Mayasich, the hero of the 1956 team, and for fellow medalist Bill Cleary, who was the gunner Riley had to have.

Neither of them could spare three months to practice with the team. Mayasich had a job with a radio/TV station in Wisconsin; Cleary had just gone into the insurance business in Boston.

So Riley had made exceptions to his original rule that you couldn't play if you hadn't been with the team all along. "No problems there," team captain Jack Kirrane would say. "Everybody knew those two guys were coming."

Problem was, Cleary wouldn't come without his brother Bobby, who'd been an All-American at Harvard and was also tied up with his insurance business. And Bobby had not been considered an exception, although he'd also been a superior player at Harvard.

With the Games only two weeks off, and the roster deadline looming, Riley put in an emergency call to Walter Brown, who was head of the AHA.

"Do you want to go into the Games with a chance to win or no chance?" Riley asked him. "The way the team is going now, we have no chance. I have to bring in two forwards, and I'm going to bring in the Clearys."

Brown was dubious. People in hockey circles, he told Riley, would raise hell. Riley said he didn't care. If they were going to win, they needed the Clearys.

"Well," Riley told Kirrane in his hotel room at Colorado Springs, where the team was going to play Denver University, "they're coming."

"Well, good," replied Kirrane, who was desperate himself for a couple of good snipers up front.

"But there might be some feeling about this," Riley mused. "Why don't you go back and tell the guys and see what the feeling is?"

The feeling, almost universal, was outrage, even among ex-Harvardians like Bob McVey and Ed Owen. They'd been working as a team since December. Now Bobby Cleary, who had not been part of any exemption, would be given a jersey; and one of them would be cut loose. If he came, they would refuse to play.

Jim Claypool, the team manager, brought the message back to Riley, who said fine, give them their plane tickets home. Meanwhile, Kirrane tried to settle his teammates down.

"Hey, I took four months' leave of absence without pay to do this," he told them. "If I have to play alone, I'm going to."

So the Clearys turned up, and two players named Bob Dupuis

and Herb Brooks were let go. The reception, at best, was chilly; the first night, the Clearys could barely get a puck to warm up with.

But the Americans never lost another game. They breezed through their preliminary matches, knocked off Sweden and routed Germany.

Then Bobby Cleary popped in a big goal against the Canadians; Jack McCartan, who'd actually been cut in training camp, played the game of his life in the American cage; the United States scored a stunning 2–1 victory; and they were a happy band of brothers ever after.

The next thirty-six hours, Riley would say, were the stuff of destiny. The Russians were dispatched in the final five minutes. The Czechs hung in for two periods the next morning, then were buried with a six-goal avalanche of Christians and Clearys.

Except for a wondrous day against Czechoslovakia in 1972 and a silver medal that grew out of it, the next twenty years were empty for the Americans.

Jack Riley's elusive amalgam couldn't be duplicated. The Cleary brothers went back to Boston and their insurance business. Jack McCartan played briefly with the New York Rangers, then spent the balance of his professional career in the minors. Jack Kirrane went back to his fire house. The 1961 National team finished seventh at the World Championships, winning one game of seven. The 1963 squad, thrown together at the eleventh hour, haphazardly managed and casually coached, placed eighth. "That team shouldn't have gone across the Charles River," said Kirrane, who came back that year for one more adventure. "Never mind the ocean. We had guys playing who couldn't make the first line on their college teams."

Predictably, the 1964 Olympic team came a cropper at Innsbruck. The Russians riddled them by four goals in the opener, the Swedes by three. "We had a bad night," scowled Paul Johnson—one of three holdovers from the 1960 team—after the Czechs had laid on a 7–1 lashing. "That makes four out of five."

In earlier years, that U.S. team would have medaled, but the Russians, Czechs and Swedes had been improving every year, catching up to the Americans, then overtaking them.

"It's the system," U.S. team manager Walter Bush would say after the Americans had skidded to fifth place, their worst Olympic finish. "The Russians are pros," he said. "We have maybe thirty-five guys in the whole country who can play this kind of competition."

The U.S. Olympic Committee would not ask for a government handout. No one amateur team, college or club, was good enough to send to the Games intact. So it was the Cincinnatus approach or nothing.

Gradually, an air of doomed gallantry surrounded the U.S. team, which was not unlike a cadre of young English officers going off to a burning Continent in 1914: We are here to die.

By the late sixties, the mission for off-year U.S. teams was something less than modest: Don't finish last.

Last place meant demotion to the "B" pool, which was filled with Italians and Austrians and Japanese, who played as if their skates were laced together.

The 1969 team, another last-minute production, did finish last, and the 1970 team had to win the B pool championship to regain the elite group. For the next decade the Americans flirted with relegation every year, scrambling to beat somebody, anybody, to stay in the A pool, all but conceding any chance at an Olympic medal.

The 1972 Olympians, well coached and organized by Murray Williamson, were luminous exceptions. They went to Sapporo seeded sixth and expected to finish sixth. The Swedes thwacked them soundly, 5–1, in the opener. The Czechs, who'd belted the 1964 U.S. team by six goals and the 1968 squad by four, were supposed to do much the same.

Instead, a goalie named Lefty Curran stood the Czechs on their ears, making thirty-nine saves in the first two periods alone. Williamson berated his players during the first intermission, telling them it was a matter of attitude, that the Americans didn't think they could win, and thus weren't winning.

So they went out and banged in three goals in the second period, Curran knocked away fifty-one shots in all and the United States won, 5–1.

The Russians nailed them—what else was new since 1960?— but the Americans ran pool on Finland and Poland and left with the silver by virtue of a 3–2 record and a better goal differential than Czechoslovakia and Sweden.

By 1975, when the United States failed to win a game at the Worlds and was relegated to jokerdom, that moment seemed light-years away. The Americans played the Czech "B" team as a tune-up that year and lost, 15–1.

"After a while," remembered Buzz Schneider, a forward on that squad, "Blaine Comstock turned around in the goal, figuring he might as well shovel 'em out."

By 1976 Cincinnatus was unavailable. With inflation on the rise and jobs growing scarce, fathers of two could no longer afford to donate four unpaid months to an uncertain quest. The servicemen of the fifties were merely a pre-Vietnam memory. Competition for players between the NHL and the new World Hockey Association had now made $100,000 salaries commonplace and the American player more desirable.

So Bob Johnson, who'd coached the 1975 team, led a quixotic mission to Innsbruck for the 1976 Games. From the beginning, the going was difficult. Several good candidates elected not to try out. Several more left the team for personal reasons. At least half of the players that would have been better than those in Innsbruck were not there.

At one point ABC broadcaster Curt Gowdy had gone to see the team play at Yale and asked Johnson how many of his players were Americans. "All of them," replied Johnson, puzzled.

"I mean, how many were really born here?" Gowdy pressed. "Not Canadians on green cards and all that." All of them, Johnson reiterated.

It was a patchwork varsity that Johnson brought with him to Austria that winter, good enough to handle most American college clubs but hardly in the same league with the Russians and Czechs.

Yet the Americans, given a bit of industry and luck, still saw themselves as medalists. Canada, protesting creeping socialist professionalism, had withdrawn from Olympic hockey after the 1968 Games.

Now the Swedes, annoyed by North American pro teams raiding their elite league for talent, had pulled out too. Only the Finns, who'd never won an Olympic medal, stood in the way of a bronze.

First, a qualifying game with the Yugoslavs loomed. "You've got to win that game," Gowdy told Johnson over dinner the previous night. "We want to televise a lot of hockey back home. We can't be in the 'B' pool."

"Don't remind me." Johnson winced.

Less than seven minutes into the game with Yugoslavia, the Americans indeed found themselves behind, then realized who they were playing against. Yanks did not lose to sub-Europeans. The final was 8–4.

They performed gallantly in the opener against the Russians, yielding three power-play goals in the first period but otherwise skating them reasonably evenly. They held the Czechs to two goals until the final twenty minutes before caving, 5–0.

Otherwise, they played well enough to stay alive for a medal until the final day. The Americans, who'd been humbled twice by Finland in tune-up games, now surprised them, 5–4, then ripped Poland by five goals.

A victory over the West Germans, the only team ranked below the United States, would clinch third place for the bronze. Instead, a behemothic forward named Erich Kuehnhackl personally shredded them; West Germany prevailed 4–1 for the bronze (although both had identical 2–3 records) and sent the Americans back to their dressing room, cursing.

Later, two U.S. players wound up in a restaurant brawl that left them bleeding and, briefly, in jail. A year later, the Americans were back in sixth place at the World Championships, and more of the same loomed for 1980 and Lake Placid.

There would be a new team and a new coach. One candidate was Michigan Tech's John MacInnes, who'd won 532 games, the most in collegiate hockey history, and three NCAA titles.

MacInnes, a naturalized citizen who had played for the legendary Vic Heyliger at Michigan in the 1940s, had dreamed of coaching a U.S. Olympic team. He was the favored candidate, well liked, respected, one of the sport's gentlemen. But in mid-1978, MacInnes withdrew his name. Diabetes and related ailments ruled him out. Bill Cleary, who'd been Harvard's coach for several years by then, was offered the job but also withdrew, reluctant to spend that much time away from his family. So the Olympic Committee looked to an intense, compulsively organized man named Herbert Brooks, who was putting together his third National Championship varsity at Minnesota.

2

THE UNCOMMON MAN

He'd grown up working-class on the east side of St. Paul, the son of an insurance underwriter, and the only thing that frightened him was failure.

So Herb Brooks ran scared, ran obsessed. The eyes told you that much. Everything that boiled and tumbled inside—the intensity, the imagination, the compulsion, the drive, the anxiety—came out through the eyes, which were at once intent, wary, focused.

Brooks coached a sport that was uncharted by design, unsuited to complex game plans and computerized tendencies, its statistics minimal.

Hockey was a sport of flow and impromptu tactics, with fresh players entering on the fly, the games often won or lost by accident—the puck ricocheting off an ankle, a stick, a skate and into the goal.

Yet Brooks, by nature, was an exhaustive planner, seeking always to control variables and reduce unknowns. Before games he would be fidgety, running himself through a continuous checklist, asking himself the same question twice a minute: What have I forgotten?

From behind the bench, the eyes would bore in on the action, the lips taut, the voice barking instructions.

"Jeez, forget it, Herb," his old college coach, John Mariucci, would tell him afterward. "The game's over."

Brooks would look at Mariucci, the eyes intent, the jaw set. "The game's never over."

There was always another challenge ahead, another chance for failure that had to be quelled. It was tonight's game, this weekend's series, the conference title, the National Championship, the next season.

In two years, Brooks took the University of Minnesota from last place in the West to the National Championship. When the final game had been won at Boston Garden, an acquaintance found Brooks sitting alone, drained, atop an empty beer case in a deserted hallway. Around a corner his players were rumpling each other's hair in rowdy celebration. They had succeeded. He had avoided failure.

Back in Minneapolis there were recruits to sign, fresh ideas to implement, other seasons to prepare for. Preparation and innovation won hockey games, Brooks believed, and both were evolutionary.

A new concept would come to him in sleep, a novel breakout pattern, perhaps; and Brooks would spring awake and scribble it down. There were always more efficient, more creative ways to go about your work. You could call it obsession, call it fear of failure. But nobody could say that Herb Brooks came to a game, a season, a job, unprepared.

So Brooks showed up for his Olympic interview in 1978 with loose-leaf binders filled with proposals, options, more proposals. He was the St. Paul insurance man again; the sales pitch was not that dissimilar.

You want to be protected against that unforeseen act of God, the 4–1 loss to Rumania? I have precisely the scheme, designed expressly to meet your personal financial situation.

Here's my short-term plan and my long-term plan, depending upon how much you want to spend. Here's my staff-line organization, my flow chart of responsibilities and communications.

I'll have a special advisory group of nine expert hockey people, to make sure we invite the best prospects to the National Sports Festival this summer. Here's how I want to select the players. Here's where we should go on trips. Here's how we do everything.

No stone unturned, Brooks had decided. He'd had an educational psychologist at the "U" draw up a psychological test for his prospects, 300 questions that seemed related to anything but hockey.

It was a small thing, Brooks admitted; but in February, when he'd have to trim half a dozen players to get down to the Olympic limit of twenty, the test might be a useful tool. Didn't they give these things to astronauts? Why overlook anything that could help you?

Wasn't that part of the NHL's problem? There was nothing wrong with the pro hockey player, Brooks believed, but he needed a more progressive environment in which to grow. All these great, educated minds in the world, Brooks thought, and hockey doesn't use them. Why? Because it's never been done before? Idiotic. We can put a guy on the moon before we can make a change in our hockey thinking. Meanwhile, people are coming over and kicking our ass.

The NHL had played the Russians in an unprecedented eight-game series in 1972, laughed at their equipment and questioned their practice and training techniques; then sat in shock when the Russians lost only one of the first four games, all in Canadian rinks.

It hadn't surprised Brooks at all. He'd been fascinated by the Russians and their approach to the game since he'd faced them on all those National teams. They'd be playing in a World Championship somewhere, and Brooks would climb aboard the Russian team bus, deliberately pretending to be lost, ignoring all the guttural grumbling, riding with them to their practice rink.

Once there, Brooks inspected every skating drill, every breakout pattern, every power play—scribbling notes, watching the coach, Anatoly Tarasov, the father of Russian hockey.

In 1979, when he was coaching the U.S. team and Tarasov was in retirement but still the gray eminence of Soviet hockey, Brooks sought him out in Moscow, bearing a jug of vodka as a lubricant.

Tarasov seemed amused by this inquisitive American who actually wanted to learn something. He'd tell Brooks a few things, unveil a mystery or two, but always held something back, thus piquing Brooks' curiosity further.

Tarasov had watched, delighted, as the Americans skated the Czechs, the Soviets' historic hockey tormentors, to a draw; then he gave Brooks a bear hug afterward.

Back in the States, Brooks wrote letters to Tarasov, seeking more pointers, further clarification. He never received answers, but Brooks had films of Russian teams playing Westerners; and he'd break them down like some Talmudic scholar, looking for hints, little secrets that might unlock the grand strategy.

Unlike their NHL counterparts, who generally dumped the puck in the corner of the rink, then scrambled in to regain it, the Russians were control-freaks, always going for the puck, hoarding it, dictating what happened to it. It made obvious sense, Brooks realized. Name a team sport where possession *wasn't* the magic ingredient. If you're always at bat, always moving 80 yards in fifteen plays and gobbling up the clock, you'll win precisely because your opponent is not at bat, is not moving the football.

Ergo, you must prize possession above all else—but creative possession, possession designed to open up something. The Russian style was fluid, the forwards always circling, the puck passed not so much to people as to places; the players always looking for the open patch of ice, for the momentary mismatch that would put two of theirs on one of yours and get them the easy goal.

They're so positive, Brooks marveled, watching Boris Mikhailov and his linemates swoop down upon the Czech goalkeeper. Nothing rattled them. Break up one play, and the Russians would regroup and come at you another way. The faces never showed anxiety or stress. If they didn't get you in the first twenty minutes, they'd get you in the last twenty, bang-bang-bang, a 4–3 game becoming a 7–3 rout in minutes.

It was conditioning, Brooks knew. The Russians had the confidence because they had the stamina. It wasn't explosiveness that produced those third-period scoring bursts. The Russians merely managed to maintain their relentless pace while their opponents were winding down, the forechecking losing its enthusiasm, the backchecking coming undone.

No accident, no secret there. The Russians, in their sports institutes, had made a science of the body and athletics; and they had developed concepts and programs that were years ahead of Western thinking.

They knew all about anaerobics, about cardiovascular exercise, about muscle groups. Their hockey workouts were models of productive motion; none of these frenetic bursts followed by periods of standing about, chin on stick.

Consequently, the Soviet National team was a marvelously tuned perpetual-motion machine, never out of synchrony, never running down. When it added six or seven late goals to a 9–0 lead, it wasn't overkill, it was inertia. Emotion never figured.

Brooks admired all that: the conditioning, the creativity, the poise. If he could add that to the classic North American hockey virtues, which were ruggedness, adrenaline and improvisation, Brooks believed he could create a hybrid. A sort of sophisticated pond hockey.

It would be his fantasy team, with skating speed, mobility, intelligence, toughness and adaptability at every position.

Later, when some of his college rivals heard what Brooks was up to with his sophisticated pond hockey, it made them chuckle. His first Gopher varsities had been big, strong, tough. "They were just destroying bodies," remembered Gus Hendrickson, the coach up at Minnesota-Duluth (UMD). "The weaving and all that other stuff—Herb didn't use that then."

The change had come on him in 1979 when Neal Broten, a baby-faced center from Roseau, up near the Canadian border, had come to the "U" and completed Minnesota's transformation from brawn to speed.

Brooks still had the muscle, but with Broten, Robbie McClanahan and Eric Strobel, he had pure aviation fuel up front, people who could go from 0 to 60 in three strides. That spring, they'd gone down to Detroit and had taken the NCAA title by storm.

That had been his third National Championship, the capstone to the rebuilding job Brooks had undertaken seven years earlier, when Minnesota hockey had hit rock bottom.

For two years Brooks had been an assistant coach at the "U," leaving finally because he hadn't jibed with the athletic director. A year later, the athletic director was gone. So was the coach, Glen Sonmor—off to be general manager and coach of the Minnesota Fighting Saints in the World Hockey Association. And the Gophers were dead last in the league.

Brooks had turned the atmosphere around immediately. Minnesota barely missed a winning record in 1973. Two losses at Wisconsin in the regional play-offs made the difference.

His varsity came off the ice after that final game at Madison and sat in the dressing room and cried. "Next year," Brooks vowed to them, "we win it all."

They did win it all in 1974, and again in 1976; and except for one rebuilding year in 1977, the Gophers had kept winning. Brooks scoured the state for talent, then sold them on his program, the sales pitch understated.

Once at the "U," recruits quickly met a different Herb Brooks. Herbie the Bastard. Herbie of the two-and-a-half-hour practices, Herbie of the endless skating drills, his eyes boring right through you, the man saying little, parceling out praise in odd lots indeed.

"The best compliment I can give you," Brooks would tell his varsity candidates, "is a jersey."

Mondays were brutal, the most demanding workout of the

week. The Gophers would have played Friday and Saturday nights. Sunday was a day off, with skating optional.

"Monday," Mike Ramsey would recall with masochistic relish, "was whipping day."

Monday was 2:30 until 5:00, with Herbie, whistle to his lips, skating everybody ragged, so tired at the end they could barely hobble down the steps to the dressing room.

One afternoon, doing loop after loop after loop inside Williams Arena, Steve Christoff made a vow to himself: No matter what happens, I'm never going to say this was fun.

So it would amuse the Gophers on hand when Brooks laid his regimen on his Olympians, and their new teammates—all these bewildered novitiates from Wisconsin and BU and UMD—would come up to them for advice and solace.

Is this real? What's he doing? Did you guys ever do this?

The Gophers would grin at each other, shrug the shoulders, roll the eyes. That's Herbie. Get used to it.

Get used to what? You never knew. Once, Eric Strobel remembered, Minnesota had lost a game to some bunch of unworthies, and Brooks had the players skate the next day without pucks.

Another time, after they'd taken a double dip at Denver, Brooks ordered up ten cases of beer and ten pizzas and passed them around.

He was always keeping you off balance that way, from the day you arrived at Minneapolis as a hotshot freshman from Eveleth or Rochester. Brooks had romanced you, told the newspapers you were the one defenseman he wanted if he wanted anybody.

Reality arrived with the first practice in the fall. "I'm not going to be your friend," Brooks would tell those assembled. "Nobody's guaranteed anything here."

Nobody, even seniors who'd skated four years for Minnesota, claimed to know him well. Just when you thought you had Brooks figured out, he'd do something that would leave you scratching your head.

"You'd see glimpses," said Bill Baker, who'd been Minnesota's captain in 1979. "I'd talk to him behind closed doors, and it would be a welcome change. Then I'd see him on the ice and he'd look right through you. You'd want to say, 'I talked to you ten minutes ago, and you were a different person.'"

Freshmen, used to positive reinforcement and lots of communication from their high school coaches, were literally left speechless. After being recruited personally by Brooks and having played a full season for him, Ramsey was checking out of his hotel room after Minnesota had won the National Championship in Detroit that March.

At the elevator bank on the fiftieth floor, he encountered Brooks, who gave him a curt nod. "I'm nervous as hell, trying to think of something to say," Ramsey would recall. "So all the way down, I didn't say anything. Fifty floors and not one word." That was deliberate. Brooks thought Ramsey was a marvelous player; he just didn't want Ramsey to know that.

Yet, all the Monday drudgery and Brooksian mysticism invariably produced a well-disciplined, beautifully conditioned, tightly knit hockey varsity.

"Every team I played on for five years always felt a common bond," Steve Janaszak would say. "Twenty guys who all hated Herb. You knew the guy sitting next to you had been through all the same crap."

Still, there was this odd magnetic attraction to the man. Some players, like Steve Christoff, actually liked the way Brooks would keep you off balance, never letting you know you had it made. Others, like Buzz Schneider, were entranced.

If you'd come from the typical working-class home, Herbie was a surrogate father laying down the law, telling you how it was, discussing your flaws and your potential out in the open.

"He knew how to hit close to home," Schneider would testify. "I'd just sit there and listen and not say 'boo.' Like I'm in church. Just shakin'."

In the dressing room, Brooks could be spellbinding before games. He always had a reason why the Gophers had to take two from North Dakota, why it was supremely important that

they nail Michigan tonight. Damn it, the players would concede, filing out of the room and into the vortex, Herbie's right.

His tirades, too, were memorable:

Brooks coming in between periods in Colorado Springs with
Minnesota losing to Colorado College saying what a goddam
country club you people are, how we didn't come all the way
out here to lose, for crissakes. . . .

Brooks storming in after the Gophers had given Michigan
Tech a couple of cheap late goals and randomly throwing a case
of soda, nearly beaning Eric Strobel. . . .

Brooks mauling the Taconite Trophy, the symbol of the Minnesota–UMD hockey rivalry, flinging it into the trash can.

He would come in and needle people, see Phil Verchota and
his army shirt and ragged jeans and climb on him—You're brutal, Verchota; see Mike Ramsey and call him an 18-year-old
prima donna, tell him to go read his press clippings.

Then Brooks might inadvertently say something funny and
the Gophers would wink at each other and howl. "You might
get a smile out of Herbie at that point," Bill Baker had noticed.
"Then he wouldn't leave it alone."

It was his joke, after all. Always, there was the control; Brooks
would make you pay for every laugh he gave you. You always
stopped short of liking him. The Gophers would win a big one,
then learn from the reporters that they'd supposedly done it for
Herbie, and they'd smile. Right. Us doing it for him.

He was very much his own man, and affection from his players was not exactly a priority with Brooks. He preferred respect.
He went his own way, currying no favor with the AHAUS (Amateur Hockey Association of the United States) people who ran
amateur hockey in America. He had no interest in or stomach
for institutional politics. He was not the Olympic officials' first
choice for coach and he knew it.

He got the interview and the offer, because he had won three
NCAA titles, and maybe also because they had to field a respectable hockey team this time.

In 1980, the Winter Olympics were being held in the United States for the first time in twenty years. The hockey games would be telecast in prime time, with Americans filling the field house and sports writers from every major newspaper peering down from the press box. A fiasco was unthinkable, and Herb Brooks would not be party to a fiasco.

This would not be a U.S. team that you'd take on tour and just as soon leave Over There. Brooks played on too many of those in the sixties; had been captain of four of them and played on the 1964 and 1968 Olympic squads.

Brooks knew how they were thrown together, how they were sent off with civic luncheons and crossed fingers, and how they came back with little more to show than victories over the Germans and Swiss, and sixth-place handshakes.

Brooks had been a fine forward himself at Minnesota in the late fifties, possibly the fastest skater in the country at the time. He had been devastated when he had been bounced from the U.S. Olympic squad in 1960. He had phoned his father back in St. Paul and complained how unfair it was, how he'd played better than several others who were being kept.

"Keep your damn mouth shut out there," his father had told him. "Say, 'Thanks, coach.' And get your ass home."

So Brooks had thanked Jack Riley and gotten his ass home. Someone pasted Bobby Cleary's head atop Brooks' body in the team photograph; and the U.S.A., with the Clearys as two of the primary heroes, went on to win the gold medal.

For the next twenty years, Brooks had a stock reply any time he was asked about it: "Must have cut the right guy." But when he put his Olympic team together, Brooks decided, it would be different. No late entries emerging from the woodwork, no regional push-and-pull, everything completely up front.

His training team would be announced at the end of the National Sports Festival, a new idea itself, with all the candidates in one room, Brooks reading twenty-six names from a list.

His taxi squad, a reserve pool of half a dozen players, would be well known in advance. If Brooks wanted to fetch someone

up, he'd fire off a letter, notify the player's college coach, and
post a copy in the dressing room. No mystery guests.

He'd coached the 1979 U.S. team that had played in the
World Championships in Moscow, so Brooks had an idea for a
nucleus. But he went well beyond that.

Brooks wrote almost every college hockey coach in the country, looking for recommendations. He had the National Hockey
League's Central Scouting Bureau do an analysis of the candidates. He had area scouts do comparisons. He picked the brains
of his advisory board—coaches from schools like Harvard and
Wisconsin and Colorado College plus a couple from the amateur International League, coaches who'd seen the prospects in
action and knew their strengths and vulnerabilities.

Brooks read all the reports, cross-matched and weighted
them. He put the names up on a big board and stared at them.
No National Football League general manager, sitting in his
situation room before the annual draft with his printouts and
phones and written assessments, ever prepared more meticu-
lously.

Everything would be better organized this time, including
the U.S. Olympic Committee. For decades, it had done little
more than gather up teams and give them uniforms and send-
offs.

Finally, after twenty years of watching more and more U.S.
teams left for dead by Socialists and bemoaning the difference
in systems, the USOC itself went systematic. After quadrennia
of raising funds with all the sophistication of a backwater
church, depending upon the patriotic generosity of Ma and Pa
Kettle, they went after corporate America and arranged for
sponsorships.

They set up a national training center in Colorado Springs
where athletes could be mustered, trained, tested and honed
for several years before each Games. Cincinnatus *was* ancient
history. You could not expect Jack Kirrane to turn up, jobless
but happy to do his duty. Not any more.

It took a long time, but finally, in 1978, the USOC had

dreamed up the National Sports Festival, a movable gymkhana that would be held during each pre-Olympic summer with virtually every sport represented; the competition, region against region.

Ever since they'd begun coming to Olympic Games in 1952, the Russians had done it that way with their *Spartakiades,* bringing athletes from all fifteen Soviet republics together in Moscow for a dress rehearsal.

It was an effective way to gauge quality and depth across the board, to shore up weak spots, to create a squad-in-embryo. But where the Russians had one *Spartakiade* every four years, the U.S. now had three.

Brooks had something to organize around, a showcase that would pit the Great Lakes against New England, Central against Midwest, for a week.

He had names, sixty-eight of them, and backups beyond them. But until Brooks got the names to sign on, he had nothing. In 1960 the stumbling block had been wives, kids and jobs. Now it was professional hockey.

In 1960 there had been six NHL teams with roughly eighteen players each, virtually all of them products of the Canadian junior leagues. There were no Americans playing in the NHL, and only a few U.S. college–trained skaters, all of them Canadians. Americans and collegians might as well have been playing in Siberia as far as the NHL was concerned. But by 1979, expansion had created twenty-one teams and 420 players, and general managers had been routinely scouting, drafting and signing American collegians for nearly a decade.

Many of the sixty-eight names had already been drafted by the NHL. One of them, 18-year-old Minnesota defenseman Mike Ramsey, was rated a certain first-round selection later that summer. Besides Ramsey, a number of Brooks' prospects had already been certified prime in previous drafts: Steve Christoff (second round by the Minnesota North Stars); Bill Baker (third round by the Montreal Canadiens); Rob McClanahan (third round by the Buffalo Sabres); and Mark Johnson, David Silk, Ralph Cox, Jim

Craig and Ken Morrow (fourth round by the Pittsburgh Penguins, the New York Rangers, the Boston Bruins, the Atlanta Flames and the New York Islanders, respectively).

Later, David Christian (Winnipeg) and Neal Broten (Minnesota) would garner enough recognition at the Sports Festival to be second-round choices in the August draft. So, was it worth it—signing on for six months to maybe finish sixth at Lake Placid —when you could be earning a year's salary in the minor (or even major) leagues and making an impression on your pro club?

Each of the dozen players Brooks wanted for his nucleus was being wooed by an NHL team, and each had the same concerns as his predecessors.

What am I going to live on? What if some faceless Czech caves in my knee? What happens to my career?

They needed assurances, assurances that a stint as an Olympian would be worthwhile, that the pros would wait, that they would have some financial protection.

To get them, Brooks first had to bury the hatchet with a New York attorney named Arthur Kaminsky who, along with a Boston associate named Bob Murray, happened to represent virtually all of the players who would eventually play on the Olympic team.

Brooks and Kaminsky had first clashed in 1975 when Brooks discovered the lawyer talking to some of his Minnesota players, and the relationship had not improved since.

By 1979, though, circumstances made both men realize they'd have to deal with each other in some fashion. Kaminsky settled on Murray, who'd played for two national champion hockey varsities at Boston University, as an intermediary.

Murray had no problems with Brooks. He would extend feelers. The preliminary soundings were encouraging, so in March, Kaminsky approached Brooks in the lobby of the Renaissance Center Hotel during the National Championships in Detroit.

"Herb, I'd like to talk to you."

"What about?"

"Look, you're the Olympic coach, and there's nothing I can do about it," Kaminsky said. "I either already represent, or will represent, many of the players who could be on that team. We can either butt heads all year and kill each other off or try to work something out."

Brooks stared at Kaminsky. "Okay," he snapped. "Meet me in my room in half an hour."

Once they were there, all the dirty laundry was tossed on the bed. Five years of antagonism, distrust and crossed wires. After an hour, when both men were verbally exhausted, Kaminsky saw his chance.

"Okay, I have a proposal," he said. "Neither one of us is going to convince the other that he is right. So let's get rid of the past. Forget it. And look ahead."

So a deal was struck. Brooks would agree not to influence his Olympians against Kaminsky. Kaminsky would encourage his clients to try out for the team, and if selected, to play; and he would help recruit other players if necessary. It was, Brooks decided later, the most important organizational meeting he'd had outside of his initial interview.

Yet, the compact only undid one tangle. The players still had to be convinced, and the key to that was Ken Morrow, a tall, rangy defenseman from Bowling Green who could have used a professional salary.

Morrow's father had passed away during his freshman year in college, and Morrow was about to be married. The New York Islanders, having drafted him higher than any other collegian in their history, were quite interested. He had played four years at Bowling Green, helping its program grow from obscurity to the NCAA Tournament in 1978. He had his degree and was ready to enter the real world. If Morrow signed, he'd be making money immediately, with a good chance for a play-off share if he was brought up to the parent club. What could the Olympic team offer him?

"Okay," Kaminsky said, "like everyone else, you'll get two hundred fifty dollars a week tax-free for living expenses, plus an extra fifty when you get married. I'll go to Bill Torrey, the

Islanders' general manager, prenegotiate a contract for you and put it in a drawer. All you have to do is sign it whenever you want. And we'll get insurance, enough to cover the signing bonus and two years' NHL salary. So if you're hurt, you won't walk away empty-handed."

The insurance was the sticky area. "We're not going to do this," the U.S. Olympic people told Brooks when he mentioned the idea. "We've never done this. Why is it necessary?"

It was necessary, Brooks implied, to avoid losing to Norway. "Hey," Brooks told them, "coaching isn't an avocation for me. It's my living."

Finally, the Olympic people agreed to pay for the first $25,-000 of insurance for whoever needed it; and said they would match anything a draftee's NHL club would pay for above that, dollar for dollar.

Then Kaminsky went to Torrey, the Islanders' astute general manager, sold him on the idea and got him to promote it among his NHL colleagues.

So Kaminsky went back to Morrow. "You've got your contract," he told him. "You've got your insurance. There's no reason not to play." So Morrow signed, and because he did, Brooks also ended up getting virtually everybody who saw himself in Morrow's situation.

Brooks got Jim Craig, the goalie from Boston University who'd been the showpiece of the 1979 World Championship team and might have signed with Atlanta. He got Jack O'Callahan, Craig's college teammate, who'd been drafted by Chicago. He got Bill Baker, who could have either played for Montreal or gone to dental school. And he got Steve Christoff, his top goal-scorer at Minnesota, who might otherwise have forgone his final college year to sign with the home-town North Stars.

So Brooks had his core, plus five other members of the 1979 U.S. National team: Cox, the nation's most prolific scorer at New Hampshire; Johnson, the All-American center from Wisconsin; and three of his Minnesota players in Eric Strobel, Phil Verchota and Rob McClanahan.

That group, plus Christian (whose father had scored the win-

ning goal against the Russians in 1960) and Ramsey—Brooks'
precocious defenseman at the "U"—were all but assured places.
Only one player whom Brooks coveted turned down his mating
call, and the hole opened by his loss would trouble Brooks for
the next six months.

Joe Mullen was a New York street urchin, raised on West
Forty-ninth Street in the Hollywood-made-infamous Hell's
Kitchen section. He had graduated from roller to ice hockey as
a teenager, and his father, Tom, had pushed a huge barrel of
boiling water over the ice surface between periods at Madison
Square Garden. Although the Zamboni machine had been invented, its entrance into New York came at least a decade after
everywhere else.

From his New York rink-rat days, Mullen moved on to Boston
College with a hockey scholarship. His first two seasons yielded
only moderate success, and during that period his draft year
came and went—with no NHL club (not even his father's employers, the New York Rangers) selecting him. "Too small, too
slow, too shy," read the scouting report. But Mullen blossomed.
In 1978, he led the Eagles to a surprise ECAC championship
and second place in the NCAAs. He was MVP in the Eastern
Championship and made All-America as a junior and senior. He
joined Brooks on the U.S. National squad at the World Championships in Moscow, and as Mark Johnson's right wing, led the
club in scoring. He had become an important factor in Brooks'
construction plans: the goal-scorer, the sniper.

Still, as an undrafted player, Mullen was eligible to sign with
any team in hockey. Though not as lucrative as baseball's free
agency, hockey's version occasionally produced fiscal windfalls
for fortunate collegians. Junior players almost never were free
agents, since the pros usually drafted all of them. For Mullen,
once "too small, too slow, too shy," the offers now came tumbling in.

There were further complications. The Mullens' apartment
had recently collapsed, and the family was in temporary lodg-
ings. Tom Mullen had been seriously ill, and the pressure was
on Joe to produce some dollars—quickly.

Brooks tried everything: phone calls to Mullen, to his New York agent, to clubs like St. Louis and the Rangers who were making offers. He even asked Kaminsky to intervene, but since Mullen was the one major player whom Kaminsky did not represent, he felt he could not interfere.

So, Mullen signed with his father's old boss, Emile Francis, now of St. Louis, and never showed up at the Sports Festival. Mullen would have been assured a spot on the Olympic team.

Mark Johnson got sick at the Sports Festival, and it meant nothing. Craig arrived with a bad hand and let in half a dozen goals in his first game. No problem. "You made the team in Moscow," Kaminsky told him.

In all, twenty players had spots in the final twenty-six, barring a dreadful performance at the Sports Festival. Their college achievements plus the analyses Brooks had received on them had convinced Brooks they were solid. The final half-dozen places on the roster would be open; whoever performed up to them would earn them.

So, for a week in Colorado Springs, Brooks and his people climbed into the stands and watched the regional teams play. Every night Brooks and his advisory committee got together and exchanged impressions.

Brooks made phone calls, seeking more background information on certain players, clearing up questions. No stone lay unturned; it was an obsession with him.

Finally, with the twenty-six names settled on, Brooks called all the candidates together in one room and read off his list:

Mark Johnson. Steve Christoff. Jim Craig. Jack O'Callahan. Dave Christian. Buzz Schneider. Ralph Cox. Phil Verchota.

This has never happened to me before, realized a 24-year-old wing from Boston named Michael Eruzione. In high school, you always knew you'd make the team. In college I was on scholarship; they had to keep me.

Not any more. Within half a dozen minutes, you would be On The Team, back in college, on your way to NHL training camp or out of hockey entirely.

Rob McClanahan. Mike Eruzione. John Harrington. Bill

*Baker. Ken Morrow. Mike Ramsey. Steve Janaszak. Mark Pave-·
lich.*

At the "U," Brooks had usually posted a list of his varsity; you
ambled by and checked for your name. Here, Brooks had arranged the names in his own peculiar order, not necessarily by
position, not necessarily by stature.

*Les Auge. Jack Hughes. Mark Wells. Eric Strobel. Dave Silk.
Dave Delich. Bruce Horsch. Gary Ross. Bob Suter.*

Brooks saved Neal Broten, his *wunderkind* freshman center
from the "U," for last. That way, he figured, lesser players announced earlier might get a little *spritz* of confidence: "Hey, I
was picked before Broten."

Brooks thanked everybody and said he'd be available for one-
on-one talks if anybody had questions, doubts, complaints. He
was determined that the reasons for everything be manifest.

Then Brooks got down to piecing them all together. This was
his fantasy team, in the flesh now. Every player could move,
could stay with any skating pace required. If Brooks had a
prejudice, it was there—he had a passion for speed. Most of
them came from working-class families; they had the lunch-
bucket ethic Brooks prized, so they could absorb five games in
eight nights, plus demanding practices, and shrug them off.

And they were all collegians and thus, Brooks presumed,
receptive to novel ideas, to unorthodox approaches to the
game. He could experiment with them, create a hybrid system
and teach it to them and know they'd see the challenge in it and
respond to it.

His forwards were aggressive and opportunistic, all of them
fine forecheckers. The defensemen were big (all save Suter
stood comfortably over six feet), mobile, physical. The goalies
had played the college game at the very highest levels and won
National Championships.

Woven together, Brooks guessed, it might be a team he'd pay
ten dollars to watch. All he had to do was weave them together.

3

A LITTLE RETROACTIVE
BAGGAGE

He told them that they were a family, that they had to be a family because they were going to be together for six months and six dozen games—living out of travel bags, dozing on jets, playing in strange rinks against inhospitables.

The problem, Herb Brooks realized, was that his Olympians were an adopted family, a busload of collegiate Hatfields and McCoys, Montagues and Capulets, all carrying their own retroactive baggage.

Half a dozen of them were from the Boston area, half a dozen more from around the Twin Cities, five from the Iron Range. Neal Broten and Dave Christian came from Roseau and Warroad, up where Minnesota, North Dakota and Canada intersect. Mark Johnson and Bobby Suter were out of Madison; Mark Wells and Ken Morrow from Michigan.

They came to the Olympic team with regional ways of looking at the world, and old college rivalries merely intensified the regionalism and sliced it different ways.

There were Range guys who'd gone to the "U" and Range guys, like John Harrington and Mark Pavelich, who'd skated for Minnesota-Duluth. Wisconsin and Minnesota had been rivals ever since someone laid down railroad track and inflated a football.

Boston University and Minnesota had a nasty brawl one minute into their NCAA play-off game in 1976, and scars from that still remained. "The puck dropped," BU coach Jack Parker would say later, "and it was war."

Both benches emptied, one player following another over the dasher like dominoes falling. It took nearly an hour for play to resume.

Chipped shoulders loomed almost everywhere you cared to look. The Boston players admitted it. They came from an intensely parochial seaport city whose ethnic pot was still unmelted and whose regionalisms were measured in city blocks.

Academics and outsiders liked to think of the city as the Athens of America, filled with libraries and museums and colleges, peopled by scholars and bluestockings and prudes who went about banning things. But it was fiction.

Boston had always been a working-class port, a docking place for the steerage class that came in heavy shoes and thick woolen coats and found employment under the Brahmin.

Boston built the nation's first subway to transport them, erected three-story wooden warrens to house them and laid down trolley lines everywhere.

One of them, the Arborway line, led to the Boston Arena, where ice hockey and neighborhood passions came together. To reach it, one climbed the steps from the subway and walked along Massachusetts Avenue past a Chinese restaurant called Mai Fong whose clock had stopped working in 1952 or perhaps 1958. Nobody seemed to remember.

Some people called it Uptown, this wedge of Boston where Mass Ave crossed Huntington and the Back Bay rubbed up against the South End. It was compact enough for one District 16 bluecoat to patrol on foot, try every door and memorize every face.

It took a couple of decades for the area to crumble, but the Arena endured long after Mai Fong's clock expired. They'd built the place in 1911 on a windy byway called St. Botolph, after the seventh-century Saxon monk from whom the city inherits its name.

But if they hadn't hung a marquee outside, the Arena could have passed for an armory, an ice house or a mortuary. Most of the time, it was a hockey rink, the draftiest, funkiest structure in the city. Any team which didn't have a place of its own played there, so the doors were always open, the marquee always crammed with magnetized letters and numbers—BOSTON CITY 2, GBI 5, MET 8—that told the daily schoolboy hockey schedule in shorthand.

The dressing rooms were always full, the rubber mats outside them always wet with melted ice shavings, the playing surface always occupied except for several minutes each half hour when a Zamboni machine was nudged out from beneath a large battered scoreboard to refresh the ice.

Thus hours blended into each other, afternoons ran into evenings—with nobody noticing. For the price of a ticket, you could arrive as soon as school let out and stay until midnight, sprawled across wooden balcony chairs worn smooth from generations of backsides.

One sank into such a lovely winter torpor at the Arena, a fine passivity. The scenery changed completely for you every few hours as one league left and another arrived: Irish city kids from Southie and Charlestown replaced by suburbanites from Arlington and Quincy.

But the aura and the smells remained unaltered. Sweat-soggy uniforms left to half dry atop radiators, then stuffed into canvas tote bags; steam heat coming from a basement boiler half a century old; popcorn cooking in oil in the lobby; and French fries sizzling at the far end.

You measured your stay at the Arena in Fry Time: six empty boxes, four hours.

Everyone was a hockey devotee in the sixties and seventies. It was very nearly unavoidable; entire leagues played all their games in front of you. College coaches did the better part of a year's recruiting from one rickety seat, watching a wing from Technical or a Columbus goaltender half a dozen times; then going downstairs to buttonhole the coach between periods.

Rivalries flourished at the Arena; dynasties were born and toppled; reputations made and undone. To make it to Boston Garden across town and the state finals, you had to win at the Arena, had to deal with the aura, with the balconies packed with entire towns, everybody peering down.

It was a provincial audience, firm in its hockey background and therefore its prejudices. Except for Minnesota and Michigan, where no proper Bostonian ever ventured—and odd corners of Rhode Island—there was really no other serious hockey played anywhere in the country.

A Bostonian learned his game on frozen ponds and on playgrounds flooded by the city, stickhandling around exposed branches and rocks, chasing the puck a hundred yards, avoiding ruts that would snap an ankle, playing until the sun went down and toes turned white.

Taken indoors, it made for a skating game, full of speed and finesse, the checking minimal, a quasi-European style. It was a European city, after all.

Generations were born, raised and buried on the same block. Boys who'd hung together on the corner as third-graders were still together as pensioners. Something there did not want to assimilate, not really.

So, old ethnic grudges and blood feuds were carried onward and institutionalized. Long after Joseph Kennedy had gone there himself, roomed with Irish boys and sent his sons there, Harvard was still perceived as the sanctuary of the Yankee Protestant.

The true Irish Catholic—or Italian Catholic, for that matter —went to Boston College, the Jesuit school at the end of the trolley line in Chestnut Hill.

When it came to hockey, which the Yankee had formalized and the Irishman taken as his own, the old resentments boiled up, whether or not the playing roster bore them out any longer.

"I shouldn't have to talk to you about Haah-vud," BC coach Snooks Kelley would tell his Cunniffs and Hogans and Hurleys before a game with the place across The Rivah. "Just the name Haah-vud . . ."

It made for fine theater—what with Snooks, a beefy man with a cheery, rosy face, standing there in his camel's hair coat with his great Hibernian grin and the rich orator's voice.

It also happened to play particularly well at the Beanpot tournament, the annual hockey class-war among the city's four major colleges—Harvard, BC, Boston University and Northeastern.

The name was ethnically apt. The Yankee ate beans out of parsimonious pleasure, the Irishman out of stark necessity. They'd conceived the tournament almost offhandedly at the Arena in the early fifties; once it was moved to the Garden and caught the city's imagination a few years later, there were not nearly enough seats.

The Beanpot popped up out of the early February slush on consecutive Monday nights, when absolutely nobody would ever want to venture beyond his living room, yet it sold out solid.

From the beginning the concept was a natural—all the unspoken passions and prejudices then simmering were given an outlet, a catharsis that was memorialized in a final score.

The stereotypes were years old; outdated, most of them; yet they were kept alive because it seemed worthwhile, and marvelous fun besides.

Harvard was supposed to be preppy, aloof, intellectual, a bit anemic. Boston College was Irish-on-the-move, hungry, muscular kids who would grow into portly lawyers and insurance salesmen and be fiercely anti-abortion.

Boston University was the place for the urban outsider, the New Yorker who wanted a taste of the Hub and didn't mind a campus bisected by trolley tracks.

Northeastern was a massive commuter school, the largest private university in America, its students working their way through on the cooperative plan, wanting the diploma for its economic value, the school's athletic image that of the persistent underdog.

In the fifties, BC and Harvard dominated hockey in the city, reaping the best of the local skaters. Kelley's approach was staunchly parochial: no Canadians need apply.

He wanted the nice Catholic lad from Arlington and Charlestown and Weymouth whose parents wanted a good Catholic education for him and would jump at a full-tuition scholarship.

Even after BU and Harvard and the rest looked more and more to Canadian players in the sixties and early seventies, Kelley stood firm.

So when Cornell came down with rosters chockablock with players from north of the border, it became a nationalistic battleground—the boy from Medicine Hat and Junior "B" versus the boy from Spy Pond and the Arena.

Harvard, coached by a Canadian (but a former Boston Bruin) in old Cooney Weiland, used its national reach to advantage. Its roster was a unique amalgam—preppies from Andover and St. Paul's; public schoolers from Greater Boston armed with 1200s in the college boards and thinking about the medical school; a hardscrabble Iron Ranger or two; here and there a Canadian like Gene Kinasewich, a scholarship kid who'd played in the Junior "A" leagues and become the center of an eligibility storm in the early sixties.

As Harvard and BC came to monopolize most of the promising local schoolboys, Boston University struck out for Ontario, thus sharpening a rivalry with BC (its Commonwealth Avenue neighbor) that was drawn distinctly enough to begin with.

Once BU drew abreast of and then surpassed BC and Harvard in the mid-sixties, their games became fierce set pieces of hockey philosophies and ideologies, staged first on Wednesday and Saturday nights in December and January, then at the Beanpot and finally at the Eastern Championships at the Garden each March.

With Ivy champion Cornell, which had a large Boston following, they packed the Garden, a vertical, smoky cockpit double the size of the Arena on Causeway Street that shared quarters with the Boston and Maine Railroad. So the rivalries were turned into urban sporting rites, the tickets bought and evenings arranged weeks in advance.

The Easterns were held on Friday and Saturday nights in

mid-March, one game at 6:15, another at 9:00. The faithful suppered heavily on Italian food in the adjacent North End, then walked over in the raw chill, filling up the balconies, crowding the corridors, debating, predicting, celebrating.

The Nationals, which usually included the two finalists, were an anticlimax. Winning the Easterns—and beating a Harvard, a Cornell, a BC or a BU in the process—was everything.

By the mid-seventies, the balance of power had swung heavily in BU's direction. Jack Kelley (not to be confused with BC's John "Snooks" Kelley), who'd brought the program up from the doldrums, had gone off to the Whalers of the World Hockey Association, giving way to Leon Abbott, who gave way to Jack Parker, a Somerville kid who'd played for Kelley, knew his system and set out to perpetuate it.

Like Kelley's teams, Parker's were finely balanced varsities filled with tireless skaters. Two of them always seemed to be on the puck, with a third circling nearby. Parker's four forward lines were all but interchangeable, his defensemen poised and imaginative, his goalie unshakable.

BU would cruise for thirty minutes, stringing you along in a 1-1 game, then pop three goals in 100 seconds. They owned Boston, turned up at the Nationals almost without thinking about it and dominated the All-East team.

Parker still foraged in Ontario, as Kelley had, but now the best Boston-Area players—who might have been lured by BC or Harvard a decade earlier—wanted BU, knowing they'd skate around the Garden ice brandishing the Beanpot and the Eastern trophy if they signed on.

Parker and Toot Cahoon, his assistant, had both played in the Arena and now haunted it daily, knowing exactly what they were looking for, fixing on the blue-chip player from the Catholic Conference.

That was the ruling power in Boston schoolboy hockey now, filled with players from Southie and Charlestown who'd gone parochial to avoid the mandatory busing that otherwise awaited them in the public system.

But there were other sources: semi-rural leagues that nobody got to, or the Boston city league, which some coaches had written off. Or the player who had nothing going for him but the intangibles; who looked too small, too slow for the classic mold, but who won hockey games for you anyway.

Parker found a goaltender named Jim Craig in an obscure corner of the commonwealth called Massasoit Junior College. No major school had noticed him. He picked up Jack O'Callahan, a defenseman who wore eyeglasses and had put Boston Latin into the tournament all by himself—but who had played to mostly empty seats.

And Parker came upon Mike Eruzione in a summer league. Eruzione was resigned to enrolling in a Division 2 school north of Boston. Nobody had asked him to do otherwise.

They all became Terriers, top dogs, overlooked no longer. Championships were their due. "Unbelievable," a teammate would tell Eruzione as they were carrying a third straight Eastern trophy off the ice.

"Yeah," Eruzione said. "And wait till we win it next year."

That was the Boston kid talking. Proud, loyal, street-smart. We'll show Them.

Some of that attitude had carried over to Colorado Springs, where Brooks was selecting his Olympians. Gary Smith, who'd been the Minnesota trainer, was Brooks' Olympic trainer. Three of the Gophers who'd played in that NCAA "brawl" game—Bill Baker, Phil Verchota and Steve Janaszak—were on his team. And four BU kids, two of whom had been involved in the fight with Brooks' Minnesotans.

"Don't go out there thinking you don't like Herb Brooks," Parker warned them, "because of something that happened between two different teams. And just because you may like me and I may not like Brooks, that doesn't mean you shouldn't like him."

Still, the Terriers had gone out to Colorado Springs defensive, worried about what Brooks might have remembered or might have heard about them.

Someone on Brooks' advisory staff at the Sports Festival told him that Eruzione was a bad liver, a troublemaker. Harvard coach Bill Cleary, the former Olympian, had been in the room and heard that and had gone to a phone to get a character reference from his good friend Parker back in Boston.

This is crazy, Eruzione thought when word reached him. I've never caused trouble anywhere I've played.

Eugene Eruzione, his father, wouldn't have tolerated it. His first question to any of his son's coaches, all the way back to peewee hockey, had never been, "How's he playing?" but "How's he behaving?"

When Eruzione saw Brooks at Colorado Springs, he sought quickly to clear the air.

"Mr. Brooks?"

"I'm Herb," Brooks informed him. "My father's Mr. Brooks."

"About me being a troublemaker . . ."

"I never heard it. It never happened. Looking forward to having you in camp."

All slates had been wiped clean as far as Brooks was concerned. He may still have had personal differences with Parker, yet he chose him for the advisory board because Parker knew hockey and would be straightforward in his assessments. And Parker's players would get a fair shot, based on ability.

Maybe we've been too defensive about this, B.U.'s Dave Silk decided. Maybe the Gophers are all right. They were invariably up front and honest, he'd noticed, even bordering on the naïve.

Minnesota had nothing of the street-corner ethnicity that marked Boston, New York and Chicago. The stock was mostly Scandinavian and the values were common—order, hard work and a passion for progress, whatever it might mean.

Minnesotans saw no reason why government couldn't be improved upon, why problems too large for cities and towns to solve couldn't be passed on to the state with a reasonable expectation that they'd be handled efficiently and honestly.

There was a simplicity to debate and thought that came naturally to people who'd lived close to the outdoors all their lives and had reached harmony with it.

Most of their northern countrymen may have taken on a siege mentality when December arrived, but the Minnesotans believed in embracing winter and building carnivals around it. So ice hockey was a natural sport for them—both the climate and the topography encouraged it.

"They've got ten thousand lakes," Dave Silk would say, "and no ocean." Fifteen thousand two hundred and ninety-one, to be exact. The question was not so much number but definition. What was a lake? The accepted bench mark, finally, was a basin of at least ten acres partially or totally filled with water.

Minneapolis alone had twenty-one lakes, and all of them froze over rather nicely, the winter temperature there being not unlike Moscow's. During World War II in fact, a local broadcaster, trying to convey just how cold it was along the Russian front, said that Minnesotans would understand.

They were playing ice polo in the Twin Cities in the middle of the nineteenth century. By 1895, when some parts of the state were still having problems with Indian raids, the University of Minnesota and the Minneapolis Hockey Club were playing for the city championship at an outdoor rink on the corner of Fourth Avenue and Eleventh Street South.

A year later, grade schools in St. Paul were playing the game; and by 1912 the city had built the Hippodrome, its own version of the Montreal Forum.

And the St. Paul Athletic Club, which played there, was the city's version of the Canadiens, with Moose Goheen as its star. By 1930, each Twin City had 300 hockey teams crowding every swatch of lake ice.

Lack of elbow room, more than anything else, kept the numbers from expanding geometrically and probably was the real reason why upstate teams dominated the state schoolboy championships for several decades.

From the end of World War II—when the tournament began —until 1969, downstate varsities won only four titles, and St. Paul Johnson, Herb Brooks' old team, captured all of them.

Not until the Twin City suburbs began putting up indoor rinks in the late sixties and early seventies did the balance shift. Suddenly, Edina, Richfield, St. Louis Park, South St. Paul—all had feeder systems and plenty of ice time to nourish them. In 1969 Edina won the state title and went on to build something of a dynasty. From that point, downstate schools won two titles out of every three.

Most of the Twin City–area Olympians learned the game on outdoor rinks, picking it up just as the construction boom was beginning. But most of them also went to high schools that had their own indoor facilities. Mike Ramsey, who grew up in Minneapolis and went to Roosevelt High, was an exception.

Before it moved to the Augsburg College rink, his varsity played its games in the Minneapolis Auditorium downtown, where chicken wire served as Plexiglas and a rowdy crew called Fred's Army, a bunch of Roosevelt upperclassmen, held forth in the upper reaches. "They'd go to every game," Ramsey recalled, "and raise holy hell." Festivities usually climaxed with one army inductee rolling down the entire flight of stairs.

The big rival was (and is) Southwest, which Roosevelt considered the rich school, the "cake-eaters." Southwest had its own indoor rink; from such distinctions do rivalries flourish.

The rivalries extended beyond league boundaries. Steve Christoff's Richfield varsity went up to Grand Rapids for a game; Roosevelt played Roseau, Neal Broten's team. Rivalries began in grade school, at the peewee level. Eric Strobel, who lived in Rochester, remembered playing against Broten in peewees and against Robbie McClanahan, who came from north of St. Paul, in bantams.

Ice hockey was Minnesota's cottage industry, a source of immense state pride. By 1980 more than half of the Americans playing professional hockey were Minnesotans. More than 4000 teams were playing the game at an organized level, 160 of them high school varsities. When the best eight convened at the St. Paul Civic Center for the annual state tournament, more than 100,000 people paid to watch.

The tournament had been a Minnesota tradition since the end of World War II, a three-day convocation that was part state fair, part psychodrama and part civil war. Miners rubbed shoulders with millers, Minneapolis executives with Duluth longshoremen. By Thursday morning the streets were clogged with school buses from Cloquet, Virginia and Edina. Every St. Paul hotel was jammed, and each of the 16,000 tickets (plus several thousand standing-room spots) was snapped up.

It was a ritual that monopolized conversation and attention across the state; if you couldn't elbow your way into the Civic Center, you watched the games on prime time television or switched on the radio.

For the participants, there was no other world for seventy-two hours. Minnesota has one division for all of its hockey teams, and thus one champion. Riding the team bus along the Interstate, a 15-year-old goalkeeper from a tiny upstate school would sense the stomach knotting, the adrenaline starting to bubble. He could be home, defeated, forgotten by suppertime. Or an immortal, at least in one corner of Minnesota, by Saturday midnight.

It was The Athletic Event of the year across the state, a concelebration of a favorite sport by a hard-working populace.

But The Team was the University of Minnesota's team, the Gophers. To a miner's son up on the Iron Range or to a dairy farmer's boy, the "U" was Mecca in Minneapolis. A leafy campus perched on the east bank of the Mississippi across from the flour mills, its square brick buildings sprouted domes and towers here and there.

In the middle of it, on University Avenue, stood Williams Arena, the imposing vault where generations of Gophers had played their hockey. It was a Canadian game, but the "U" had made a cult out of using the Minnesota player, only rarely venturing into Ontario and Manitoba.

The home-grown product, bursting with state pride, was the natural quarry: the working-class kid, unselfish and unspoiled, playing for the "U." His U.

How could you turn it down? Grand Rapids would be playing Greenway up on the Range, and word would filter down to the players' bench: He's up there, Herbie's watching tonight.

"Herbie" was Herb Brooks, the Minnesota coach, and that was his recruiting style, low-key, making the good eye contact, the voice assured, the handshake firm. Sometimes you didn't know he was after you until he popped up face-to-face one day.

Buzz Schneider, who played on Brooks' first Minnesota varsity, had gone to the state schoolboy tournament as a spectator during his senior year, bringing extra tickets to hawk outside.

A neatly dressed, low-key insurance salesman, seeing Schneider in his Babbitt letter jacket, had approached him.

"You Buzz Schneider?"

"Yeah. Want to buy some tickets?"

"I'm Herb Brooks."

The approach was deliberately subtle, designed not to overwhelm. Brooks had been something of a schoolboy legend himself at St. Paul Johnson. He had grown up working-class on the East Side, the son of an insurance underwriter. He'd played at the "U."

He believed in the "U," and he believed that you, Buzz Schneider, and you, Robbie McClanahan, belonged there. You were the only forward, the only defenseman, the only goalkeeper he really wanted.

Wooed that way, a number of latter-day Minnesota legends who'd been looking elsewhere decided to stay home, to be Gopher S. McClanahan, who lived a couple of hockey rinks away from Brooks in the northern suburbs, was being pursued by every school in the West plus Harvard and Cornell out East.

He'd all but settled on Michigan Tech, a fine school with an excellent hockey tradition nestled on the Upper Peninsula. But Brooks had gotten McClanahan to go to his big recruiting weekend at the "U," and McClanahan had taken it all in—the lawns and the sprouting domes and Williams Arena; had talked to some of the Gophers; had seen the other latter-day schoolboy legends wandering around being convinced; and had changed his mind. "This," McClanahan concluded, "is the place to play."

The "U" was exactly that, the collegiate repository of everything that was intellectual, social and athletic in the state of
Minnesota. "We're the main U," Brooks would remind his players. "The others are just small colleges."

Minnesota-Duluth was a branch school one-seventh the size
of the "U," a functional, modernish campus sitting on a hill
overlooking Lake Superior and billing itself the Minnesota of
the North.

The two schools played each other at least four times a year:
twice in Duluth, twice in Minneapolis, always on consecutive
nights with the results a given—at least in one man's mind.
Herb Brooks did not lose to a branch.

The alternative was too painful for a Gopher to consider. One
year, Buzz Schneider remembered, Brooks had his players
skate ten Herbies in practice, up and back, after losing to UMD.
Lose to Duluth, and his father would hear about it back on the
Range, Bill Baker knew. All those snickering comments at
work: "Hey, what happened to the Gophers?"

Baker came from Grand Rapids, a working-class town on the
eastern end of the Range, a three-hour drive northwest of the
Twin Cities. Bob Dylan, troubador for the sixties, grew up in
Hibbing, Minnesota, not far away. "I'm North Dakota–Min-
nesota midwestern," Dylan once told a magazine interviewer.
"I'm that color. I speak that way. I'm from someplace called the
Iron Range. My brains and feelings have come from there."

There was a proud, communal sense on the Range, enforced
by the terrain and the climate. You pulled together because
there was nobody else up there.

People didn't bother locking their doors on the Range. Huge
stacks of cordwood were left to dry on front lawns and nobody
worried about theft. The Mesabi Range offered hard work and
plain talk, and that much had barely changed in a hundred
years.

The geography, the mere remoteness of the place, made for
that. Except for Duluth, more than an hour's drive southeast,

there was no major city within several hundred miles. Something as simple as driving back from Minneapolis after a hockey game took on Donner Party overtones if a blizzard blew up past midnight two hours along Route 65. "Put your car in a ditch," said Bill Baker, "and you're there."

Range towns were compact, self-sufficient by necessity.

The area had begun as the rawest of frontiers before the turn of the century, a twisting strip 110 miles long crisscrossed by railroad track and filled with ore.

Each village along the Range was a virtual company town, the wooden houses built without foundations so an entire settlement could be moved quickly if a new deposit was found underneath.

Fires swept through them frequently; the town of Virginia burned down twice in seven years before residents decided to switch to stone, brick and concrete.

Mining companies set up shop every few miles, employing a stewage of untutored immigrants—Irish, Slovenes, Croats, Jews, Italians, Scandinavians—anybody who'd taken the trains westbound from Ellis Island until the money ran out.

The life was brutal, the rewards minimal. In 1906, a day's labor of ripping a ton of ore from an open pit and loading it onto freight trains for Duluth brought a man $1.65 and a bit of free political advice ("Vote for Taft or don't report for work").

For recreation there was drink (the town of Hibbing had forty-five saloons for 7500 people), prostitution, thievery, brawling, murder.

That was during the best of times. The worst—like the panic of 1893, the Depression, and the recession of the 1980s—sent shock waves along the Range.

By the sixties, when most of the natural ores had been stripped from the earth and the steel companies began looking elsewhere, the Range reached a crossroads. Unemployment was climbing; when miners weren't working, nobody else was either.

Finally, someone realized that a lower-grade substance called taconite, which was plentiful on the Range, made for acceptable iron once it was pulverized and sifted.

By the seventies, most people were working again; but they'd been reminded that prosperity on the Range was cyclical, at best tenuous.

When the steel industry was booming, a job with U.S. Steel looked terrific to the average high-school graduate from Mountain Iron. Get a twenty-thousand-dollar job with full benefits? Buzz Schneider's classmates thought. Hey, why not?

But by the middle of 1982, when the recession was still bottoming and the automobile and heavy-construction industries were on their backs, unemployment on the Range was over 85 percent in some places. Some of Schneider's friends had been out of work for nearly a year, their unemployment benefits exhausted. And word had come back from those who'd gone to other states in search of jobs that there was nothing Out There, either.

At least on the Range you had friends. There was room in the back yard for a vegetable patch; game in the fields; trout in the lakes. "We'll get by somehow," was the rallying cry. "We'll just have to cut corners."

You survived best if you appreciated a dollar's value and acquired enough handyman's skills to fend for yourself when the economy went flat.

So, most Rangers could remodel a house, build a cabin from the ground up or repair anything that moved. For recreation they hunted, fished and played a unique form of hockey.

It was hockey alfresco, played on a frozen lake until dusk made the puck invisible. A Ranger began skating almost as soon as he was ambulatory, bringing a sandwich, a couple of oranges, a dime for a Coca-Cola and two thick magazines as makeshift shin guards.

Most towns had one indoor rink; an hour's ice time was rare and precious. More likely, Range children did what Bill Baker did. They went down the hill to a makeshift outdoor rink and played until supper. After supper, they went back. "When it got to be nine or nine thirty at night, my mother would flip on the outside light," Baker remembered. "That's when I knew it was time to come in."

Range children shoveled off a swatch of ice to create their rink and stayed out there for a dozen hours a day with the thermometer often reading below zero, the puck so brittle sometimes it would shatter. Half might go in the goal, half might skitter off elsewhere, touching off a debate: goal or no goal?

It was scrimmage hockey, the most primitive form of the game, played ten to a side. But it instilled a respect for fundamentals and a terrific hockey sense.

You learned to stickhandle (one of the lost arts) just to be able to thread your way through nineteen other bodies. You learned to look for teammates because there simply wasn't the skating room to bust free.

The limitations and the inventiveness they engendered produced a recognizable Range style. You could tell a Range team, Bill Baker believed, just by watching it play for a while.

Where city teams were explosive and high-scoring, with a flair for wheeling in and out of zones, Rangers were methodical, basic—checking fiercely, grinding it out.

Almost any Range town produced the same kind of player, hewn from the same background and ethic. But when their high schools played each other, the atmosphere was a throwback to the frontier days.

The Range might stretch and curl for miles, but many of its towns huddled close together, pellets on an iron necklace.

Half a mile out of Virginia, Eveleth's water tower loomed. Stay on Routes 169 and 53 long enough, and you saw them all —Buhl, Chisholm, Hibbing, Coleraine, Grand Rapids and the rest.

Virginia was four miles from Eveleth, Hibbing six miles from Chisholm, Gilbert four miles from Virginia. On a weekend night, entire towns would turn out to watch two high school teams play.

There was no college hockey for miles. Making the local varsity was the achievement of an adolescent's life.

Invariably, passions ran high and spectators would fall to brawling in the stands and walkways, the players on the bench turning around to watch.

They were proud towns, and some, like Eveleth ("The City of Meterless Parking"), had long hockey traditions. They'd been playing the game seriously at Eveleth since 1922, when townspeople built the Hippodrome and formed a high school team.

From 1948 through 1951 Eveleth simply dominated the state, winning four straight Minnesota high school championships and ripping off victory streaks that reached fifty-eight and seventy-eight games.

Anyone in the town could recite the appropriate trivia. In 1942, when there were only six goaltenders in the National Hockey League, three came from Eveleth. The U.S. Hockey Hall of Fame, perched on a rise overlooking Route 53, has four Eveleth natives in it. Three players and the coach from the 1956 Olympic team that won the silver medal were out of Eveleth.

When Buzz Schneider, who lived in Babbitt, wanted to see a hockey game, his father drove him the 47 miles to watch the Eveleth Rangers. "I thought that was the NHL," Schneider would say.

Only International Falls, 100 miles north at Canada's doorstep, has won more state schoolboy titles. Eighteen times since the end of World War II when the championship was formalized, either I. Falls or a Range team went downstate and brought it back.

Grand Rapids, which had only finished third in the Iron Range Conference during the regular season, went down and won it all the year after Bill Baker was graduated. When the players came back, they said it hadn't been such a big deal; that Virginia or Eveleth could have won the title, too.

The Rangers were like that, squabbling among themselves during the league season, then uniting behind their champion when they went downstate for the tournament.

They made an expedition out of it, piling into buses for the four-hour ride to The Cities on Thursday, watching their game, piling back on for the return trip, then doing it all again on Friday and Saturday. Nobody seemed to mind. IRON RANGERS, the bumper sticker read. WE'RE NOT TOO SMART, BUT WE LIFT HEAVY THINGS.

When UMD, its roster top-heavy with Rangers, played the "U," the games were four-hour wars filled with chopping, mucking and shoving. Later, when Mark Pavelich and John "Bah" Harrington were playing for UMD and Brooks had his roadrunners, the games were flat-out, end-to-end skating jousts, terrific hockey. But Minnesota always won them, by a single goal as often as not, or managed a tie.

For twenty-one games over five years while Brooks was there, the "U" maintained its mastery. The reward was the Taconite Trophy, which Brooks kept over some pipes in the dressing-room lavatory and periodically abused.

That was approximately the way, players guessed, that Herbie felt about UMD itself. In 1970, when Duluth was looking for a head coach and Brooks was available, they told him they already had their man and hired someone named Terry Shercliffe.

So the Taconite Trophy was a suitable receptacle for the Brooksian wrath. After observing several years' worth of dents, thuds and abrasions, Bill Baker chuckled. "They're dying to beat us," he thought. "But they don't know what they're going to get."

The spell had finally been snapped the winter before Brooks took charge of the Olympic team, when UMD emerged from the slough of four bad seasons and finished third in the league with their strongest team ever, led by Harrington, Pavelich and Curt Giles, later of the Minnesota North Stars.

Harrington had dreamed of the night when, the Gophers finally vanquished, he could skate over magnanimously to a crestfallen Brooks, say "Good game, coach," and skate away.

The chance came on a Saturday night in November at Duluth. The Gophers had escaped on Friday night in overtime, just as they had a half-dozen other times during the streak. But Saturday belonged to UMD by a single goal.

Harrington had found Brooks, had been magnanimous and had dashed off to celebrate. Outside on the team bus, as the driver was turning over the engine for the three-hour ride back down Interstate 35, Brooks stood up to address the representatives of the main "U."

"Congratulations, gentlemen," he told them. "You've just given (UMD coach) Gus Hendrickson another two years on his contract."

Gophers did not lose to a branch, any branch. Gophers also did not lose to Badgers, particularly at Madison.

The badger had been the Wisconsin state symbol since the nineteenth century, when the lead-mining boom began. The surface mines, with all the earth dug up and piled alongside, looked like badger holes. In winter, when icy winds turned hands numb, Wisconsinites tunneled underground for shelter. Just like badgers.

They were fascinating folk, at once practical and radical. They invented Kleenex and malted milk and the typewriter. The Gideons placed their first Bible in Wisconsin. The Ringling Brothers pitched their first circus tent there.

Wisconsin gave you Joe McCarthy with one hand, Bob La Follette and progressivism with the other. It believed that government did not have to be corrupt, that you could dream up public policy at your state university and have it translated into law at the State House down the street.

But Wisconsin had not been a hockey state, not until Bob Johnson arrived. There was only one indoor rink in Madison, a smoky, rowdy den on the east side called Hartmeyer Arena.

For twenty-seven years the university had no hockey team; when the program resumed in 1962, the Wisconsin varsity lugged its gear into Hartmeyer like everybody else.

The high school programs were primitive, a fallow area for anyone hunting Division 1 material. But there was potential there; and Johnson, a natural salesman with unfettered enthusiasm and energy, was the right man to develop it.

Johnson was actually a native Minnesotan; he'd played both hockey and baseball at the "U" in the fifties. He'd spent three years coaching hockey at Colorado College with reasonable success. In 1966, he came to Madison.

He started there with little more than a desk and seventeen players. When he went to Minnesota and Canada on recruiting forays, Johnson sold prospects on the idea of what Wisconsin hockey *could* be.

A new 8000-seat coliseum would be ready in a year or so. The Badgers would be joining the WCHA before long—no more Gustavi Adolphi or St. Anonymities on the schedule. "Madison's a terrific place to go to school. You're going to love it there."

Once he'd sold the players, Johnson began on the citizenry the same way, going to civic groups and business luncheons and telling them how fantastic it was, a great game to watch. Come to three games, just three. If you don't like it, if you don't think it's a great game . . .

Madison is a prosperous city of 170,000 crammed onto an isthmus between two lakes at the bottom of the state. The territorial legislature had set it apart in 1836 as the site for both the state capital and the state university, meaning for one to feed off the other.

In the sixties, the university was the Berkeley of the Midwest, fiercely anti-war, a major stop on any liberal politician's itinerary. In the eighties, you could still find graffiti scrawled on an administration building that advised you to "Engulf Patriarchy."

Yet, the university lived in harmony with a city that might have been a model for middle-class America. *Life* magazine, once the weekly reader of the middle-class American, dispatched photographer Alfred Eisenstadt in 1948 for a look at "The Good Life in Madison."

He brought back pictures of clean, tree-lined streets, rosy-cheeked children skipping off to fine schools, trim houses, well-groomed parks, lakes bristling with pleasure boats and teeming with perch. It was America of the dreams, of the Fourth of July picnics, every immigrant's picture of the U.S.A.

"Is it the best place in America to live?" *Life* wondered. Except for mosquitoes and downtown traffic, everything seemed pretty much ideal.

Geography had blessed the city with hills overlooking graceful shores, so city fathers arranged for an expansive square with facing shops, placed a pillared State House in the center and let Madison spread from there along either side of the isthmus. The university they placed down by Lake Mendota and decided it should become all things to all Wisconsin people, helping the politician to govern and the farmer to harvest.

Heavy industry was discouraged. Milwaukee could keep the breweries; "udder cola" was good enough for Madisonians. The locals wanted no slums, no illiteracy, no leaden skies, so they planned them away.

By the end of World War II, Madison had 805 acres of parks, ten beaches, 30 miles of scenic drives, 23,000 trees, seven libraries, two newspapers and a civic symphony.

It also had a blended populace reminiscent of New York or one of the lakefront cities. Southern Wisconsin had been old Sac and Fox Indians' territory; the Black Hawk Wars were fought not far away. In the seventies, the state still had the largest Indian population east of the Mississippi.

Madison had Englishmen and Cornishmen, Germans and Scandinavians, Irish and Italians. They wouldn't have melted in Boston; in Madison they made for a great composite cheddar, the people for whom Henry Ford built his automobiles, whose complexions Procter & Gamble sought to burnish, for whose sensibilities Norman Rockwell painted.

"Few people who have ever lived in Madison," *Life* concluded, "ever move away of their own free will." Madison was also the mecca of Badgermania. Drive anywhere in the city and you saw Bucky Badger in shop windows, on clocks, on store signs, strutting confidently with his toothy grin.

Nobody had more blind faith than Badger fans. For years, they came out every Saturday, 70,000 strong, to watch sorry football teams lose by eight touchdowns to Ohio State and Michigan. One Big Ten championship, one trip to Pasadena for the Rose Bowl every twenty years or so was all anyone expected. Now they had a hockey team to cheer for, and Johnson made it all come true for them. Dane County Coliseum, the largest college rink in America, opened; and attendance doubled overnight.

Wisconsin did join the WCHA in 1969-70, knocked off Denver, the defending national champion, and went to the Nationals in Lake Placid that first year. They finished a respectable third there, losing by a goal in the last few minutes to champion Cornell. Roughly a hundred Badger fans, a portent of things to come, accompanied them and made enough commotion for a thousand.

Three years later, they went to Boston and took it all. Wisconsin fell four goals behind Cornell in their semifinal, stormed back to tie the game with five seconds on the clock, then won it in overtime. Then they brought down Denver the next night for the championship.

Johnson had a photo sequence of the Cornell game tying goal mounted and framed and hung in the hallway at home. A decade later, he'd still show the highlight film for visitors, puttering about his office, his eyes lighting up when he heard the announcer say, "They're going wild in Boston, they're going wild in Boston."

Badgermania really took hold that year. Nearly 4000 fans went with the varsity to Boston, garbed in red and white from scalp to socks. And when the Badgers trailed Cornell by four, the fans hung in, their frenzy and volume increasing. They held Wisconsin in a game that should have been conceded by that point; they simply wouldn't let their team die.

They wore candy-striped overalls, scarlet cowboy hats and

buttoned-down caps with large white *W*'s; red parkas, red windbreakers, red T-shirts.

They chanted as one and they drank as one, liberating every dingy tavern along Causeway and Canal streets, demanding Heileman's Old Style Beer but settling for anything.

The fans became a fixture on Wisconsin road trips, buying up every motel room along the South Bend strip when the games were at Notre Dame, planning their ski trips around the Denver weekend.

They were a sagging chamber of commerce's favorite fantasy, a reasonably well behaved caravan that descended on your town for anywhere from forty-eight to seventy-two hours and absorbed rooms, meals, beverages and souvenirs; then vanished to return next year.

After they'd helped salvage the 1978 NCAA tournament at Providence (which, with Bowling Green and two Boston teams, had loomed as a promoter's nightmare), a chamber of commerce type actually did go out to Madison and present a trophy to the "World's Greatest Fans."

That view went unshared by Brooks, who tartly called them drunken bums (You were forbidden to sell alcohol, Brooks would point out, at Big 10 games) with little appreciation for the game. When the Gophers made their next appearance in Madison, Brooks found the fans had created an enormous computer printout showing Brooks holding a Budweiser can and a straw.

If Madison was his favorite place to win, Brooks was their favorite visitor, the man they loved to ride.

The newspapers would have been building up the confrontation all week, fanning fires that needed minimal stoking anyway, and when the Gophers arrived, it would be Looney Tunes for two days. Eight thousand six hundred believers packed the saucer-shaped Coliseum to the roof both nights, howling and booing, hanging out rubber chickens and taunting Herbie's goaltender with their accusatory "Sieve . . . sieve . . . sieve" chant, complete with pointing fingers.

Back in Minneapolis, the favor would be returned, insult for insult. Mark Johnson had skated onto the ice at Williams Arena (which was imposing in its own way, usually packed to its dingy rafters with six or seven thousand Gopher fans) as a freshman and been overwhelmed by the immediate outpouring of hostility, the denizens shouting at his father all night long.

Once, a Gopher fan had come up to Wisconsin's team doctor and coughed in his face. "I've got the flu," the fan informed him. "And I hope you get it now, too."

Tales of drunkenness and cruelty invariably filtered back, the indignities merely assuring turnabout treatment for the next meeting. "Their fans were nasty to our guys, we've got to be nasty to them," Bob Johnson recalled. "That's how it was."

Beyond the parochialism, the undiluted Badgerism and Gopherism, there was a personal thing between Brooks and Johnson. Both men would deny it if you asked them, but it was there.

They'd both graduated from the "U" and both were driven, compulsive people. But there were important differences, too. Where Brooks was tight-lipped, blunt, often cryptic, Johnson was hyperactive, garrulous, unabashedly boosterish. Brooks was mysterious, enigmatic, always keeping you off base. With Johnson, no guessing was necessary; if you didn't know what he was doing and why, he would tell you—a dozen times.

So when Madison people heard that Brooks would be coaching the 1980 Olympians, some of them told Mark Johnson they were afraid he'd have problems with Brooks, that he might pay for being a Badger, that he'd be caught in a squeeze between his college-coach father and new Olympic coach.

That hadn't happened. He'd hit it off right away with Brooks, who recognized immediately that Johnson would be indispensable to his squad. Still, Johnson and Bobby Suter, his old high school rival and Wisconsin teammate, were conscious of being the only Badgers among all those Gophers. They had to make the Olympic team—everybody back in Madison was counting on them.

So the regionalism, intentional or not, was there. Someone would go on about Quincy Market in Boston or Stub and Herb's in Minneapolis or Tuna's Bar in Eveleth; and Bah Harrington would say it: Don't get regional.

Mark Johnson would talk about the big football game at Columbus on Saturday, how the Badgers just had to win it, and somebody would jump on him. Let's not get regional.

There is strength in your differences, Brooks told his players, but don't beat yourself. That was to become the cornerstone of his credo. Don't beat yourselves on the ice, don't beat yourselves in the locker room, don't beat yourselves in your social interactions.

You could beat yourselves with cliques, with Gopherism, with Badgerism, with Terrierism. Brooks wanted none of it.

4

WALTZING
THROUGH OSLO

The best cure for regionalism was a three-week European tour. The team had had a few weeks off after Colorado Springs, then spent a week at Lake Placid to regroup, work out and prepare for five dozen games in five months.

Europe would be an ideal place to start, to develop the camaraderie Brooks wanted to see. The Olympians would play ten games in sixteen days over there, bouncing from Holland to Finland to Norway, taking overnight trains and climbing aboard buses.

The food would be strange, the faces unfamiliar, the languages alien. Nobody would know a Gopher from a Badger in The Hague. They would merely be twenty-six kids in U.S.A. jerseys lugging their gear through a different hotel lobby every morning. "Low-budget team," Jack O'Callahan would conclude. "No porters."

They would be 4000 miles from home, trying to learn a new kind of hockey with Brooks pushing them every day and nobody to turn to except themselves.

Certainly not to Herbie. "I'm going to come to the rink, do my job and be gone," Brooks had determined. He would keep his distance and use his assistant, Craig Patrick, as the go-between.

"This is my plan," Brooks had told Patrick. "And this is your role: to keep everyone happy, to be close to the players and solve all their problems. And to tell me when a little thing might be becoming a big thing.

"You're not going to be treated all that well," Brooks told Patrick. "At least not in front of the players. On the ice, it'll be Patrick do this, Patrick do that."

The idea was to get the players to feel that Patrick was virtually one of them, that he had to put up with the same aloofness, the same Drill Instructor's bark that they did.

Patrick accepted all that. The role would not be that unfamiliar, anyway, because Patrick had been one of them just a few months earlier, captain of the U.S. National team that Brooks had brought to Moscow.

He'd been playing the game at their level since the late sixties, when Patrick had been a member of Denver's two National Championship varsities.

He was part of the Patrick clan, which was as close to a royal hockey family as the United States had produced. The patriarch, Lester Patrick, had been involved with the game since the beginning of the century, first as a player, then as guiding hand of the New York Rangers for two decades.

He was the Silver Fox—the face chiseled, the bearing imposing. When the Rangers won their first Stanley Cup in 1928, Patrick, at 45 and well beyond his playing days, had been the hero, coming from behind the bench to tend goal midway through the second game.

His regular there, Lorne Chabot, had been carried off unconscious after a puck had damaged an eye. But the Montreal Maroons refused to let Patrick borrow a replacement from another club.

"Boys," Patrick told his players, "I'm going to play goal. Check as you've never checked before and help protect an old man." The Rangers had rallied around him, and with Patrick batting down whatever got through, managed to win the game in overtime and went on to win the series.

They were the Broadway Blues, the toast of the town in a day when Manhattan stayed awake until dawn. For ten years, the roster remained virtually intact; and until World War II depleted the ranks, the Rangers made the play-offs thirteen times in fourteen years and won two Cups. And for fourteen years Lester Patrick was the man who coached them and ran the franchise as general manager.

His sons, Muzz and Lynn, followed him, each playing for the Rangers, then coaching them. Later, Lynn Patrick would go to Boston as the Bruins' general manager, and finally to St. Louis, where he got their expansion franchise off the ground and into the Stanley Cup final the same year.

Craig was Lynn's son, and the Bruins the club he identified with as a child growing up in Wellesley, an affluent suburb west of Boston.

The Bruins played the game he wanted to play, the professional game, and when he reached high school age, Craig went to Montreal to board with a family there and play hockey Canadian-style.

He wound up attending a Catholic high school ("Even though I wasn't Catholic"), played for a team sponsored by the Montreal Canadiens, and thus, according to a hockey version of *droit du seigneur,* became Canadien property.

He might have stayed in that system and followed the traditional road to the NHL, but the Patricks had always stressed education. Hockey was fine, but there was little money in it and no real security. There was no pressure, or even desire, to have Craig carry on the family tradition, if that was indeed what it was. So Lynn Patrick called up an old friend, Murray Armstrong, the coach at the University of Denver, and Craig headed west, not without reservations.

He had no idea whether WCHA hockey was worth the trouble, and he suspected it probably wasn't. He'd played the game at a pre-professional level in Quebec, and now fretted that he might be frittering away four years on a college varsity that would be better spent in Junior "A."

Instead, Denver University hockey was better than Patrick

had dared hope. The 1968 varsity, which won its final twenty-two games and allowed only one goal in the National Championship tournament, sent eight players to the NHL, a staggering number in an era when the number of collegians in professional hockey had been calculable on one hand.

"This hockey," Patrick came to conclude, "is as good as any hockey anywhere." After graduation, Patrick spent two years in the army, played on two U.S. National teams, then reached a career crossroads. Did he play with the 1972 Olympic team? Or did he try out for the California Golden Seals and go professional?

Once he made the California roster, the Olympics vanished. Patrick spent nine years as a pro, going from California to St. Louis, then to the Minnesota Fighting Saints of the World Hockey Association; and finished up with the NHL's Washington Capitals.

Patrick had retired from the Capitals that year ("There was no great desire for my services") and decided to get one more U.S.A. jacket before looking for a coaching job.

"You know of anything available?" he'd asked Brooks, who'd been his teammate on the 1970 National squad.

"Don't know right now," Brooks told him, "but there might be something with the Olympic team."

When they'd returned to the States after the 1979 Worlds, Brooks had offered Patrick a dual assistantship as coach and general manager. "To improve your résumé," Brooks explained. "This way, you can apply for either coaching or management jobs when this is over."

Patrick would room with Brooks on the road and be privy to anything that was worth knowing. He would be indispensable to Brooks, a sort of alter ego. The praise, the reassurances that Brooks wanted to give his players yet dared not, could be dispensed by Patrick. So Patrick's prime mission was to hang out with the players, to keep their confidence up, to share beers with them and offer a sympathetic ear.

"How'm I doing?" Dave Silk might ask him.

"You really want to know?"

And Patrick would lay it out straight: Herbie thinks your skating's got to get better. But he likes the way you've been working.

The encouragement, especially on grim days, had to come from Patrick, because Brooks wanted to be able to push, yet still remain isolated.

Such was Patrick's role. Brooks would be the martinet. He knew what his players muttered to each other when they saw him approaching: "Here comes the Ayatollah."

It was going to be the loneliest year of his life, away from his family and apart from his team. Brooks had prepared for that, and he wasn't looking for sympathy, but there were times when the role gnawed at him.

This was the hockey team Brooks had always wanted to coach. The players had all the qualities he admired, everything that would have made them marvelous people with whom to drink and gossip.

That was why Brooks treated them somewhat differently than he had his college varsities. He would stand still for a little more back talk in practice, Neal Broten noticed.

And when the day was done, the players would be on their own without having to worry whether Brooks would be checking on them, looking for a report on last night's dissipations.

They had to have room to breathe, to blow off the steam that Brooks would be creating in them daily. "Hell," Brooks would say, "I've been a hockey player. I know their chemistry. They want to work hard, then go out and have a good time."

Brooks had been driving his players since day one at Colorado Springs, turning legs to neoprene, shredding egos, nudging them further. Dave Silk called it "being put through the Herb Brooks machine"—this way the man had of taking and stripping you of everything you'd ever built up and remolding you to his own specifications.

He'd laid it on all at once: the new system with its continual motion, its weaving and regrouping, the conditioning drills, the blank face, the distance and the Herbies, a semi-sadistic series of start-and-stop skating sprints designed to build wind, strengthen leg muscles and test resolve.

Some of the non-Gophers like John Harrington, who'd always responded best to a boot in the backside, gravitated immediately to Brooks. Others, like Silk, were baffled and frustrated.

"I'll show him," Silk finally decided on one of the bad days. "I'll skate till I drop. Then he'll be sorry."

Silk had come out of Boston University with a reputation as a sniper, a natural scorer who played reliable defense and always gave you 100 percent.

"Put him in Boston Garden against New Hampshire," said Jack Parker, "and you'd get two hundred percent."

Silk had planned on going to New Hampshire, a bucolic state school an hour's drive north of Boston, with a strong hockey program. When he heard that, Parker, who'd never gotten a high school prospect that UNH really wanted, all but wrote Silk off.

Then Silk had gone up to Durham to chat with Charlie Holt, the coach there, who was delighted that Silk had signed a letter of intent.

"You know, Dave," Holt told him over ice cream at the campus dairy bar, "up here at U.N.H. we don't have a win-at-all-costs philosophy. If we win, fine. If not, that's okay too."

For Silk, who'd always applied a cutthroat philosophy to his hockey, it was inconceivable that losing could be okay.

"Is that right, Coach?" Silk had replied. Then he finished his ice cream, shook Holt's hand, got into his car, stopped at the first pay phone on the way back to Boston and called Toot Cahoon, one of BU's hockey assistants. "Still got that scholarship?" Silk asked.

He'd thrived at BU right away, scoring thirty-five goals in his first thirty-four games, always pumping himself up highest for the big ones with Boston College, Harvard and UNH at the Easterns. Twice, when BU went to the NCAAs, Silk had ended up on the All-Tournament team. After his sophomore year, the New York Rangers drafted him.

"If you need a guy to get the puck out of your zone late in the game," Parker had told Brooks, "he'll do it for you." Silk prided himself on that, on taking the hit to make the play, on picking up his wing and sticking with him, on getting the big goal, on paying the price.

He'd always worked hard in practice, busting a gut for a thump on the back. So here he was, sprinting down the ice during the first Olympic practice and hearing Brooks shout, "Skate, skate."

"Jesus Christ," Silk thought, turning around. "I *am* skating." He was no Eric Strobel, Silk conceded, and his style wasn't exactly hydraulic. But he got from point A to point B and did what was expected of him.

Yet Brooks, with visions of Russian wings swooping down in overdrive, fretted that Silk might not be fast enough. "I don't know if you can't skate or won't skate," Brooks told him. "But I intend to find out. I'm going to work you every day and you're not going to like it, but it's going to make you better."

After a few weeks of this, with Silk desperate for an encouraging word, he heard someone murmur, "It's getting better." Silk whirled around and saw . . . nobody. He looked again and noticed Brooks skating away, his back turned. Goddam, Silk thought. How do you like that? Silk felt omnipotent then. "Of course," Silk would say, "he got on me again the next day."

If there was consolation to be derived from all this, it was that Brooks was that way to everybody. It didn't matter if he'd recruited you out of high school himself, if you'd played four years for him at the "U" and won him championships. If anything, several Gophers thought, he treats us worse.

That was Brooks' plan, to push his players and challenge them and withhold the praise and push them again. "I admire your talents," he'd told them right off. "And I'll push you because I admire your talents."

But he would not get close to them, and he told them so. As long as they didn't drink in the hotel bar, got in at a reasonable hour and stayed within the laws of the Republic, Brooks would leave them alone off the ice.

"I'm not taking you," Brooks told his team, "to any damn dance."

To get close was to breed favoritism. To breed favoritism was to destroy the team fabric, to risk the regionalism that had undone other U.S. teams, to return to the days of the College All-Stars. To do that was to lose three of five games at Lake Placid and blow the medal round.

So Brooks yelled at Ramsey, his "19-year-old prima donna." He yelled at Verchota because he knew it would build a fire under Verchota and because he'd always yelled at him.

And he yelled at Steve Christoff, who could have signed with the North Stars instead of signing on for this aggravation. "I don't care who your agent is," he told Christoff. "Lou Nanne [the North Stars' general manager] will send you down to the 'I' so quick your head will spin."

The "I" was the International League, the never-never land between amateur and professional hockey that Buzz Schneider and Mike Eruzione had just escaped. Christoff was not going back to the "U." The threat of the "I" was the only scourge Brooks could wield.

Christoff was used to the prodding by now. He'd been a high school All-American at Richfield, a middle-class suburb a few miles southwest of Minneapolis. He'd led Brooks' varsity in scoring for the past two years. The Boston Bruins had considered drafting him in the first round after his sophomore season; when they didn't, the Minnesota North Stars had snatched him up in the second round.

Christoff skated beautifully and shot the puck accurately and hard. He was a natural scorer who'd produce a goal and an assist nearly every game. When he put thirty-goal seasons back to back at the "U," he was the first man to do it in more than twenty years.

Yet Brooks said Christoff hadn't been progressing, that he'd expected more from him. Much was expected of him, possibly because Christoff had expected much of himself.

From the time he was old enough to skate, his only desire had been to play professional hockey. Assigned a paper for a ninth-grade social studies class, Christoff interviewed Walter Bush, the North Stars' president, and his general manager, Wren Blair —and had written about his own future in hockey.

He'd been untouchable as a peewee, literally scoring at will. At Richfield, he scored thirty-nine goals in twenty-one games as a junior; nobody could remember what the record was, so they made that the record.

The next year, with a bad ankle, Christoff scored eight goals in two games against archrivals Edina East and West, and ended up bringing Richfield to within a goal of the state championship.

He was a natural for the "U" and had been lined up for it ever since his junior year, when Brooks had told him he could watch all the Gopher games he wanted. Once there, Christoff quickly made his mark as a man who could play either center or right wing, an interchangeable part that could give any line outstanding versatility.

After Christoff's sophomore season, his teammates voted him Most Valuable Player. But once the North Stars drafted him and the World Hockey Association offered him a contract, Christoff's interest in college hockey—and college—waned.

By most standards, he had a fine junior season, leading the "U" in scoring again, finishing fourth in the league; but even Christoff seemed dissatisfied.

When the Gophers lost that year, critics would blame the goalie or blame Christoff: "Rif wasn't into it tonight." "Rif" was the nickname, short for "Riffraff."

He was intense, saying little but seeming to smolder inside. The eyebrows, heavy and dark, always seemed knitted into a frown, the face done up in a half-scowl.

He always looks pissed off, Bah Harrington thought.

Christoff's great natural talent was his burden. Because he was so skilled and fluid, moves that were ordinarily difficult came rather easily to him. Because he was such an effortless skater, he didn't look as though he were trying when he skated faster than others. When he skated on a par with his opposing number, it looked as if he weren't trying at all.

At the 1978 Sports Festival, Christoff had had a go with Jack O'Callahan. He'd developed a reputation as a good fighter, a man not to be provoked.

He was precisely the kind of player Brooks wanted, which was why Brooks drove Christoff relentlessly. "Christoff, you're playing worse every day," Brooks told him, from Holland to Helsinki. "And right now, you're playing like the middle of next month."

Brooks harped on Eric Strobel, too, but it somehow rolled off Strobel.

Brooks had played for Eric's father, Art Strobel, in his expenses-only days with the Rochester Mustangs, had eaten dinner frequently at the Strobel house when Eric was spraying food from a high chair.

He'd recruited Eric personally, coached him for three years at the "U" and yet felt frustrated by him. Somewhere, Brooks guessed, was potential he just couldn't pull out of Strobel, no matter how much he badgered him. I go easy on him, Brooks thought, and he still floats.

The talent was undeniable, visible the moment you put Strobel on the ice. Nobody in America burned as much raw octane; defenders were left behind as if rooted.

Strobel would float, then kick on the afterburners, blitz in for a goal, then float again. This made for dazzling nights when Strobel would pop in four goals. It also made for puzzling stretches of emptiness, two or three games full of missed connections, pucks whizzing over the crossbar.

Brooks would holler at him, saying he wasn't working hard enough, that he was going through the motions. And Strobel would shrug. What do you want from me? It's just my personality. Hockey comes easy to me.

Teammates called him Breeze and loved to watch him in semi-action, moving slow, mind at ease, off to Sergeant Preston's, his favorite Minneapolis bar, for a few hours of hanging out.

He's our Californian, Jim Craig thought. Strobel came to you from the pages of a teen-idol magazine. Lots of blond hair that poked out of his helmet earholes and flopped against his neck when Strobel was really wheeling.

His nose was unbroken, his face unstitched, his expression unruffled, pleasant, a little distant. If there was another solar system in the vicinity, friends thought, Strobel probably had the charts to it.

Bill Baker, who'd been captain of the Minnesota varsity, was at once baffled and amused by him. The Gophers would be playing down at Madison with 8600 hostiles jeering at them, Herbie jittering like an overwound mainspring, everybody's adrenaline shooting off the scale, Baker's face showing the strain.

And during intermission, in would breeze Strobel, unconcerned and reassuring: "Hey, guuyys, what's the matter? We're only down by threee."

The nonchalance was genuine; three goals were nothing for Strobel. He was a game-breaker; he'd scored four against Colorado College one night, three in an NCAA semifinal. He'd cruise the neutral zone, someone would get him the puck, and in four strides Strobel would be in overdrive, past everybody.

His high school coach at Rochester Mayo likened Strobel to Montreal's Yvan Cournoyer, the fabulous Roadrunner himself. Teammates would tease him about his thighs, which were not unlike small tree trunks; only Eric Heiden, the Olympic speedskater, had larger ones, and Heiden's were measured on some superhuman scale.

Strobel had the good genes, after all. His father had been something of a legend with the minor-league Minneapolis Millers when the Millers were not that far below the National Hockey League, and actually did play for the New York Rangers before he gave it up.

Eric had followed in the same groove; at age 4, he'd been playing cards with the Rochester Mustangs on bus trips to Green Bay. He was the best athlete at Rochester Mayo, and in

1976, the jewel in the biggest recruiting mother lode the "U" had ever found.

Strobel played for Brooks right away as a center, but when Neal Broten arrived a year later, Brooks put Strobel out on the wing. It was irresistible, the thought of all that combustion on the same line. Nobody could stay with them, and Strobel blossomed. He scored thirty goals in forty-four games, but just as the Gophers were preparing to storm Detroit for the NCAAs, Brooks came to him. "Look," he told Strobel, "we need more balance. I'm moving you back to center."

On a different line. It might have bothered him previously, but Strobel had adopted a new credo by then. As a freshman, he'd been in the middle of everything, always getting his hair mussed and his mind blown by the turbulence.

Then a sophomore named T. J. Gorence, who went on to a career with the Philadelphia Flyers, took Strobel aside. "The best place to be," Gorence told him, "is off to the side."

Strobel came to believe it, and adopted this as a philosophy of life in general. Life's little unpredictabilities weren't worth ulcerating over. Herbie could have you centering the first line today and twiddling your thumbs as fourth-line right wing tomorrow.

"Screw it," Strobel decided during his third year on the varsity. "I'm just going to go out and do my own thing." Now, away from the "U," he could sit back and inspect the latest Brooksian experiment with a suitably detached air.

"Too many mind games," Strobel had concluded. "What can you do but sit back and watch Herbie work?"

Brooks wanted maximum effort every night. If anybody still doubted it, they were convinced after the Oslo Waltz. The team had swept through Holland, beating the Dutch National team 8–1 and 11–4. They'd come out of Finland with four victories in six games over nine days, traveling by train from one end of the country to the other.

Now they were wrapping up their Grand Tour with two games in Oslo against the Norwegian National team. The U.S.A.

would be playing Norway for certain at Lake Placid, and Brooks knew the European mentality. Blitz them tonight, he figured, and they'd all but concede you the game in February. "Set the tempo now," Brooks said. "Don't waltz. Let them know we're going to be hell to deal with."

So they went out and waltzed like Arthur Murray while Brooks burned behind the bench. "Hey, if you don't skate tonight, gentlemen," he warned them between periods, "we'll skate after the game."

Aww, the gentlemen thought, it's just one period. We'll skate better in the next one. They did not, and Brooks said it again. Skate now, or skate later.

Still, the Norwegians, the *Norwegians* for godsake, were leading the U.S.A. with only a few minutes left. Finally, Ralph Cox, who could get you the big goal almost on command, tied it up and they got out of it 3–3. Routine.

So the Americans shook hands with their obliging hosts and began skating off to the dressing room. "Wait a minute," Brooks said, pointing to center ice. "Back there."

For Herbies. At first the spectators thought their guests were putting on some sort of skating exhibition, and they cheered. Then, when it became obvious that all this up-and-back was some kind of punishment tour, they booed.

Finally, after everybody had drifted out, the rink workers flicked off the lights and left the crazy Americans skating in the dark.

Buzz Schneider and Mike Ramsey, who were watching from the stands in street clothes because they'd been ejected from the game for fighting, went up to Patrick and asked him whether they ought to get back into uniform and join their teammates.

"Don't worry about it," Patrick told them. "They're going to be done soon." But the Herbies continued, darkness or not. Doc Nagobads, who'd been Brooks' team doctor at the "U," was appalled. "You'll kill those boys," he admonished Brooks. "They have to play again tomorrow."

Finally Brooks called off the Herbies and had the players do loops to unwind and cool down. While they circled, sullen and mutinous, Mark Johnson whacked his stick on the boards, trying to break it and maybe break the tension as well.

Then he whacked it again and the stick did break and Brooks went bonkers. He said he didn't know it was Johnson. It was too dark to see anything much more than shapes.

"If anybody breaks a stick on the boards again," Brooks shouted, "I'll skate you till you die." But it was the lassitude, the cheap confidence, that really angered Brooks. "Here's my credit card," he growled at his players. "Call Kaminsky. Turn pro. But I'm not going to let you embarrass yourselves with a half-hearted effort." There would be no more waltzes. Norway went down 9–0 the next night, and the tempo was set. On one side of the ocean, at least.

5

VISITORS AT HOME

For a month on the Continent they'd been overnight guests with passports and curved sticks, playing their games, drinking their beer, moving on.

It was the end of September now, and the Olympians had settled into transient quarters near Minneapolis. They were home to box scores and burgers, yet they were still aliens in their own rink.

The U.S. team was going to play what passed for its home schedule in the Met Center, the same Met Center that happened to contain the Minnesota North Stars.

So, as a kind of perverse housewarming, a game had been arranged, the first of four in a row with National Hockey League clubs, who were likely to be (a) annoyed by the idea, (b) somewhat unsettled by it, and thus (c) a trifle belligerent.

None of them more than the North Stars, who'd come into the league as an expansion franchise in 1967 and had gained only an uneven acceptance.

Six teams had entered the league that year, doubling its size overnight, and Minnesota was to be the glamour expansion franchise. Some of the new locations seemed haphazardly chosen (Los Angeles, the country's second-biggest market, made sense—but Oakland?), but there was no controversy about Minnesota.

It was natural hockey turf, the sport's most serious American hotbed, where spectators knew icing from offsides. But they also knew quality from mediocrity, and the Minnesotans' discriminating palates soured on the North Stars within a decade.

They were a decent expansion club at first, and in 1971 Minnesota took two play-off games from the champion Canadiens. No expansion team had ever won a Stanley Cup game from an original franchise.

That was the high point—consistent capacity crowds of 15,000, great excitement, pride and support. But by 1978 it had all collapsed. The "No-Stars," as they were derisively called, were mired in last place, their attendance halved.

The ultimate embarrassment involved the team from the other American hockey hotbed. Thirty-five times in a row they went into Boston Garden and were manhandled by the Bruins, who came to regard them as prime chumps. The telling moment had come in 1977 when John Wensink, the Bruins' curly-haired bouncer, skated over to the Minnesota bench and offered to take on all comers. No North Star had moved.

So, drastic measures were in order. Club management hired Lou Nanne—a former Gopher who'd been the sole local hero among Canadian discards on their original team—and gave him a free hand.

Nanne built quickly and shrewdly, helped somewhat when the owners of the moribund Cleveland Barons bought the semi-moribund North Stars and merged the two rosters.

One wag said it was insignificant, since "adding one pile of crap to another pile of crap only produces a larger pile of crap." But Nanne combed the pile for useful elements, found a few serviceable players and traded his spare parts for draft choices.

Beyond that, there was the benefit of finishing last in a system where last drafts first. When Minnesota was locked in a death-or-death duel with Washington for the bottom of the league in 1978, Nanne found ways to get tryout players and semicripples into his lineup.

The North Stars did manage to finish last, and plucked a forward named Bobby Smith, the all-time scorer in the Ontario

junior league. Craig Hartsburg and Tom McCarthy, two more
first-round building blocks, arrived in 1979. By 1980 Minnesota
was a club on the rise, young and talented, eager to reclaim lost
status with its fans.

Now this bunch of college kids was taking up residence, the
American flag wrapped around their shoulders. "They think
you're after their paychecks," Brooks warned them, and it was
true. The North Stars held the professional rights to three
Olympians—Neal Broten, Steve Christoff and Phil Verchota. If
they looked impressive against the men they were drafted to
replace, the Olympians might indeed be drawing NHL salaries
by the spring.

So, the word seeped in during the afternoon before the game
that Herbie's Kids should keep their heads up if they didn't
want them separated from their shoulders. Particularly one
Philip Verchota.

Nothing personal, of course. Just a little matter of turf. The
U.S. Olympic team was no longer in its Hands-Across-the-Sea
mode, playing friendlies with harmless Dutchmen or pacifist
Norwegians.

That became clear thirty-five seconds after the puck was
dropped that night: Verchota was on his back, his two front
teeth dislodged. He'd gone into a corner, and a Minnesota defenseman named Brad Maxwell had gone in with him. The puck
came out, Maxwell and Verchota came out, Maxwell dropped
his gloves, "and," Verchota testified, "he beat the bloody shit
out of me."

"Welcome back to the U.S.A.," thought Jack O'Callahan. The
Met Center fans, disgusted, booed the North Stars ("Yeah, what
about last year?" somebody shouted) and adopted Herbie's Kids
for the rest of the evening. Meanwhile, Verchota's teammates
were mystified.

Incredible, thought Bill Baker. They think Phil's our goon.
Baker, who'd roomed with Verchota for three years at the "U"
(where they were dubbed the Odd Couple), knew how ludicrous that was.

On the ice, Verchota looked like a grenadier on wheels, a

square-jawed, broad-shouldered wing who easily could have played at 220 pounds.

Cal Stoll, the Minnesota football coach, had wanted to put 30 pounds on Verchota and make him an outside linebacker. As it was, at 6–2, 195, he was intimidating enough.

"You'd see this look in Phil's eyes," remembered John Harrington, who'd had to face Verchota at least four times a year in college. "And you'd be afraid to go into the boards with him."

Off the ice, though, Verchota was like a teddy bear on Quaaludes. Once Brooks had put his Olympic team together, former rivals were stunned to discover Verchota's true nature.

He was actually amiable—get Verchota chuckling and it would trigger an avalanche, a cascade of belly laughs, and his living pace was down somewhere around 16 rpm.

"Come onnn, Philll," Mark Johnson would groan, trying to jump-start him. "Let's gooo."

"Aww, leave me aloone," Verchota would grump. "I'm sooo tired."

Verchota had arrived at college mellow, Baker remembered, and grew more laid-back every year. After one of Herbie's cartilage-grinding practices and a substantial dinner, Verchota would flip on the television, flop onto the couch and go inert for the evening.

Baker would come by later, see Verchota lying there and maybe suggest a few beers at Stub and Herb's, a campus hangout.

"Aww, Willie, I'm too tired," Verchota would drawl. "Why pay two dollars for a beer when we've got a whole case here?" So Baker would leave, and when he returned, Verchota would still be supine, watching some program he didn't even like simply because he was too exhausted to change the channel.

At daybreak you could trace Verchota's progress to bed by following the trail of discarded clothes littering the floor— boots, socks, ragged jeans, green army shirt.

After the season Verchota grew a full beard, tied on a bandanna and downshifted even further. He'd go back to Duluth for the summer, get a job painting houses on contract and work out at UMD.

Once, Harrington, who'd played at UMD, lifted weights there for an afternoon alongside Verchota without recognizing him.

"What did you and Phil talk about?" the trainer asked Harrington afterward.

"Phil who?"

"Verchota. That was Phil Verchota."

"In the beard and the bandanna? That guy was Phil Verchota?"

He was always surprising people that way. Although Verchota had been an excellent schoolboy athlete, a state discus champion, a tight end/defensive tackle in football and a rugged hockey center, the grenadier rampant was only game-deep.

What people missed was the intellect: Verchota was a Williams Scholar at the "U" and twice won the hockey team's student-athlete award. Both his parents were teachers, and he himself was inquiring and reflective.

Verchota gave and received a crunching body check as well as anyone, yet the gratuitous violence in the game troubled him. It was unsettling, he said, to find out at 4:00 in the afternoon that somebody you'd never met was planning on taking your head off by 7:31.

"How would you like to be a businessman," he asked, "and go to work eighty or one-hundred days a year knowing at any given time you'd have to fight?"

That was how it would be for a week, anyway, as the Olympians ran an NHL minigauntlet. After mugging Verchota, the North Stars went on to claim the evening 4–2. The next night, in Des Moines, the St. Louis Blues laid on a 9–1 lashing.

The Atlanta Flames made it 6–1 three nights later, and the Washington Capitals closed it out, 5–4. Oh-for-four—not that much more had been expected.

It would not be easy any night, Brooks had told his players. The pros, as he'd told them, were guarding their paychecks.

The minor leaguers, halfway between the NHL and oblivion, knew that scouts were watching both teams from the stands, that judgment was being passed.

So, when the Olympians went next to Portland to play the Maine Mariners, Philadelphia's prime farm club, the Mariners emptied the bench onto them. Somebody belted Jack O'Callahan, and O'Callahan's eye swelled shut before he even left the ice.

O'Callahan shrugged it off. That was his way, and it amused his teammates. He'd be sitting in the dressing room between periods, John Harrington would notice, blithely ignoring a swelling upper lip or a trickle of nasal blood. If you mentioned it, O'Callahan would grin. "Oh, yeah. Had my head down."

He was a bright, hard-nosed Bostonian. Lumps were part of life.

O'Callahan had grown up in the shadow of Bunker Hill with a brother and a sister, not far from the projects. His father worked for Boston Edison. If you grew up in Charlestown, chances were maybe 50–50 you'd either go to college or to jail; and O'Callahan had friends in both places.

He preferred the idea of college, so he went to Boston Latin, the oldest public school in America. By the time he left he'd made All-State in hockey and had put together Ivy-level college board scores.

By Charlestown standards, O'Callahan had begun skating unfashionably late—age 9. He started with a fifteen-dollar pair of Hyde skates whose blades kept breaking because his ankles tilted so badly; but by the time he was a high school senior O'Callahan *was* Boston Latin.

He never left the ice, playing defense beneath a helmet and eyeglasses because he couldn't afford contact lenses. Both Harvard and BU wanted him, and when O'Callahan chose BU, the Latin School headmaster was appalled. "You have to go to Harvard," he told O'Callahan. "You don't understand."

But the financial package was better at BU. The hockey program—two Eastern titles going on four in a row—was better, too. O'Callahan thrived there. By the end of his freshman year he was already something of a team leader. At the NCAAs that year Parker noticed O'Callahan's poise and determination anew in the Minnesota game, how they seemed to grow as the game grew in intensity. "This kid," Parker told himself, "is going to be something."

Parker had always liked Townies, had valued their hunger, their taste for the corners and their charming insouciance about cosmetic injury.

By the time he was graduated, O'Callahan reckoned he was missing three front teeth, a few back molars, maybe a dozen in all. The doctors kept telling him that the scars from nearly 100 facial stitches would fade, but O'Callahan was philosophical about them.

"Some of them came from just growing up in Charlestown," he'd say. "Some of them came from not keeping my head up. And some of them came from keeping my head up and not caring anyway."

O'Callahan was philosophical about most temporal things. When he'd captained Boston University for two years and was, thus, something of a spokesman, he'd provided absolutely un-varnished quotes which, once printed, infuriated partisans up The Avenue at Boston College or over at Harvard.

You never learn, his elders would tell him, after O'Callahan would say that Harvard should be used to losing by now, that they'd been losing all year.

"Yeah," O'Callahan would concede when you brought the image up to him.

I know. The perennial wise guy. What the hell, he figured. If you felt it, you had to say it. You had to be honest. So after home games, the Terriers would be stretched out in personalized director's chairs in their carpeted dressing room with disco music ricocheting off cinder-block walls, and O'Callahan would be telling the Boston sportswriters that BU had better get it together. That they were going to get their heads handed to them, that they hadn't been truly pumped for a game in two weeks. "That's OCee for you," his teammates would say. "Telling it like it is."

O'Callahan delivered it without Novocain and didn't mind taking it the same way. The black eye would fade. The score—U.S. Olympic team 4, Maine 2—was permanent.

Word passed quickly. You could try and mug the college kids, but you were likely to pay for it on the scoreboard. The Maine game was the beginning of something: the Olympians played eight more games in October and won all of them, four by shutouts.

Yet, it was a peculiar way to operate. They were America's team. Their jerseys said so.

But they were aliens in every rink they played. They came back to the St. Paul Civic Center to play the "U," and Robbie McClanahan, who would otherwise have been a senior there wearing the big *M,* thought how strange it was to hear the Minnesota band play the Rouser and to be on the other side, beating the Gophers 8–2.

It was assistant coach Brad Buetow's varsity now, at least until the end of the season. Though Brooks had the option to resume his job, he was thought to be restless, unlikely to return.

It had been "Herb Brooks Appreciation Night" in St. Paul; his departure almost eerily seemed assumed. He was here tonight; he'd be going to Chicago tomorrow with his traveling show—a bit of peripatetic Americana suitable for the Freedom Train and a niche next to the Bill of Rights and the Emancipation Proclamation.

It would be a six-month grind, with more games in fewer days than any team, amateur or professional, had to deal with, and with 80 percent of them on the road.

There was no championship to play for, no standings kept. The Olympians were the Philip Nolan of hockey teams, a club without a league. So Brooks, as he'd done at the "U," devised a theme for each night, a reason why the team had to strap their hats on and get after it.

He drew up a chart with quotas that had to be met: so many

points from games with college teams, so many from the NHL games, so many from the minor leagues. Just so there'd be a measuring rod of some kind. That's Herbie, the Gophers thought.

It was an unrooted, disorienting way to live, but it was even more so if you weren't on the Olympic bus, if you were, instead, on Herb's Taxi.

He'd chosen twenty-six men at Colorado Springs and given them jerseys, but only twenty would dress for a given game. Several would have to watch every night from the stands in civilian clothes; Brooks rotated those, everybody sitting out at least a few times. Others would be sent to the "I" or the Central League to get work, to stay in shape and wait for the phone call or the letter from Brooks that would summon them back.

Beyond that, Brooks had a list of half a dozen collegians— Aaron Broten (Neal's younger brother) and Timmy Harrer at the "U," Bill Whelton at Boston University, Donnie Waddell at Northern Michigan, Dan Lempe at Minnesota-Duluth, Craig Homola at Vermont—whom he reserved the right to call up.

The team had to be formally fluid, Brooks believed. What if he committed now, in October, and found that he'd made a mistake on somebody? What if a player simply didn't play up to expectations, didn't improve the way he'd been projected to? What if someone got himself hurt? Or some college kid came on like gangbusters?

If you wanted a hockey team comprising the best twenty amateur players available, Brooks reasoned, you had to keep the roster open. Anybody might be cut; anybody might be brought in for a look.

But unlike 1960, Brooks continued to promise, nobody would be coming out of the woodwork. Letters would be written and posted.

And if a team member was being sent down to open space, Brooks would have a face-to-face chat with him, explaining everything, promising to stay in touch. So there'd be no rumors, no unnecessary bitterness, no mysteries.

Not that there wouldn't be a Rod Serling touch or two. The day before Halloween, the Olympians found themselves in Flint, home of the Generals. And a man named Mark Wells found himself asking: "Who am I playing for tonight?"

Wells was one of the twenty-six, a tenacious dark-eyed center who'd made the European trip but had been sent down to the "I," the dreaded "I," to stay in shape and stay on call.

Now he'd been a General for a month, unsure of where his loyalties lay this night. So Wells had asked his general manager, who'd asked Brooks. And Brooks had decided that Wells, this night, should be an Olympian.

Brooks liked Wells' tenacity, liked his style. He'd come up the same way Ken Morrow had, growing up in the Detroit area, bypassing the marginal high school hockey program to play Junior "A."

If you were serious about your hockey, Junior "A" was the only viable avenue out of the Detroit area, and for years there wasn't even a league. There was the NHL club (the Red Wings) and its junior team. Period.

For a quarter century, the Red Wings were professional hockey's glamour franchise in the United States. They played in a building called The Olympia on a beautiful boulevard named Grand River, and from 1933 to 1957 the Red Wings won a dozen NHL championships and seven Stanley Cups.

With time, the Olympia, the neighborhood and the Red Wings all deteriorated. Yet Detroit hockey, despite tenuous roots, managed to persist and prosper.

Geography and climate were factors, but more critical was a group of local businessmen who supported the extensive youth programs like benevolent despots—and continued to develop the product which local high schools, devastated by shrinking tax bases and revenues, simply could not handle.

In Massachusetts the teams were the towns—Needham, Arlington, Melrose. In Minnesota they were the towns on the Range—Hibbing, Eveleth, Virginia—and the schools in the cities—St. Paul Johnson, Minneapolis Roosevelt, Duluth East. In

Detroit, though, it was Paddock Pools, Little Caesar's and Adrey Appliances.

They were the junior teams, a natural outgrowth of the Junior Wings, which had been sponsored by the NHL club. If you were a promising teen-age player in and around the city, that was your ambition, to play for the Junior Wings. Both Ken Morrow and Mark Wells had come up that way.

But by the mid-seventies there was a need for something more extensive. Dozens of players were suspended in limbo, too talented for their high school varsities but not good enough to earn one of the twenty spots on the Junior Wings.

So the locals formed the Great Lakes Junior Hockey League and ran it not unlike a Junior "A" league in Canada. There were five teams, six more in a feeder league, administrators, coaches, scouts, an annual draft, a weekly newsletter.

It was the logical progression for amateur programs that began for eight-year-olds and continued through the age groups (peewees, bantams, midgets) well into adolescence. AHAUS, the national amateur hockey organization, ran programs like that in all of the country's hotbeds.

In Minnesota and Massachusetts, high-powered high school programs siphoned off the best players at 14. In Michigan, the schoolboy varsities were little more than token programs. The junior league offered the best road up.

AHAUS provided some money to them, but the sponsors anted up most of the operating cash, paying as much as $20,000 a year for ice time, uniforms, sticks, travel.

A Yugoslav immigrant named Mike Illitch, who'd built a chain of Little Caesar's pizza parlors and would later buy the Red Wings, sponsored one club. Chuck and Bill Robertson, who installed swimming facilities and filtration systems, sponsored Paddock Pools. Mike Adrey, who sponsored a 200-team youth baseball league statewide, had his own hockey club.

The whole concept depended on voluntarism. The coaches were Lansing bankers, school administrators, blue-collar businessmen; all signed on for free.

Every club carried twenty players between ages 16 and 20 with twenty more on its feeder team in the "B" league. Each May, team officials assembled in a hotel and conducted their own NHL-style draft, with the last-place club choosing first.

They would have already scouted the 15- and 16-year-olds at the midget level plus the players in the feeder leagues; the draft would continue until each club had taken forty players.

Everything was funneled toward the five "A" teams, who played two league games a week in local rinks, each team having a road and a home date. By the end of a season every boy would have played at least forty-five league games, plus as many as twenty-five play-off games and exhibitions.

For the 16-year-old from Ecorse or St. Clair Shores who had outgrown his high school program and didn't want to go to Ontario to play in the junior league there, the Great Lakes League was an attractive option.

He could live at home and play good hockey—a lot of it—at no expense and progress toward the NHL, a major college, or both. Scouts from both attended games regularly, so once a year the league alerted them, matched up all its teams and held a college-pro day.

Booklets filled with the vital data—height, weight, birth date, school, academic counselor, grade-point average—were printed and passed out.

In an average year, more than two dozen scholarships might be offered, and players would move on to the big three Michigan hockey schools—the U. of M., Tech and State—or other colleges in the WCHA and the CCHA, the two major Western leagues.

Michigan college hockey had been underrated for years, yet its tradition was unsurpassed. U. of M. had been the ruling dynasty during the early fifties, winning five National titles in six years, and its overall total of seven is the most in NCAA history. Tech, hidden up on the peninsula at Houghton, in the heart of the state's copper country, won three championships, and State grabbed a title as well, in 1966.

For them, college-pro day became what the Eastern Massachusetts schoolboy tournament was for the Boston colleges or
what Minnesota's state championship was to Herb Brooks and
Gus Hendrickson—the most compact and fruitful hunting
grounds imaginable.

Pro scouts found it worthwhile, too. They could take early
notes on a 16-year-old, watch him develop in college, then draft
him after his sophomore year. Morrow was chosen that way. So
was Wells.

You didn't need to overachieve in a low-key varsity program
or play the expatriate in London or Kitchener. You could learn
the game as one of Little Caesar's legions and know you'd be
noticed. It was, Paddock Pools' Chuck Robertson liked to say,
the best of both worlds.

Wells flourished there and developed into a fine center-ice
man, a resolute forechecker who skated well, passed the puck
nicely and had a terrific scoring touch.

At 17, playing for a fifth-place club in a Canadian junior
league, Wells ranked among the league's top ten scorers.
"Then, I got my head beat in," he remembered wryly. "They
wanted to let me know I wasn't going to stay in the top ten."

The University of Michigan had been talking to Wells since
he was 16, but they finally backed off and signed someone else.
"Boy, would I like to have you," said Ron Mason, the coach at
Bowling Green, but he only offered Wells a partial scholarship.
At first, these slights annoyed Wells, then they merely stiffened
his resolve.

"Gotta show this guy I can play," he concluded, then did just
that. His teammates voted him Rookie of the Year after his
freshman season. Wells won the conference scoring title the
next year, went on to pile up 232 points in his four seasons at
Bowling Green and ranked fourth in the nation as a senior, with
eighty-three points.

But after Minnesota had put Bowling Green out of the
NCAAs that year, mainly by shutting down Wells, Brooks had
made a point of calling him by name ("Hello, Mark") in the

handshake line afterward. That had pleased Wells, who thought it might be a point in his favor going out to the trials.

He'd made the team almost solely on his performance at Colorado Springs, surprising everyone; but as soon as they'd gotten back to the States from Norway, Brooks sent Wells down. He'd hurt an ankle over there, and Brooks told him that he needed some work.

At first, Wells had taken it badly. If you don't want me totally, he thought, forget it. The Montreal Canadiens owned his NHL rights; he could sign with them and concentrate on his professional career.

Still, ever since Wells had seen Mark Spitz win seven gold medals at the 1972 Summer Games, the Olympics had been a dream. Brooks had been conciliatory about it, calling him and suggesting that they work it out together; that there was still a good chance for Wells, just no guarantee.

During his month in Flint, there were times when Wells felt completely out of touch, a man in exile. He would frequently call Kaminsky, his lawyer, to find out if he had any chance to return, any chance of another look. Kaminsky tried to reassure him. Brooks was installing his system, drawing impressions, forming conclusions. He was still not set. But Wells felt he was on a different planet.

Is there somebody really watching me? he wondered. Finally, to preserve his sanity, he decided there had to be. Otherwise, how would Herbie know?

Tonight, there'd be no doubt. Still, Wells found himself a stateless person, consigned to his own dressing room, a tiny cubicle that belonged to neither team.

He played well, scoring two goals and setting up another, but how much did it mean? The Olympians had buried Flint, 15–0, the rout mounting so rapidly that Brooks finally told his people to lay off, that there was no need to ruin the franchise, to turn the fans away.

I played fine, Wells told himself afterward, stripping off his uniform in his cubicle. But maybe they couldn't tell. The score was kind of high.

Soon, Brooks and Craig Patrick came by.

"Mark, do you like it here?" Patrick wanted to know.

How am I going to answer this one? Wells wondered. "I like it here because I'm doing very well," Wells said carefully, "but..."

"You're staying here."

On Herbie's big yellow taxi.

6

GREEK GODS
AND MAGIC MEN

Back on the bus it was early November now, and Brooks the psychologist had been studying his experimental group dynamic for several months, looking for the pecking order to emerge, watching how players and roles matched up and pondering how it all might be of use.

Mike Eruzione was his captain. At 25, Eruzione had been only a 50–50 bet to make the team at all, but he'd played well at Colorado Springs and was now a regular left wing.

Bill Cleary, who'd watched Eruzione devastate his Harvard team for four years, told Brooks, "He'll give you that older player." "He'll be a catalyst."

So when the players voted for captain, the ballots were counted and it was Eruzione, some of his teammates, laughing about it later, called it the Idi Amin vote with the result not necessarily reflecting the tally.

Maybe Herbie wanted Eruzione all along, a couple of players mused. Maybe he rigged the election. Brooks denied it flatly, even though he'd done his best to get the point across, choosing Eruzione more often than anybody else for the rotating game captaincy and selecting him particularly for the biggest games.

So Eruzione would perform the traditional captain's role as intermediary, carrying gripes upward and bringing back rationales. But Brooks also made him his confidant, explaining the method to the madness so Eruzione could go back to the team and say, "Hey, it's not as wacky as it seems. There's a reason for all this."

There were other natural leaders, half a dozen of them, that Brooks could use in various ways to stabilize the team, to perk it up, to absorb its collective share of abuse.

Mark Johnson, who was 22 going on 42 if you were measuring maturity, possessed unhurried and dependable rhythms. Brooks thought he'd make a fine metronome up front and had told him so toward the end of the European trip.

He'd summoned Johnson to his hotel room, where Johnson found Brooks sitting on the floor, looking typically inscrutable.

"You're the guy," Brooks told him.

Johnson was puzzled. "I'm the guy to do what?"

"When you go, we're going to go. Just keep doing your thing."

That was all. Johnson left, at once gratified and stunned. "Here I am worrying about just making the team," he thought, "and Herbie throws this curve ball at me."

Back in his room, Brooks wondered for a moment whether he'd done the right thing. "I think," he mused, "I just blew his mind."

But it was true. Johnson *was* the guy, and it seemed foolish to keep him in suspense about his status.

He was "Magic," Magic Johnson, and he could flick on the red light any number of wondrous ways. Dave Silk had coined the nickname, using the Los Angeles Lakers' quicksilver guard as a model, and it had stuck.

"He can make the puck talk," marveled Mike Eruzione, and it was very nearly true. Johnson would glide out for a face-off, the jaw set, the shoulders slightly hunched; and he would see everything unfolding before him.

Intuitively, Johnson sensed motion around him, sensed where his wings were, where the open spaces might be, where the goalie was or wasn't looking.

It was a terrifying thing, Steve Janaszak said, to play Wiscon-

sin and see Johnson skate out for the power play with the
Badger fans chanting and the drums booming.

Here we go again, Janaszak would think. Looking down the
gun. The Badgers would set up their pinball machine around
him, and at its vortex would be Johnson, cruising, sitting, waiting.

"No matter where they moved the puck, you knew it was
going to him," Janaszak would say. "Then . . . bang . . . right in
the top shelf." What made Johnson unstoppable was that he did
it on the fly. Didn't tee it up, just got the puck and shot without
stopping it.

He was voted Wisconsin's most consistent player, but no bal-
lot was necessary. No player in the country produced at the
same level Saturday after Friday after Saturday. Each weekend
Johnson's five points would come, in one form or another.

Once up at Duluth, Bah Harrington had bet an assistant
coach a six-pack of beer that Johnson wouldn't score against his
line.

"The first night he doesn't get a point," Harrington reported.
"So we're all pumped up. The second night he gets three goals
and two assists. Dominates us. You'd shake your head. How does
he do it?"

Johnson had always been irrepressible that way, had always
been able to crank his abilities to whatever level was de-
manded. At age 10 he was skating with a mélange of varsity
players and adult rink-rats in the Sunday games his father was
always organizing.

By 16, he was good enough for the 1976 Olympic team and
actually did play on the squad in its pre-Olympic schedule for
a while as a spare. Forty-five minutes before the plane was to
leave for an exhibition tour of Europe, Johnson heard himself
paged over the high school loudspeaker.

"Pack your bags," his father told him. "You're coming with
us." It was understood that Mark would not be going to Innsbruck and the Games. Hell, he wasn't shaving yet.

He was a fourth-line wing on a team that temporarily needed

one. And he played well enough to earn a permanent spot on the squad. Even the other players agreed with that. But when the team returned to the States with Mark still aboard, Bob Johnson began hearing the murmurs from the stands: "Which one is the coach's kid?"

When the team lost, it became: "No wonder. Guy has his kid on the team."

"Mark doesn't need this," his father decided, and sent him back to Madison Memorial. "Lead your team to the league championship," he told his son. So Mark did.

Memorial ran a record blitz on everyone that winter, winning its twenty-two games by a margin of 209–20. Then, with Johnson pulling them out of a 3–0 hole, Memorial went on to beat Superior in overtime for the state title.

A gifted child, Johnson had performed at a different plateau all season. He set a league scoring record, once popping in five goals in the first period of a 19–0 tattooing of Beloit. He'd scored three more before the coach sat him down with ten minutes to play.

It was a foregone conclusion that Johnson would play for Wisconsin, and a foregone conclusion that he would play right away. Coach's son, Robbie McClanahan figured, the first time Johnson faced Minnesota. Of course he'll play.

His first year, Johnson scored eighty points (then a record for freshmen) on an NCAA champion squad. In 1977–78, he had forty-eight goals (and thirty-eight assists) and made All-America. And, in Johnson's junior year, he rolled up ninety points, made All-America again and was voted College Player of the Year. No one had ever scored 125 goals in his first three years of major college competition; cracks about "the coach's kid" had become obsolete.

Obviously, he would have played anywhere, would have had wings clamoring to be matched with him. Later, whenever Brooks wanted to perk up a slumping forward, he simply put him with Johnson for a few nights of spoon feeding.

The Magic Man had all the good midwestern virtues—team

spirit, a sense of himself, a zest for hard work and a faith that it would pay off. He came over the dasher for his shift and cooled things out nicely, dealing the puck off calmly, creatively, settling down his linemates.

Then, the evening's work done, Johnson would slip back to the hotel for a cheeseburger. He had the Olympic team made from the beginning, though Johnson never thought so.

Brooks had assured Bob Johnson, his old rival, of that. Mark had played on the 1979 World team, broken his wrist in the second game, and it didn't matter. He'd gotten sick at the Sports Festival, and it didn't matter. Not only was Magic Johnson on the team, he was the team. Now he had Brooks telling him so.

Johnson was a self-starter, serious, disciplined, absolutely reliable. He functioned quite nicely without the whip, so Brooks mostly left him alone.

Neal Broten was 19, a *wunderkind* just out of his freshman year, so Brooks paternalistically called him Neal and left him alone, too. With Jim Craig, his goaltender, Brooks was empathetic, even avuncular. And he seemed to go out of his way to avoid alienating Ken Morrow—partly in appreciation of Morrow's critical role in helping recruit the team, partly because it was smart coaching.

Brooks had had a rule at the "U" about facial hair; it was *verboten.* Now he had a rule for his Olympians. But Brooks conveniently believed in the constitutional ban on ex-post-facto rules. No beards unless, of course, you happened to have a beard when you joined the team. Who was the only pre-hirsute Olympian? Ken Morrow.

"If the beard is your personality," Brooks rationalized, "you can have it. The beard is Kenny's personality. The beard *is* Ken Morrow."

Later, when Brooks was fretting about shoulder injuries, he laid down the law: Everybody wears shoulder guards. Get 'em sewn on. I'll be checking. Morrow thought the idea ridiculous and didn't bother. Somehow, Brooks never got around to checking Morrow's shoulder guards.

You didn't have to motivate Kenny Morrow, Brooks realized early on, so he largely let him be. If something was bothering Morrow, his coaches had usually picked up on it, called him aside for a quiet chat and ironed things out.

He was something of a gentle giant off the ice, happy to sit in a corner and drink his beer and be along for the ride. When something amused him, Morrow's face would light up with the most delighted, benevolent grin imaginable. "Look at him," teammates would say. "Kenny's just a big kid."

There were times, sitting at home before a big game, when Morrow would wonder about himself. Why am I here? Am I that talented? But once he climbed into his car, Morrow could sense something change in him, feel the water starting to boil.

Putting on his gear, he'd be transformed, the confidence unshakable now, his appetite for ice time boundless.

At 6-feet-4, 210 pounds, Morrow was easily the team's most imposing defenseman. Jim Craig and Steve Janaszak would peer out from the cage, see Morrow on sentry duty and be enormously comforted.

He looks like a Greek god, Craig thought, with the beard and the calm expression and the aura of control.

You couldn't beat Kenny Morrow, John Harrington decided. Once he gained control of the puck and started moving out of his zone, you could begin backchecking because nobody was taking the puck away.

And if you had the puck, breaking in with a couple of wings, and thought you had gotten by him, Morrow would turn, reach and bust the play up. Nothing flashy, ever. The man simply made the play that had to be made the way the instruction manual said it should be made.

He always seemed to be a level above everybody else, even though Morrow hadn't come from a major hockey hotbed and hadn't gone to a college with a long hockey tradition.

He grew up in downstate Michigan, in Flint, where the high school hockey program was so primitive that Morrow didn't bother going out for it.

Instead, he joined an amateur traveling team that played in

Marquette, in Chicago, in Sault Ste. Marie. It was hockey the way Canadian teen-agers grew up playing it, and by the time he was a senior, Morrow was skating for the Detroit Junior Red Wings and helping them to a national title.

He might have continued on that road—the New York Islanders drafted him a year later, and Morrow could have signed, worked his way up through the farm system and made the NHL that way.

But he was drawn to Bowling Green, a college of 14,000, ninety minutes south of Detroit and not far from Toledo. It had a rural-looking campus, a comfortable atmosphere and a hockey program that was beginning to do something.

Nobody had ever come out of Flint and played college hockey at any major level. At first, Morrow wasn't sure he could make the varsity. Instead, he and Mark Wells, his best friend on the Olympic team, helped Bowling Green become a national power by 1979.

Morrow made All-America that year, the first CCHA player ever chosen, and wound up going to Prague with the U.S. National team for the Worlds.

It was a bizarre experience, Morrow remembered. Someone had been hurt, and Morrow received a call telling him to get on a plane and get himself to Czechoslovakia. He'd walked off the jet at noon, by four o'clock was in uniform against the Russians, and by seven had lost, 9–4. So Morrow had originally been skeptical about the Olympic program.

But when Morrow decided to join, Brooks built his defense around him. Morrow was the personality anchor back there, Brooks thought, the buoyancy factor. When Brooks was looking for someone to partner Mike Ramsey, his ebullient 19-year-old, he chose Morrow, knowing Morrow would slow Ramsey down and back him up.

"Jack," Brooks asked O'Callahan, his hard-nosed Bostonian, "do you know what a whipping boy is?"

O'Callahan nodded.

"Well, you're going to be my whipping boy. Whenever I say

'Jack,' I'll be talking to you. When it's 'OCee,' I'm talking to everybody else."

O'Callahan as lightning rod—it was another way for Brooks to keep in touch yet keep his distance. He wanted a window on his team, but the view would be indirect. Outside of the rink they would not see him, and he preferred not to see them. The pecking order—the "comradeship," as Brooks put it—would have to develop on its own, as the team found its own social rhythms.

After a while, small groups had begun falling together naturally for evening field trips that transcended zip codes and college ties. Eruzione might go out with Baker and Strobel one night, with Christoff and Johnson the next.

If you tended to hang with your linemates, you invariably hung with a dozen faces over a month, because Brooks was always shaking up his lines.

Still, you usually saw entries, two guys that invariably traveled together. Mark Wells and Ken Morrow were like that. They'd played together since their junior days, were roommates in college and felt comfortable with each other. O'Callahan and Silk, old Boston University teammates, were naturals; and you'd usually see Hughes, an old Harvard rival, in their company, too.

Johnson, a Badger, became fast friends with Robbie McClanahan, a Gopher. "Mark Johnson's a hell of a guy," McClanahan found himself admitting to a Madison newspaperman. "I never thought I'd be saying that."

And if you saw Dave Christian, you saw Neal Broten. They lived only a few miles apart up in northwest Minnesota, Christian in Warroad, Broten in Roseau. They also shared a few ideas about pregame meals: McDonald's was just fine.

"Neal's twelve going on nineteen," amused teammates would say. Mike Ramsey was younger by a year, but Broten *looked* younger—cherubic face, hair down over his forehead, eyes all wide. His voice had barely made it to puberty.

"He'd have one beer ('Oh, Christ, a beer') and be goofy," Bah

Harrington said. Out for the night, Broten appeared a younger brother invited to join his older brothers—just this once.

Folks up in Roseau had been watching that scene on hockey rinks for years: Broten as a third-grader had played evenly, or more than evenly, with sixth-graders.

He was a 98-pound high school freshman on a state tournament varsity, already circled in recruiters' programs as a wonderchild. As a sophomore, Broten once killed off a two-man penalty without an opponent ever touching the puck. As a senior, he was the best player in the state, far and away. There were magnificent hockey instincts there, made exceptional by Broten's sheer speed.

Only Eric Strobel could match him stride for stride, and when Broten arrived at the "U," Brooks moved Strobel out on a wing and put the two together.

Brooks, who rarely puffed his freshmen, said that Broten was the smartest hockey player to come to Minnesota in 20 years and immediately put him at the point on his power play. "There's nothing I can teach this kid," Brooks told intimates.

Broten rolled up more than 70 points in his first year at the "U," breaking a record for assists that had stood for a quarter-century. When the Gophers beat North Dakota for the national championship that year, it was Broten who potted the winning goal. Yet he was aware of his place, the younger brother among Bakers and McClanahans and Janaszaks, the varsity's elder statesmen. "All I did was keep my mouth shut and take my shifts," he said.

He'd never be an elder statesman at the "U," not if the Minnesota North Stars had anything to do with it. They'd taken him in the second round of the 1979 draft and saw him as the prototype of the homegrown player that had become central to Lou Nanne's rebuilding plan.

But Broten thought he needed more time to develop strength and savvy. He'd play for the Olympic team, then go back to the "U" and play with his brother Aaron, his old Roseau High linemate, who was going to be a freshman. Then he'd see what happened.

Brooks had made him no commitment in Olympic terms, yet there quickly was no question that Broten not only would make the team, but would be the second-line center behind Mark Johnson.

He'd been the dominant player at the Sports Festival, scoring four goals on Jim Craig in half a game. Wings who'd been centers loved to play with him because it was a challenge to keep up with Broten and a delight to receive the passes he'd craft. Nobody moved the puck with quite as much imagination and verve as Neal.

He was always "Neal," to everybody, Brooks included. Older players with good professional futures themselves had a special reserve of admiration for his abilities and, more, his potential. If he's this good now . . . what will he be like at twenty-three?

His talent and his approach to his work were still in the uncomplicated stage. "Nothing bothers him," Johnson had observed. "Absolutely nothing. Other guys get uptight before a game. Neal puts the skates on, and there he goes, a hundred-five miles an hour. Like he's skating on one of those outdoor rinks up in Roseau."

For Broten, the Olympic year and all these trips to Chicago and Houston and Calgary were a magic mystery tour, complete with expense money for steaks or, more likely, Quarter-Pounders with Cheese.

It was that way for all of them, courtesy of the schedule-maker. The Olympians had played one home game in October, facing the Canadian National team on the fourteenth. They played another on November 4 against the Birmingham minor-league team, then didn't see the Met again for two weeks.

It was Houston on the seventh, Birmingham on the eighth, wake-up calls in strange hotel rooms, early flights, sullen opponents, noncommittal spectators.

So there were times, in Eveleth on a Saturday night or in Flint on a Tuesday, when it was a good thing to "get regional," to follow Mark Pavelich to Tuna's Bar or ask Kenny Morrow where to find a decent pregame restaurant.

When the team found itself in Boston on a Friday night before a game at Harvard, Eruzione brought a bunch of his comrades home for a typically massive Italian meal, with a dozen different things bubbling on the stove and every kind of pasta known to man.

"We ate in his mom's bedroom," marveled Eric Strobel. "They moved the bed out and put in a big table. And we all chowed down. Must have been fifty people in there."

Most of them Eruziones. They sat there for a couple of hours, everybody shouting, laughing, eating, introducing each other and eating some more. And in the middle of it was Michael, completely at home, his expression saying that it was all perfectly normal. Even the jet screech.

They were in Winthrop, a beach town that juts out of Boston like an appendix. The wide-bodies leave Logan Airport for San Francisco and Rome and pass directly overhead roughly ten seconds after take-off, rattling windows and drowning conversation.

Residents shrug and accept the jets the way they accept working two jobs to pay bills and the northeast wind.

The Eruziones lived in the middle layer at 274 Bowdoin Street, sandwiched between clans of cousins. "If I didn't like what my mother was cooking," Michael remembered, "I'd go upstairs and eat in my aunt's house."

No problem there. There was always something simmering on the back burner, always something clean to wear. Eugene Eruzione juggled three jobs to take care of that: a day shift at Watertown Arsenal; nights hustling drinks and pizzas at Santarpio's Restaurant at the mouth of the tunnel in East Boston; weekends as a welder.

You didn't depend on the government. And you didn't tell Eugene Eruzione that you wanted an allowance. "You like having money in your pocket?" he told his six children. "Go work for it."

There were other unwritten house rules. If you join something, stick with it. Respect authority. And be happy, because you're not going to be rich.

Mike Eruzione slept in a room with three siblings and bought his first baseball glove with S&H Green Stamps. Competitiveness came naturally to him.

The yard behind the three-decker was the neighborhood playground and Fenway Park, all in one. If a tree branch blocked a foul line, the tree branch was sacrificed.

"We cut the apple tree down because you couldn't tell if it was a home run or not," Eruzione would say. "That's the way we were. We used to play block ball. Saw a baseball bat in half and pitch baby blocks. Or play curtain-rod hockey in the house. Once we brought up all the storm windows to make it more realistic, and I checked one of my cousins right through the glass. Twelve stitches in his elbow."

Hockey, ice hockey, was merely something Eruzione did to pass winter afternoons. As an 8-year-old he'd borrowed a sister's white figure skates and gone down to the golf course at the end of the street to skate on frozen sand traps.

He'd skate for four or five hours, then have his grandmother thaw out his feet in the oven. Winthrop had no indoor rink. To play peewee hockey, you went to Revere or East Boston and paid fifty cents to skate in a league with 12-year-olds.

Winthrop High didn't have a varsity until the sixties. They played their games in Lynn Arena, a rink left over from World War II in a North Shore city left over from the Industrial Revolution.

Several games would be played concurrently, the teams alternating periods, which suited Winthrop's varsity well. It had only one serious line and Eruzione centered it.

He was a peppy, irrepressible skater, cruising, darting in quickly, punching in goals out of a scramble, living up to his name. Eruzione, after all, meant "eruption" in Italian. Busting in from nowhere, like Bugs Bunny popping into a cartoon frame, was his specialty.

He liked playing ten minutes of a twelve-minute period, catching his breath in the dressing room, then going out and doing it again. Eruzione wanted to be depended upon, wanted to play the position that could decide a game.

In baseball season he was the pitcher and shortstop. During the fall, he played safety. If the bases were loaded, Eruzione wanted to be up at the plate. If his team was losing 6–0 in the closing moments of a football game, he wanted to be running back the punt.

He had everything coaches say they want in an athlete—drive, resiliency, discipline, team loyalty and an instinct for the big play. Eruzione's teams won conference titles, qualified for the state tournament. He easily made the All-Scholastic squad.

Yet the only college to show interest was Merrimack, a small Division 2 power on the North Shore that specialized in rooting out the overlooked player on a championship team.

Eruzione would have given anything to go to the University of New Hampshire, but Charlie Holt, the coach there, wasn't interested. (Later, after Eruzione had tormented UNH for four years as an opponent, Holt would institute the "Mike Eruzione Rule," i.e., if someone wants to come to New Hampshire badly enough, you take him.)

Boston College, which never recruited anybody *but* Americans, wasn't interested either, nor was Northeastern, even though they hadn't won anything in years.

What's wrong with me? Eruzione wondered. I always thought people looked for good athletes, he mused. I said, "Hey, I'll work hard. I'll kill penalties."

Maybe they'd missed him in the shuffle. Winthrop had lasted only one game in the tournament that year. Maybe the recruiters wanted another look.

Eruzione went to a Maine prep school called Berwick Academy, in the hope of getting the second look, but, still, a year later nobody but Merrimack cared. So he sent in his $250 deposit and went off to play in the summer leagues like everyone else.

There were several leagues like that, pseudo-formal arrangements where college players, schoolboy wonders and overripe amateurs could stay in shape, try a faster track or recreate bygone moments.

One night when Eruzione scored half a dozen goals in a typical 15–7 all-skate, Jack Parker, then a BU assistant coach, happened to be calling the lines and noticed him.

An intermediary was dispatched. If Eruzione was interested in Division 1 hockey, at least one Division 1 school was interested in him.

Eruzione laughed. "Come on," he told the intermediary, "cut the crap."

"No, Jackie's really interested."

So Eruzione put on a sport coat and went over to Commonwealth Avenue to meet Parker. A few months later he was sitting inside BU's arena, an unknown recruit watching the varsity run through a practice. You can't make this team, Eruzione told himself.

Until he did, he'd have to provide his own skates. Team rule. He bought some red Hyde Jelineks, because they were fifty dollars and Eruzione could afford that. Then he came to practice thinking, These guys are going to laugh at me.

Nobody laughed, and Eruzione made the team. He never was BU's most gifted skater or best shooter, but things happened when Eruzione was out there. Goals were scored when none seemed likely, gears were shifted, momentum reversed.

Years later, Parker would remember the Eastern finals that year—and the game with Harvard when his only two penalty killers were whistled off to serve simultaneous penalties late in a close game.

"I'm looking down the bench and everybody's staring straight ahead," Parker would say. "Everyone knew I was in trouble."

The only player looking at him was Eruzione, the freshman, with his typical "I'll-go, I'll-go" expression.

He was dying to get out there, Parker realized. So he sent Eruzione over the dasher to kill the penalties. Harvard failed to score, and BU won another title.

What he brought to a team was intangible, which is why Eruzione never made All-America, never was named Most Val-

uable Player in the ECAC tournament in a day when BU owned
it.

Instead, the hockey writers annually named him New England's best defensive forward. "A sympathy trophy," Eruzione
guessed. "Well, we've got to give him *something.*"

The National Hockey League, which had never been enam-
ored of eastern college kids with mere intangibles, barely gave
him a glance. So Eruzione went off to hockey's version of Merrimack, the International Hockey League, and the Toledo Goal-
diggers.

The "I" was lunch-bucket, button-your-chin-strap hockey. To
survive and prosper in Toledo, you kept your head up and got
durable. Just possibly, an NHL scout would notice you on a
Wednesday night in Saginaw. More likely, you compared the
welts and scars against your bank book after a few years and
decided to make a living somewhere else.

There was one other choice. Since the "I" was technically an
amateur league, you could still try out for the Olympic team
when the cycle came around. By the summer of 1979, after two
years of ducking swinging sticks and stray elbows, Eruzione
decided it was the only real option left to him.

The best shot he had at the NHL had vanished the year
before when the New York Rangers let go general manager
John Ferguson, who'd liked Eruzione's street instincts and enthusiasm. Ferguson had invited Eruzione to the Rangers' training camp in 1977 and he'd done well. Still, the Rangers' scouts
couldn't agree on his future, and the word came down—Try a
year in Toledo. Ferguson also threw an extra $1,000 Eruzione's
way—in exchange for giving the Rangers an option on his services.

Even though he had a fine season at Toledo, the only reward
was an invitation to the Colorado Rockies' camp. Yet somehow,
even the worst team in the NHL had no room; and it was on
to the Philadelphia Firebirds, in the AHL, for a short stay, then
back to Toledo.

By the summer of 1979, the "I" promised Eruzione little

more than another winter of keeping his head up. So he was down to two options, an assistant's job at BU under Parker or the Olympic team. "If I don't try out," Eruzione told Parker, "I'll never forgive myself."

Brooks, like Parker, had valued Eruzione's intangibles. And the same qualities that had gotten Eruzione on the team—his discipline, his maturity and perspective, his eagerness to skate himself into the floor—had gotten him the captaincy.

Brooks would land on him from time to time, just as he landed on everybody else.

"I'm going to send you back to Port Huron."

"It's Toledo, Herb."

"Whatever."

He wore the captain's *C,* and he had Brooks' ear; but to his mates Eruzione was more of a comrade in arms, their man Rizzo who'd seen it all. "He'd been through all the battles and all the wars," Bobby Suter said of him, "and he never got upset."

Eating dinner with three or four dozen people, the decibel level up there with the jet-screech, was standard procedure for him. The midwesterners thought it was a terrific socio-cultural evening. Mrs. Eruzione had even insisted upon washing Bill Baker's dirty laundry. All this Boston stuff they found intriguing, particularly if you got the Bostonians hanging together.

"Go out with Pavelich or Verchota," said Mark Johnson, "and you'd have to take charge. Go out with O'Callahan or Silk, and they'd take charge."

Particularly in the big cities. "OCee" would turn up for the evening in shades and a turned-up collar, ready to do a disco, maybe three or four discos. "Hollywood's here," teammates would proclaim.

Jack Hughes and Dave Silk would be alongside, and if Silk noticed that O'Callahan's collar had drooped he'd stop him: "OCee, your collar's wrong." And turn it back up, Charlestown-style.

When they were on the town, time and money tended to lose

meaning. Once, Strobel had joined O'Callahan, Hughes and Silk
at Sergeant Preston's, his favorite Minneapolis hangout. They
sat over beer from two in the afternoon until five. Strobel left
for an hour, returned at six, then left to watch a hockey game.
"I came back at eleven," Strobel would say, amazed, "and they
were still there. They must have spent three or four hundred
dollars."

On the road, the Boston guys might troop out to a golf course
and rent electric carts as a matter of course. "They'd drop fifty
or sixty bucks and think nothing of it," said Bill Baker. "They
spent a lot of cash. More than us."

The Boston guys delighted in defying convention, in astonish-
ing friends and bystanders. Most of the team lived in an apartment complex in Burnsville, south of Minneapolis and a good
forty-five-minute drive from the airport in morning traffic.

Their plane would be scheduled for 8:00 A.M. At 7:20, Bah
Harrington and Mark Pavelich would walk down the hall,
packed and ready; peer in and see O'Callahan, Hughes and Silk
still sacked out.

Yet, at 7:59, the Bostonians would amble down the jetway,
boarding passes in hand, relaxed and fully alert. "How'd you
guys get here?" Harrington would ask, mystified.

"Well," Silk would reply, "we just drove."

Driving with "Hollywood," Hughes and Silkie meant twenty
minutes at eighty miles an hour: twenty minutes of median
strips and shoulders, twenty minutes of craziness on Highway
13 in Craig Patrick's station wagon. Everybody rode with them
—once.

"Holy Christ, guys," Schneider would yelp, his hands grip-
ping the dashboard as O'Callahan did his Formula One number.

"Please," Gayle Schneider begged him, "don't go with those
guys."

The Boston guys were terrific guides in any town with a
subway and a 4:00 A.M. closing time. They were not much good
at all in a soybean field or in the middle of a frozen lake.

So they came to have an appreciation for the Minnesotans in

that regard, particularly for Bill Baker, who embodied the good pioneer values.

He'd been a regular defenseman at Minnesota all four years and made All-America as a senior, and if you were looking for a Gopher straight from Central Casting, it was Baker.

He was rangy, quiet and intense, with blond hair and sea-water eyes. In the summer, when Baker let the hair grow, he looked not unlike Vitas Gerulaitis, the tennis player, but a six-foot-two, 205-pound Gerulaitis. If Leif Ericson was somewhat of a Viking god, then you could easily picture him looking like Bill Baker.

He'd be reserved in a crowd, keeping fairly much to himself; but in a group of three, Baker was marvelous company, a fine running mate. Everybody, said Jim Craig, wanted to be Billy Baker's friend.

In the dressing room, he was a *de facto* team leader, going about his work with a sort of calm obsession, winding himself more and more tightly as game-time approached. He came from the Range, but after four years at the "U" he knew every Gopher by heart. If you wanted a sense of what the Minnesota guys were thinking, Jack O'Callahan said, you listened to what Baker was saying.

He was very bright, an automatic admission to almost any college in the country, but Baker also had the Range ethic. It was no surprise that every major hockey-playing school in America sent him a letter.

He'd visited Harvard and was intrigued by it, but the "U" pulled at Baker hard. "I lived and died for getting those envelopes from Herb with the big Minnesota 'M' on them," he remembered. "You'd come home from school on the day of a game and see the envelope and it would pump you right up."

It was an honor, Baker believed, to be recruited by the "U." Once Brooks said publicly that he wanted Bill Baker, that Bill Baker was a natural Gopher, it was beyond doubt.

Everything he wanted in a university Baker could have in Minneapolis: a good dental school and a terrific hockey program filled with working-class kids just like him. The school was near enough to Grand Rapids that his parents could drive down after work on Fridays and watch him play.

That had been as important as anything else. The Bakers were a close family, spending their weekends together hunting and fishing. Actually, Bill's mother had taught his father how to hunt; on Sundays both parents, and Bill and his sisters, would pack up their gear and go out in search of trout and bass.

The catch would be a nice supplement to the family freezer, because money had never been in lavish supply around the Baker household. His father ran an ice business, managed an apartment complex, sold used cars and did shift work at a local paper mill to make ends meet.

If something broke, the Bakers fixed it themselves. If they wanted a cabin, they built it from the ground up. A four-year scholarship to the "U," and the possibility of dental school beyond that ("It's such a sound business," Baker had reasoned), was a dream come true.

He'd postponed dental school to play for the Olympic team, but he still managed to squeeze in some outdoor life. On days off or after practice, Baker would take a teammate or two and go off in search of fish and/or game.

Once Mike Eruzione tagged along on an ice-fishing expedition. "He shows up in a Windbreaker and a U.S.A. hat," Baker, appalled, would relate. "No gloves, no boots, nothing. 'I'll be all right,' he says."

Every rod-and-gun trip with these characters, Baker came to realize, was semi-manic. He'd taken Schneider and Mike Ramsey out hunting pheasant, then realized he had one partner who couldn't tell a rooster from a hen and another who could barely tell one end of the gun from the other. And these were Minnesotans, fellow Gophers.

They'd come upon a flock of pheasant in a soybean field, and Ramsey, in his eagerness, began running towards them without his gun. "Bird up," Baker shouted, and the pheasant passed over Ramsey's head while he was frantically jamming shells in —backwards.

There were more than a dozen birds there, Baker figured. Somebody's got to hit something. Presently, Schneider, his adrenaline pumping, fired and watched a bird fall.

"Hey, Buzzie, you shot a hen," called Baker, who'd gone over to inspect. Hunters are not supposed to shoot hens, says the law. "Oh, Jesus, Willie, what'd I do," Schneider moaned. So Baker stuffed the bird in a pocket and they'd moved quickly on.

So much for cross-cultural phenomena. But it was making for exactly the kind of comradeship, as Brooks called it, that he'd wanted.

Such adventures were impromptu by nature when the team was back in Minnesota. On the road, with the players crammed into the same bus and quartered in one hotel, a binding instinct took hold. When they returned to home base for a few days of regular practices and relaxed hours, the Olympians scattered randomly.

Though most did live in Burnsville, the rest were off in a variety of arrangements. Eruzione and Ralph Cox shared a place; some of the local Minnesotans, happy to have the option, decided to live at home and save the money.

Jim Craig was a Bostonian, but wanted to save the money. His mother had passed away not long before and his father had been unemployed. So Craig moved in with Doc Nagobads, who'd just retired as team physician at the "U" and was handling that job for the Olympic team.

Craig came from a family of eight, of whom three were still at home with his father. He liked that atmosphere, and missed it, so living with the Nagobads solved several problems at once. He could retain a family feeling and still send money home.

He was used to bunk beds and close quarters and lots of faces around the dinner table. But in a way, that had also made Craig something of a loner. He liked being around his teammates, yet something in him wanted to be off by itself. "When you're one of eight," Craig would say, "you want to find a little spot where nobody bothers you."

He played the loner's position, out there alone in the cage, the mask covering his face, absolutely nobody to talk to. Forwards and defensemen could come off the bench, work their shift and return to the bench for advice, reinforcement, thumps on the back. Craig, a chatterer by nature, was isolated out there with his ice shavings. So he kept up a steady stream of talk with his defensemen.

If you came back into the U.S.A. zone to retrieve the puck, you picked up Craig's voice at the top of the face-off circles, warning you, directing you, yelling encouragement, admonitions, corrections.

The problem, as some teammates saw it, was that the stream rarely ended. Off the ice, Craig would still be chattering. At Boston University, where there'd been a rough and easy camaraderie on those championship teams, the retort had been simple, at once humorous and serious: "Hey, Jimmy. Shut up."

But the Olympians, who hadn't known Craig nearly so long, weren't sure what to tell him. Brooks, a loner by design, empathized with Craig. He's misunderstood, Brooks thought. But he means well. Jimmy always means well.

Brooks had believed in him ever since the World Championships in Moscow the previous spring, where Craig had performed beautifully on short notice.

The Americans had been beaten by Canada and tied by Finland in the preliminary round. Advancement to the medal round, with the Czechs on the horizon, seemed doubtful.

So Brooks, looking to give his first-string goalie, Jim Warden, a rest before the final five games, tapped Craig for the Czech game. "Don't feel bad," Brooks told him, "if they score ten."

Instead, Craig had held the Czech sharpshooters at bay, the U.S.A. had managed a 2–2 tie and Craig's spot on the Olympic team had been assured.

He'd gone to Colorado Springs with a bad hand, the stitches newly removed from a gash, and had been shelled for half a dozen goals in half a game. It made no difference; he was Brooks' man.

Any time the Americans had ever done anything in the Olympics, Brooks knew, their goaltender had been the difference—Willard Ikola in 1956, with a silver, Jack McCartan for the gold medal in 1960, Lefty Curran, the silver in 1972. So he wanted Craig feeling secure and confident, and went out of his way to forge a close relationship with him.

Craig missed his family—his father particularly—and he quickly came to have that kind of attachment to Brooks. He'd sit up front on the team bus and listen to Brooks theorize, pumping him for ideas. Brooks had given him a book, *The World's Greatest Salesman,* and Craig had all but memorized it.

He'd always craved feedback from his coaches, always come around looking to chat, looking for ways to improve. He developed a strong and useful relationship with Warren Strelow, the team's rotund goalkeeper coach, whom Brooks had personally selected with the intent of providing Craig with professional individual coaching. Recognition had always come slowly to Craig, when it had come at all.

He'd been a superior goaltender for his high school back in Easton, an old mill town in southeastern Massachusetts not too far from Boston. Craig had played fifty-seven games there, and his team had won fifty-three, yet he never made the All-Scholastic team. Oliver Ames won most of its games by seven or eight goals, the reasoning went. Craig saw maybe half a dozen tough shots a game. How could you judge him?

Holy Cross had noticed him, but Craig's college board scores fell short. So he went up to Norwich, a military college in Vermont, and decided in one day it wasn't for him.

He'd wound up at Massasoit Junior College, hoping to play there for a semester or so and then transfer to a Division 1 school. BU had found him there, expressed interest, but said there'd be no guarantee of a scholarship.

Jack Parker already had one goaltender in Brian Durocher. He was wooing a second, an All-Scholastic from Weymouth named Mark Holden. If Holden went to BU, Parker would have used up his available scholarships.

"I've seen Durocher," Craig told him. "And I've seen Holden.

And I'm going to be your goaltender."

Parker had raised an eyebrow. He's a lit-tle bit cocky, he thought, but very shortly, Craig was his goaltender. Holden had decided to go to Brown, and Durocher had lost his first four games.

So Parker started Craig in the fifth game. Craig lost it, but didn't lose another all year. BU won the Easterns again, and Craig became Durocher's co-equal. They shared the job the next year, and Craig played in the NCAA finals and beat Boston College. By the winter of 1979 the job was his, and he made All-America.

Now, his position on the Olympic team assured in advance, Craig found himself at a crossroads. The Atlanta Flames had drafted him several years before and seemed eager to sign him. Even if they sent him to the minors, it probably meant $22,000 a year, and he could send some of that home.

Instead, after some soul searching, Craig had opted for the Olympic team and the delayed payoff. He clicked with Brooks right away; thought he was a terrific coach with fascinating ideas.

Except for the psychological test.

Most team members, particularly those who'd played for Brooks in college, cocked an eyebrow ("That's Herbie") and filled them out. Some, like Mike Ramsey, took it as a Byzantine joke. "You know me," Ramsey told his roommates, handing over his half-completed questionnaire. "Just put down whatever you think I would."

Others, like Dave Silk, were worried about it. "I've always had a reputation for being a little bit twisted," Silk mused. "What if I fill this thing out and it shows that I secretly want to kill my coach?"

So Silk stuffed his questionnaire in a suitcase and figured he'd say it was in the mail if Brooks ever asked. But Craig refused to take it at all.

"It's got nothing to do with hockey," he told Brooks. "It's a lot of bull, psychology."

"Well, here's the reasons why I think it's valuable," Brooks replied. "Here's what it might show."

"Nahh," Craig decided. "I'm not taking that test."

"Fine, you don't have to," Brooks said. "You just did."

"I did?"

"And you flunked."

Craig decided to take the test.

So he was on the team and, by choice, on his own. Not that it was unusual. After three months, the sense of comradeship that Brooks was looking for was still embryonic, the team socially splintered any number of ways. It took Bill Baker's birthday party to bring them all together.

Thanksgiving had come and gone. December promised three weeks on the road and uncertainty beyond that. Baker had a mess of game from successful forays into Minneapolis-area soybean fields.

"The eastern guys might like a taste of pheasant," he guessed. So the function room at the Burnsville apartment complex had been reserved. Baker had done up the pheasants; Gayle Schneider, Buzzy's wife, had fixed a turkey. There was wild rice, birthday cake, a punch concocted by Jack O'Callahan and Jack Hughes, and only a few dozen more beers than necessary.

Around one in the morning, the soiree began unraveling. Mark Pavelich, who normally wouldn't say boo to a goose, began flinging pheasant bones. Cake began adorning the walls. Then Bobby Suter, who had his freshly broken ankle in a cast and was looking for a release valve, began pouring beer onto Mike Eruzione. Pavelich joined him.

Moments later, Baker watched Eruzione storm out of the room. His favorite disco shirt was a mess, his hair plastered down so damply that you could see his bald spot. I've never seen him this mad, Baker thought.

"Rizzie, calm down," Schneider told Eruzione, barely able to keep a straight face. "It's just a party."

But Eruzione was beyond mollifying. He'd brought his girl friend, ostensibly to impress her with the *savoir-faire* of his comrades. Now he was gluey with cake and drenched with beer.

"I don't need to put up with this aggravation," he told Schneider. Then he took his girl friend by the arm. "C'mon Donna," Eruzione said. "We're outta here."

Next morning, the caretaker had been livid. There was a wedding party scheduled for the room that night, and the place was still littered with half-eaten chunks of bird, gobbets of rice, smears of frosting. It smelled like Milwaukee on a wet day.

So Baker and friends ordered up another keg of beer and had a clean-up party. And when Eruzione arrived at the dressing room for practice, he received the full falsetto chorus: "We're outta heah Donnah, we're outta heah Donnah."

It became a rallying cry. Something for the boys to organize around, home or away.

7

A CLOUSEAU CHRISTMAS

He never knew who . . . or what . . . hit him. Bobby Suter had been playing his best game of the year, had just crossed the Canadian blue line and was winding up for a slapshot. Then someone thumped him, Suter's skate snagged in a crack and he fell heavily.

Later, when the doctor came in with the X rays confirming the break, Mark Johnson would remember the expression on Suter's face—disgust, disappointment, anxiety all blended.

"The tough kid from the East Side," one Madison newspaper had called Suter, a bouncy fireplug with shaggy blond hair who enjoyed disturbing the peace. Lenin would have loved him. Agitation was Suter's specialty: an elbow in your short ribs, a stick across your ankles, a quick sapper attack . . . then gone.

"Skate up from behind, whack you and skate away smiling," Mike Eruzione would say. It was the wide-open grin and the eyes, bugging out from beneath the mop of corn silk, that were the warning signals.

Steve Janaszak called it Suter's "Don't-mess-with-me-I'm-crazy look," and everybody around the WCHA had seen it a dozen times. A weekend with Wisconsin was grim enough, having to deal with all those howling candy-striped fans and a whirling Mark Johnson.

But the package also included 120 minutes of Suter japing

you, always getting in the last elbow, the last punch, the last word. Especially against Minnesota.

"Who are those 'Sutter' brothers?" a mispronouncing Brooks had wondered after a double dose of Bobby and his older sibling John, and Suter had loved that.

He'd relished annoying Herbie's big wings at the "U," savored disrupting somebody as fine-tuned as Robbie McClanahan and messing up his game.

Something about seeing the jerseys with the splay-legged *M* and Brooks pacing the bench would set Suter off. "Every time we played the Gophers I went whacko," he would admit. "It was win, and win at any cost. I probably cheap-shotted every one of them."

There was something of the Dickensian street child in Suter, who could have been the Artful Dodger's impish right-hand man. At Wisconsin he easily set a record for penalty minutes, 377 in four years, the equivalent of sitting out more than six full games.

One night against North Dakota's frontier bruisers, Suter spent fifty minutes of a sixty-minute game in the box.

Two nights before selections were made, Kaminsky took Suter for a postgame snack.

"Bob, I gotta be honest with you," he told him. "I don't think you have a chance in hell to make this club. You can't just go all over sticking Minnesota players left and right."

Suter grinned sheepishly and muttered something about that's how he played. Kaminsky shrugged his shoulders and said that they would just have to see what happened. He wasn't optimistic.

Suter had not been one of the original twenty defensemen invited to the Sports Festival. But when Notre Dame's Jeff Brownschidle opted out, Brooks took into consideration the fact that he did score 16 goals the previous season for Wisconsin and invited the scrappy defenseman.

So Suter turned up at Colorado Springs—and went a little wacko. Displaying his usual aggressive, chippy style, he piled up tons of penalties, seemingly taking special delight at chopping away at the Gopher players.

Yet Suter had made the team because he had two virtues Brooks valued most: a bucketful of East Side working-class gumption, and flying skates.

None of Brooks' defensemen rushed the puck quite like Suter, who came busting out of his zone with legs pumping, found somebody open or blasted the puck himself. One night against Denver, he'd had a hand in seven goals, setting up four in one period alone.

Later, after they'd played alongside Suter for a while, Gophers like McClanahan and Steve Christoff decided they'd underestimated him. It was marvelous fun to have a Badger-wacko on your side, to wind him up and watch him jap somebody else for a change.

Added to a bunch of defensemen who were mostly tall, rangy and silent, Suter provided a nice trace of volatility, a sprinkle of cayenne.

"There's a devil in him someplace," Brooks realized. "He'll smile, but something's lurking back there that wants to explode." Suter was just crazy enough to believe that the ankle would heal in a couple of months, that he could go back to Madison and see Doc Clancy, lace on a skate with a cast inside and be back on the ice in two weeks.

"I don't want you going off and saying it's done," Brooks told Suter, knowing he wouldn't. "You're going to come back and you're going to play. I'll give you my word, you'll be able to pick up where you left off."

Meanwhile, Brooks had some patching—and juggling—to do. To fill the hole on the roster, he called up Donnie Waddell from the taxi squad. Waddell was an affable defenseman from Detroit and Northern Michigan University who'd been well on his way to making the team at Colorado Springs when he slid violently into the end boards and broke his ankle.

But unlike Suter, he never came back to full strength. It was a perversely capricious quirk of timing. Break a bone in July, you lose out. Break it in November, and you can still go for gold.

Still, Brooks was dissatisfied with the team's puck movement out of its own end, which was crucial to his grand plan. If you couldn't break out of your own zone, all the weaving and swirling meant nothing.

All of Brooks' defensemen were adequate skaters (some more than adequate) and good stickhandlers, but none had the speed and quick release that marked the Bobby Orrs, the Denis Potvins, the Larry Robinsons—master defenders of the modern age.

But one of his forwards did—Dave Christian. Brooks liked Christian's unique passing ability, his mobility, and above all, the hockey sense that gave Christian an innate feel for the game. The club had plenty of that at center with Mark Johnson, Mark Pavelich and Neal Broten. If Brooks could shift some of that to the blue line, he reasoned, the offense would hum.

Christian had played some defense in high school back in Warroad. At North Dakota, he'd manned the point on the power play. Brooks had toyed with the idea of moving Christian back there even before Suter's injury. Now, with a critical pre-Christmas tournament only two weeks off, Brooks decided to experiment.

So, for the game against the Adirondack Red Wings eleven days into December, Brooks put Christian back at defense, then let Craig Patrick run the bench and went upstairs to watch from the stands.

"He touched the puck," Brooks would recall, "and it was bang-bang-bang. And I said, 'That's it.' "

"Herb," Jimmy Craig concurred after the game, "there's our guy."

If you were going to start a hockey team from scratch, Craig thought, Dave Christian would be the cornerstone, the first man you'd pick. Other Olympians had more raw speed, a better shot, purer defensive skills. But none of them matched Christian in versatility.

He'd played for a small high school in northwestern Min-

nesota that couldn't put much more than two forward lines and
four defensemen on the ice. So Christian routinely logged between thirty-five and forty minutes of playing time in a forty-
five-minute game, simply switching back to defense when he
grew tired.

In college he'd skated his regular turn at center, then gone
back to the point for power plays. Brooks had used him at right
wing; when he'd mentioned defense as yet another possibility,
Christian had shrugged. As long as he was playing . . .

The hunger for ice time, the hockey sense, the quickness and
mobility were genetic. "Every move he makes," mused the
coach at Roseau, the next town over from Warroad, "you say,
'There goes Billy Christian all over again.' "

If the Patricks were the royal family of American professional
hockey, the Christians were their amateur counterparts. One of
Dave's uncles, Gordon Christian, had won a silver medal as a
wing on the 1956 Olympic team. His father Billy and uncle
Roger had been linemates for the 1960 squad that had beaten
the Russians at Squaw Valley.

The gold medal had been put in a glass case and placed on
the coffee table at home, but beyond that there'd been little
mention of 1960 around the Christian house. Dave Christian
read about it on his own, how his father had scored the winning
goal against the Russians with barely five minutes to play, how
Roger had scored four against the Czechs in the gold-medal
game the next morning, three of them in the decisive third
period.

The brothers played together again on the 1964 team, then
returned to Warroad, formed their own hockey stick company
and kept playing—back with the amateur Warroad Lakers now,
traveling through Manitoba.

Warroad might have been a Canadian town; you can drive to
the border in less time than it takes to reach either Roseau or
Williams, the nearest Minnesota outposts. It had been a Chip-
pewa village in the nineteenth century, perched next to the
Lake of the Woods, the gateway to the wild rice fields that the

Sioux wanted badly enough to fight a war over.

The Sioux, who were prairie dwellers, would invade
canoe, coming up the Red and Roseau rivers. The village v
situated along their war road. Thus the name.

To reach Warroad from the east, you come through Baudet
which bills itself as the walleye capital of the world ("Home
Willie Walleye"). If you drive west from International F
along Route 11, the road passes so close to the border that y
can glance out the window across the Rainy River and see t
Maple Leaf flying.

Route 11 is a crumpled two-lane blacktop ribbon thread
through unchanging farmland. Every two miles looks like t
last two miles; except for having to pull out every ten minu
or so to blow by a lumber truck, a motorist can pass an afterno
without seeing a soul.

Roughly every twenty miles a town rises up out of the fl
—a main street with hardware store, gas station, tavern, din
a few smaller arteries running off it—then disappears. Willia
follows Baudette along "11," Warroad follows Williams.

The town is working-class. The stick factory and Marvin W
dows sit at opposite sides of State Street. American flags li
East Lake Street. There is no daily newspaper; most folks g
the Grand Forks *Herald.* For recreation they fish (night cra
ers, minnows and leeches are available almost everywhere) a
they play hockey, using Christian Brothers sticks.

Dave Christian began skating as a toddler, learning his
ther's game on the frozen river ice behind his house. By 15
was already living up to the legacy, the dominant player on
team as a sophomore.

Brooks, who'd played with the Christians on the 1964 U
squad, wanted David for the "U" and offered him a thre
quarters scholarship.

But Christian, who felt he deserved a full ride, had gone
instead to North Dakota, where his uncle Gordon had played
the fifties. The program, after the glory years of the sixties, w
on its way back from a mid-seventies slump. The geography w

better, too. Minneapolis was a stark six-hour drive downstate from Warroad. Grand Forks was two hours southwest.

The league, schedule, itinerary and level of play was the same, and Christian developed quickly there. After a fair freshman year, he scored twenty-two goals as a sophomore (two of them beat Minnesota in the season finale and gave North Dakota the WCHA championship), got himself drafted in the second round by the Winnipeg Jets and reached a crossroads. He was Billy Christian's son, and an Olympic year was on the horizon. There was no doubt Dave Christian would try out for the team.

Beyond that, he was unsure. If he played well at Lake Placid, the Jets would be likely to offer a contract. Would he take it? Or go back to school for two years?

Christian decided he'd worry about it later. Nothing much ruffled him. You'd see Christian hanging out with Neal Broten, his old rival from Roseau, and they seemed like two kids at play. Or up to mischief. Christian might not say much, but teammates knew better. If the desk clerk rang your room at 3:00 A.M., it was assumed that "Koho" had put in the call.

Robbie McClanahan claimed credit for the nickname. Koho was a brand of Finnish hockey stick, perhaps the Christian Brothers' prime rival. So, "Koho" it was, and several players professed to be in awe of him. Brooks had given Christian no guarantees, but nobody thought any were necessary. He was going to play . . . somewhere.

With one move, Brooks had changed all the odds. For the defensemen, who didn't worry so much about the four-line, left-right-center Rubik's Cube possibilities, Christian's arrival among them was easy to assess. "There goes one spot," Mike Ramsey concluded.

For the forwards, it merely beclouded things further. It was terrific news for the centers—unless, of course, Brooks decided to change one of his former centers from a wing back to center. If he did that, it was terrific news for wings.

What there was little enough of at the moment, was any news

at all. The Christmas tournament at Lake Placid, their international dress rehearsal, was less than a week away now and the
tension was growing. The Games themselves were two months
off, the time getting closer when Brooks would be making decisions on people, forming reasonably permanent lines.

Or, worse, if he was dissatisfied, he might be dipping into his
taxi squad and posting letters.

So when the squad got to Lake Placid and settled in for a
couple of weeks, he sat down with each player individually and
gave an unvarnished assessment of status and potential.

He'd done it once before, just after the twenty-six names had
been announced at Colorado Springs during the summer. Now
the evaluation had more of an edge to it. If I were picking the
team tomorrow, Brooks would begin . . .

You'd be on it, he told his Bakers, Morrows, Craigs, Johnsons,
McClanahans. You can still lose it. But if you keep doing what
you've been doing, you're on.

You're borderline, he told his Harringtons, his Hugheses, his
Coxes. Right now you're my fourteenth forward, my seventh
defenseman. You've got to keep working hard. We'll see.

No promises. The only constants were the system, Herbie's
whistle and uncertainty. The bodies, in a whirl of red, blue,
green, yellow and black jerseys, were mixed and remixed daily
as Brooks experimented with a seemingly infinite number of
combinations.

"Herbie's lines were like those Chinese sticks," Phil Verchota
would say. "Throw 'em up in the air and see how they come
down."

Brooks would enter the dressing room before a game and
remake the lines on the spot: Neal, you play with Strobel and
Eruzione tonight. Christoff, you're with Verchota and Silk.
Pavelich—you guys stay the same.

"You guys" meant Buzz Schneider and John Harrington,
Pavelich's colleagues from the Iron Range. "Nobody can play
with you and Harrington anyway," Brooks was fond of telling
Pavelich.

So it became a litany. Everybody else would mix and match, but it was Youguysstaythesame. They did complement each other in an uncanny way, Brooks had observed, both on and off the ice.

Pavelich and Harrington had played alongside each other at Duluth and had brought UMD up out of the ruck that season. For two years they'd skated on different lines; the previous winter, in fact, they'd scuffled one day in practice.

Pavelich, a darting, elusive center, was always deking and diving. Harrington was always chasing him all over the ice, grabbing for him. Finally Pavelich had popped, told Harrington he was tired of having a stick in his face and began swinging.

A week later, coach Gus Hendrickson had put them together. Hell, he figured, nobody else could play with Pavelich anyway. "We have a system," Hendrickson liked to say. "And Pav just kind of plays."

That style was perfect for Harrington, who'd developed his own sort of rhythm. He was a scrappy, hard-nosed right wing, a drifter who'd go for the puck if he thought he had even a 40 percent chance of getting it.

"I'm in better condition than anybody else," Harrington reasoned. "I'll get back." His stamina, grit and gambler's instincts made him a fine penalty killer.

Once, at UMD, Harrington had scored two shorthanded goals against Michigan on the same shift and would have had a third if he hadn't been tripped from behind. Together, Pavelich and Harrington made for a shinny symphony, hockey by the seat of one's pants.

Their system, Harrington said, was "See ya at the other end of the rink." It was unorthodox, Harrington admitted, but they would always get down there somehow. They'd scramble all over the ice, move the puck around like a billiard ball, but they *would* get down there.

Pavelich came from Eveleth, Harrington from Virginia, four miles apart on the Iron Range. They'd played against each other in high school, but where Pavelich had gone straight to UMD,

Harrington had opted for the Air Force Academy.

His tenure there had been the briefest possible: one day to determine he despised it, a second day to be processed out. Colorado College, the other school in town, wouldn't let him transfer.

Nobody else had really recruited him, so Harrington turned up at UMD. His parents, thinking of that lovely, free four-year Academy education up the flue, frowned.

"Well, I want to play," Harrington told them. "I'll go to UMD and that's the way it's going to be." He'd walked on there, and Hendrickson promised Harrington a scholarship if he made the varsity. He'd gotten himself on, had a decent freshman season, then tore shoulder ligaments the next fall.

"The highlight of my junior year," Harrington would relate, "was being asked back after my sophomore year." Hendrickson played Harrington on his "hustle line" that season, using him to bog down opponents' scoring lines and to kill penalties.

But when Hendrickson matched him with Pavelich the following year, both players prospered. They scored sixty goals between them, finished third and fourth in the WCHA scoring table and pushed UMD to its best season ever. Yet they had gone undrafted in previous years, so no NHL club was watching either with any particular interest. So, even though he was a free agent, Harrington had gone to Colorado Springs with absolutely nothing guaranteed.

"You're an average player," Brooks told him. "An average stickhandler, an average skater. Average. The only reason you're here is because you work so hard."

Harrington was spunky and inventive, a true Ranger on the ice, a nonstop talker off it. If Pavelich was laconic, Calvin Coolidge's Minnesota grandson, Harrington more than made up for him.

There's always excitement around him, Mark Johnson noticed, and it was not coincidental. Harrington loved japing people, finding out their sensitive areas and deftly inserting a needle.

Then he'd stand there with his hands in his pockets, Jim Craig would say, with his short hair and his choirboy look. "Who, me?"

"Don't tell me about Davey Christian being a shit disturber," Phil Verchota would say. "Bah's no better."

Nobody called him John. He came from a family of six where nicknames were applied along with diapers—T.P., Tootie, Mugs. One brother, ten months older than Harrington, couldn't pronounce "Baby." So John became "Bah" and it stuck.

At first, Harrington hated the nickname and the confusion it caused. "This is Bah Harrington." "Oh, hi, Bob." Finally, after reading his name that way in newspaper stories, Harrington had reconciled himself to it.

He became the line's official spokesman, almost by default. Schneider, after all, was an inconsistent talker—sometimes a mile a minute; other times, complete silence—and Pavelich never said anything.

"I didn't know if he couldn't talk," Brooks would say later, "or wouldn't talk." Watching Pavelich dodge newspapermen on the way to the team bus was like watching a gerbil negotiate a maze. "No, that's okay," he'd mumble, deking and diving. "Thanks, but I've got to go."

Pavelich was happiest when he was playing his guitar or off by himself fishing on the North Shore. Trout were unlikely to ask impertinent questions. An hour spent with him in the corner of a bar generally produced half a dozen empty beer bottles, four semismiles and two monosyllables.

Taped interviews were futile—How did you record a nod? His philosophy, as expressed once to a Minneapolis sports writer, was uncomplicated: There's no pressure on the ice, but a lot of anxiety off it.

So Pavelich stayed on it as long as he could. He'd been the all-time rink-rat ever since his Eveleth days when he'd skate the varsity practice, then work out with the "B" team, go home for dinner, then go outdoors and skate again.

That much never changed. When Pavelich went off to Duluth to college, Hendrickson would pass by an outdoor rink and see him cruising along it, all alone and completely content.

That was his game, skating and stickhandling and passing. Shooting was something Pavelich did when there was no other alternative. Making the play was his passion, and his passes, Schneider said, came right from the heart. Pavelich's greatest strength came from his smallish stature. Much like a downhill skier in a severe tuck, his five feet and seven inches was even more compressed when he skated. The result was an incredibly low center of gravity that made Pavelich almost impossible to knock off the puck—or to move out of the corners. So he possessed terrific puck control, a key element in the Brooks grand plan.

He was a natural center, the eyes moving, skates flashing, always finding you and putting the puck square on your stick. Diagrammed plays eluded him. "Buzzie, I'll get it there," Pavelich would assure Schneider. "Don't worry about it."

If linemates were sometimes left without warning, opponents were befuddled. Pavelich would come wheeling in, the stick whipping left, right, left. Sometimes he'd fake a defender in, then out, then back in—and collide with him because the defender would still be going for the first fake.

"Why don't you just fake him in, out, then go to the net?" Hendrickson would ask him. Pavelich would shrug. "Gus, I don't know. I just play."

The better the opponent, the bigger the challenge, the harder Pavelich pushed himself. A mediocre team brought a mediocre response from him, left him uninspired.

Nobody went through the motions like Pav did when he wasn't into it, Harrington said. The boredom was that obvious. But when the game was critical, you could see the excitement in his eyes. Pavelich would begin chattering about it, dreaming up his plan of attack.

Otherwise, he left the game alone. Pavelich literally could not sit through one as a spectator, and except for an admiration for Bobby Orr, did not follow the NHL. The idea of playing for the U.S. Olympic team had never intrigued Pavelich; he only went to Colorado Springs because friends, family and coaches badgered him into it.

Once there, he'd come late to practice or not show up at all. "Pav," said Hendrickson, who was coaching the Minnesota team in the Sports Festival, "don't you want to play?"

Pavelich had shrugged. "I don't care."

He'd stayed with it, though; and now, four months later, Pavelich and Harrington were still free-forming it, still managing somehow to meet each other at the other end of the ice.

Once there, it was Schneider who cashed their check, Schneider who put the puck away. He was the lone holdover from Innsbruck, the man who'd played on four guaranteed-quixotic U.S. National teams all the way back to 1974.

If the Russians knew any American player, they knew Schneider, who'd played against them a dozen times and usually tweaked their noses.

The first time, in 1975, he'd burned Tretiak for the hat trick. Nothing magical about it, Schneider had concluded. He'd simply been circling, looking for the puck. When it came, he'd leveled it on net as always. "Piece of cake," he'd tell you, winking.

Schneider had always had the slapshot, and Brooks had honed his skating at the "U," making him wear a leaded vest. Schneider was durable, reliable, tough-minded. Yet professional clubs kept passing on him.

Schneider had had a chance to go with the Pittsburgh Penguins after the 1976 Games, but there had been a management snaggle and he'd gone to camp without a contract. He had a five-game trial with Birmingham of the World Hockey Association, but never played another game in the pros.

The next year found him in Hampton, Virginia, in the Southern League, then back with the U.S. National team. By the end of 1977, Schneider was playing with Milwaukee in the International League, the same "I" whither Brooks was always threatening to ship Steve Christoff and to which he actually had consigned Mark Wells.

Mike Eruzione, a former U.S. National teammate, was with Toledo then. One night, playing Milwaukee, he felt himself being hooked from behind. It was Schneider, newly made a defenseman and mystified by it.

"Buzzy," Eruzione said, "what the hell are you doing?"

"Rizzie, I don't know what I'm doing."

Afterward, they'd sat down over beer. "When are we getting out of here, Buzzy?" Eruzione wondered.

"Any time," Schneider said. "Let me know. We'll pack our bags and go together. We'll go play for Herbie."

There were nights when Schneider told himself he was crazy. He was half a dozen years out of college, married and still kicking around in the minors. A couple of times Schneider did throw it in and hang up the skates for a while. But he always came back.

By 1979 he was at another crossroads. A West German team was offering him a $30,000 contract, an apartment and a car. Brooks was offering him another U.S.A. jacket.

"Herb, I don't know what to do," Schneider had said.

"Buzz," Brooks had replied, "let's take a walk."

If he played well at the Olympics, it could only up the ante if Schneider wanted to go back to Europe. The NHL might even notice. A last hurrah with Rizzo, Schneider mused. Another feather in your cap. Why not?

After four years of bouncing among four leagues, it would be good to be back with Brooks, the man who'd gotten him out of Babbitt. Schneider had been a gifted schoolboy athlete there—the Babbitt Rabbit. He'd played quarterback and safety, kicked field goals for the football team—and handled third base well enough to earn a tryout with the Kansas City Royals.

For college, he'd looked at Denver, at North Dakota (where his father had played) and at the "U," where Brooks had just arrived. Herbie had recruited him sight unseen; Schneider was honored. How could you turn down the "U"?

Now, he was a Conehead. A married, mature, 25-year-old Conehead. That was the line's nickname, the Coneheads. Pavelich thought Schneider had coined it. Schneider and Harrington credited authorship to Pavelich, who was always watching *Saturday Night Live* and loved the Coneheads, extraterrestrials with skulls like MX missiles who spoke a bizarre form of computerese and told the curious that they came from France.

On Herbie's team, Pavelich's line were the extraterrestrials. "We were the idiots," Harrington mused. Brooks would be working the power play in practice, rotating everybody around, but somehow Pavelich & Co. would end up as alien beings at the far end of the rink, as much a part of the proceedings as the cones, "those orange pylons," said Schneider, "that just stand there and do nothing."

"Man, we could be doing anything down here," Pavelich realized one day, after a typical half-hour's quarantine. "We're just a bunch of Coneheads."

Yet Brooks did keep them together, and finally Harrington decided it was a good sign. Brooks did seem intrigued by them. He'd send the Coneheads over the dasher and something would happen. They'd get down the ice somehow, Harrington would muck around in the corner and poke the puck out to Pavelich, who'd get it to Schneider for a 25-foot blast.

If the team scored seven goals, the Coneheads always had the two you couldn't quite remember afterward. But they always seemed to have two. So the Pavelich line stayed together while Brooks fiddled elsewhere.

The Christmas tournament would be the prime testing ground for the players and a crucible for the system, for Brooks' sophisticated pond hockey.

They'd been playing the system for more than three months now, listening to the skeptical comments from scouts and hockey insiders ("What the hell are you guys doing?"), but Brooks thought it was all beginning to come together.

There was some cohesion now, some intuitive sense of the weave and the motion, all of it bolstered by the conditioning base. And it was showing up in the results. The 1976 team had lost to almost as many college teams as it had beaten. This team had waxed every varsity it played.

The Central League teams had been confounded by the system. "I hate that European style of hockey," an Oklahoma City player named Alex Pirus had said after his mates lost to Herbie's maddeningly elusive kids. "They're always weaving and doubling back to keep possession, and you never get to touch the puck."

The CHL was one of two prime minor leagues for the NHL. Compared with the other, the American league, it was more for kids on the way up than veterans on the way down. The talent was decent and the skating fast; several CHL clubs were possibly as good as the poorer NHL squads.

So people began taking notice when the Olympians faced off against League champion Salt Lake City, which was loaded with high drafts, mostly graduates of Canadian Junior hockey.

Lou Nanne had helped arrange that, lobbying the CHL board of governors to agree to an eighteen-game schedule with the Olympians (two games with each club), with the results counting in the CHL standings.

So the games were for money and the special incentive of sticking it to a bunch of pampered college kids; each CHL team couldn't wait to pounce.

Instead, the pouncers became the pouncees. Salt Lake fell 7–5. Then Indianapolis 1–0, in a brilliant hockey game. Next, Birmingham 5–2. By January, the Olympians had blitzed the League, winning twelve of fourteen and tying one. Then, having proved the point decisively, they eased off a bit as Brooks experimented and substituted liberally. Still, the final tally was 14–3–1, an .805 percentage; few, if any, NHL clubs would have fared better. Added to the 4–2 victory over AHL champion Maine, it made the Olympians the *de facto* minor-league champions of 1980.

But the Swedes, Russians and Czechs would not be confounded that way. They had seen this hockey for decades; no surprises for them. So if the U.S.A. did well at the Christmas tournament, Brooks would cast his die and stick with the system. If not, there was still time to go back to something more comfortable, more traditional.

Not that he'd be getting a terribly realistic perception. If Lake Placid in December was a dress rehearsal, it was an off-Broadway production.

Everybody else's stars would be in Moscow for the annual Izvestia Tournament. See a score from Moscow—U.S.S.R. 6, Finland 3—and you had something of a morning line on the Olympics. The understudies were sent to Lake Placid to check out the accommodations and Herbie's Kids.

Run a finger down the Russian roster—Efstifeev, Bystrov, Kabanov, Tivmenev—and you didn't see a familiar name. Only the Americans and Canadians had sent the varsity. If we don't win this, thought Jack O'Callahan, we might as well go home at the end of January.

Yet, other U.S. Olympic teams had been embarrassed by European junior varsities, which weren't that far behind the big squad. At least four or five of the Swedish and Czech skaters in Lake Placid had previously played with their National "A" teams.

So the Americans approached the Christmas tournament as if it were already February, because in most respects, it was February. The uniforms, building, anthems and playing styles were the same, now and then. They even had gold medals on hand.

Except that this was Christmas season and the team was penned up in a Holiday Inn on a hill overlooking the village. "We've got to get a tree," Robbie McClanahan and Mark Johnson decided.

They found one and decorated it and gave it an honored spot in their motel room. Then it vanished, and McClanahan ("We paid good money for that tree") went wild. The Gophers, remembering how McClanahan had been at the "U," loved it.

"That's Ricky," they said. Mark Johnson and Bobby Suter had administered the nickname because McClanahan reminded them of an old Badger teammate named Craig Norwich.

Norwich had been a meticulous sort, careful about his clothes and his appearance. He was a wealthy kid from Edina with brains, good looks and All-American hockey ability. They'd dubbed him "Ricky," thinking perhaps of Ricky Nelson or maybe taking it from Richard, Norwich's middle name. McClanahan, cut from similar cloth, struck them the same way, so McClanahan was "Ricky," too.

Everything had to be perfect with him, teammates said. Bah Harrington had been amazed at McClanahan's stick ritual, how he'd line up half a dozen new ones before a game and go over them with everything short of a micrometer, cutting off the tops, smoothing down the burrs, taping the knob just so.

Once, when McClanahan had his back turned, Harrington had filched an armful of his sticks and hidden them, just to watch McClanahan flip out.

His Minnesota teammates had been doing that for four years. McClanahan came out of North Oaks, a tony residential section a few miles north of St. Paul. So they called him a rich kid and ribbed him about his Calvin Kleins. They knew McClanahan's parents had moved there twenty-five years earlier, before the prices had spiraled, knew McClanahan wasn't all that much better off than they were. But he was good-looking, bright, with broad intellectual interests, drawing most of his close friends from pre-law and pre-med, not from the rink or the weight room.

Teammates loved to see his reactions, knew he'd always rise to the bait. McClanahan would come in and fix his sticks and they'd jap him about it. He'd fold his clothes and they'd jap him about that. He kept a Tupperware container handy for his false front tooth, and they japped him some more.

McClanahan called his fetishes "preparation." Teammates called them compulsion. Recruiting him, Brooks was exasperated by McClanahan's obsession with every little detail. Finally, Brooks realized it was a virtue, that it was much of what made McClanahan a fine hockey player.

On the ice, he was a tireless worker, a technical perfectionist, the best two-way collegiate player in the country. Brooks used him on the power play, tapped him to kill penalties. McClanahan could outskate everybody save Neal Broten and Eric Strobel, and he had a fierce discipline and resolve. His biggest weakness the first two years at the "U" was scoring. He just didn't seem to have the knack. So he worked hard at it, shooting hundreds of pucks a day. By December he had become the team's second leading scorer.

Twice his teammates at the "U" voted him their most determined player—first one in the locker room (the stick ritual, after all, took time), last one off the ice.

So it was no surprise that he and Mark Johnson were natural linemates and companions. They shared many of the same qualities and interests. But McClanahan took one trait just a bit further. You just didn't mess with McClanahan's sticks or his yuletide fantasies.

The disappearing tree was nothing less than a crime against the Christmas spirit, the players agreed solemnly. Better get Inspector Clouseau on the case.

There were several prime suspects. Brooks, of course, was one. What wouldn't the Ayatollah stoop to during the sacred holiday season? Neal Broten was another. Someone had seen the tree in Mike Eruzione's room, so he was a likely perpetrator. Dave Christian, he of the bogus 3:00 A.M. wake-up call, had to be on the list. It would have been easy for him to trick the desk clerk into giving him a key to McClanahan and Johnson's room.

So every day for a week, new clues appeared on the dressing-room blackboard. The tree had last been seen at 9:30 A.M. The stand had been seen cast onto the ice on Mirror Lake. Bill Baker reported having seen the tree pass through his room. A trail of tinsel led to Eruzione.

All relevant information was passed on for Clouseau to digest. Then, after a week, a new twist developed. A tree, similar in size and shape to the missing one, had been seen floating ominously in the lake itself, its top branches bobbing.

McClanahan had flipped out afresh when he saw that. "Kept

us amused for two weeks," Baker would say. Meanwhile, out on the arena ice, the Americans were running Europe's understudies ragged. They'd knocked off the Swedes by two goals with a late flurry, Strobel, Harrington and Eruzione scoring bap-bap-bap in a span of seven minutes.

They'd spotted Canada an early goal, then shut them down, 3–1. They'd blanked the Czechs, 3–0. Then they'd waited for the Russians. To break the tedium, Harrington, Eruzione and Dave Silk had been lying around a motel room, spouting Brooksisms—the thoughts of Chairman Herb, aphorisms he'd been laying on them for so many weeks now that they knew them by heart.

"You know," Silk mused, "we should get a notebook and write some of these things down." So Harrington ducked out and bought a spiral notebook and a ball-point pen. "Brooksisms," he inscribed. "As told by Coach Herb Brooks of the 1980 U.S. Olympic Hockey Team and retold by John Harrington, Dave Silk and Mike Eruzione."

To wit:

- If you want to play this game effectively, you'd better report with a hard hat and a lunch pail. If not, you better watch some old guys ice fishing.
- Fool me once, shame on you. Fool me twice, shame on me.
- Let's be idealistic, but let's also be practical.
- You guys looked like a monkey screwing a football out there.
- Don't dump the puck in. That went out with short pants.
- In front of the net, it's bloody-nose alley.
- Throw the puck in and weave, weave, weave. But don't just weave for the sake of weaving.
- Go up to the tiger, spit in his eye, then shoot him.
- We went to the well again and the water was colder and the water was deeper.
- Gentlemen, you don't have enough talent to win on talent alone.

- You can't be common, because the common man goes nowhere. You have to be uncommon.
- We were damned if we did and damned if we didn't.
- For lack of a better phrase . . .

Harrington stuffed the notebook into his hockey bag. From then on, whenever Brooks would unveil a new aphorism, Harrington, Silk and Eruzione would catch each other's glance. And after the game they'd ask Harrington, "Did you get that one in there?"

It was all part of the lore, which was now growing daily. Since they'd returned from Europe at the end of September, the team had been reading about itself in morning newspapers in Salt Lake City, Buffalo and points between, whenever they stopped by for their one-night stand.

The assessments generally followed a theme: They're our boys and we're proud of them, but don't expect too much. Maybe a bronze medal. Terrific kids, though.

Now they were at Placid, and the Russians had sent a second-string club to deal with them. It irked the Americans a bit, Eruzione would admit, and made them want to send a message back to Moscow that this was not your basic, haphazard "B" pool U.S.A. team; that if you wanted to beat us, you sent your best. Maybe you blitzed us, but you had to respect us enough to at least send Mikhailov, Tretiak and Maltsev.

What the Russians had sent seemed little better than a select junior team. The Swedes beat them. The Czechs beat them. And very quickly, the Americans were beating them, 2–0.

But it wasn't going to be quite that easy. Within eight minutes, the Russians tied up the game, then went ahead. The night was in doubt until the final fourteen minutes, when Johnson banged in a rebound and Strobel streaked in for another goal half a minute later. Finally, the Magic Man had flung the puck into an empty Soviet net in the final few seconds and it was 5–3.

So the Americans were champions of the dress rehearsal. Someone named Walter Wasservogel from the International

Hockey Federation draped gold medals around their necks.
They stood for the Anthem. Then, half a dozen of the stars
trooped off to a press conference.

They were the Undergraduates. Underage and Underrated.
Fourteen of them were 22 or younger. Ten had college eligibil-
ity left. "I think some of 'em are so young they still believe in
Santa Claus," Brooks had become fond of cracking.

Someone asked them about that at the press conference; and
four of the six had raised their hands solemnly, yes, they did
believe. Youngest of the believers was Mike Ramsey, who'd
only had one season at the "U" before Brooks tapped him for
the Olympic team. A year earlier, he'd been a precocious freshman from southeast Minneapolis, buried on the junior varsity.

Now the Buffalo Sabres were clamoring for him, waving a
professional contract and saying they'd wait three years or
longer if they had to.

Scotty Bowman, the Buffalo general manager, had watched
Ramsey at the Sports Festival and had come away deeply im-
pressed. "He's the type of athlete you put together in your
dreams," Bowman decided, and it was true.

He was "The Rammer," 6-foot-3, a hundred ninety pounds
("and still growing," he'd tell people), the best athlete in the
city. Ramsey was a state tennis champion, an All-City football
player, the best hockey defenseman in Minnesota.

The Michigan schools were after him. So was Bob Johnson at
Wisconsin, who couldn't believe that Ramsey wouldn't at least
come down to Madison for a look. "That's like going to a used-
car lot," Johnson told him, "and buying the first one you see."

Yet if any of Brooks' players had been born to be a Gopher,
it was Ramsey. He'd grown up near Minnehaha Falls, the youngest of three children of a bakery deliveryman, and learned his
hockey on the outdoor rinks.

Ramsey had gone to Minneapolis Roosevelt and been something of a fixture at Gopher games. How could he not have gone
to the "U," even if it meant taking a number and waiting his
turn on the JV?

Eight veteran defensemen loomed ahead of him, but midway through the season Brooks brought Ramsey up to the varsity, and the rest of the year passed in a whirl.

Before long he was one of Brooks' four regular defensemen. Then he was named to the NCAA All-Tournament team as the Gophers won the title. Next, it was the Olympic team (which Ramsey had thought he was too young to make).

Then the NHL draft. Scotty Bowman, who'd just left Montreal after winning a fourth straight Stanley Cup, hadn't been able to scout any top prospects that year. But he had talked to Kaminsky about Ramsey and decided to go to the Sports Festival to inspect him in person.

After a few days there, Bowman sat down next to Kaminsky at a practice. "I'm going to take Ramsey," he said.

"Where?" Kaminsky asked him. "If not on the first round, I think others will nab him."

"On the first," Bowman replied. "Number eleven. But I want Jimmy Roberts and Roger Neilson (his assistant coaches) to fly out here for a look, just to verify. But I'm sure they'll agree."

Then, in August, Bowman did it. No American-born, college-trained skater had ever been chosen that high, and Ramsey was stunned. Jeez, he thought, things are happening pretty fast here.

Ramsey was only 18 when he came to the Olympic team, a year younger than anyone else, and when Brooks growled at him, that was the theme.

"Go read your press clippings," Brooks would tell him. "You're an eighteen-year-old prima donna."

Ramsey would grin. "What am I gonna be next year, Herb?"

"You'll be a nineteen-year-old prima donna."

He was an effervescent manchild, rawboned and broad-shouldered, sleepy-faced yet brimming with intelligence and physical energy. Defense was a natural position for him.

The Rammer loved to carry the puck, upper body bent slightly forward, chin thrust out a bit. He loved to wind up and fire, to rock rushing wings into the boards with thudding body checks. "This kid," Steve Christoff decided at first glance, "is all over the ice."

He'd been jolted dramatically out of adolescence in just a few months, but Brooks still considered him a kid.

So just in case Ramsey, or any of them, still kept the faith with Santa, the team held a Christmas party before they left for home. Mike Eruzione, a right jolly old elf, passed out the presents, which each player had been assigned to buy for another, with idiosyncrasies in mind.

O'Callahan, the man from Hollywood, got oversize sunglasses and a cigar. Eric Strobel and Eruzione both received miner's helmets with domelights. They'd collided in practice one day and Eruzione had busted a bone in his hand.

Jim Craig was given a giant jawbreaker and a wad of cotton, to plug three orifices at once. Harrington, keeper of Brooksisms and the team's Herbthropologist, found himself with a poster of a monkey scrawling graffiti.

Mark Pavelich, the compleat angler, got a bucket and a rod made from a hockey stick. Donnie Waddell, still struggling with his post-pubescent complexion, was furnished with a tube of Clearasil.

And so it went, everybody receiving something perversely appropriate, re-bonding the comradeship. It was good to see, noticed Brooks, who actually came by for a few beers and was presented with a whip. Because the next month was going to be brutal.

8

26 INTO 20

Life Olympus-style was beginning to resemble the flip side of an old Willie Nelson record by mid-January, something about five months on the road with sore bones, dishwater coffee and what you call your terminal boredom. Five months on the road, and Lord Killanin still another month over yonder.

"We have a tired hockey team right now," Brooks was admitting after a semisleepy Tuesday night decision over Wisconsin. "A mentally fatigued team."

Fatigued by the whole concept of Oklahoma City to Tulsa to Wichita in three nights; fatigued from dueling decapitating minor leaguers whom you'd never see again; fatigued by playing and beating lower-case Russians but never The Russians.

They'd just flown from Kansas back to Minnesota, eyelids at half mast, and some officious stewardess had come back and harassed America's adopted sons about the cowboy hats they'd stuffed under some first-class seats. If they weren't removed, she said, it would be a $4000 fine. Government regulations specifically require . . .

So somebody had gotten one of the hats and begun passing it around, trying to raise the $4000 because it was simply too much of a mortal aggravation to move the goddam things.

They were beyond it now. They'd played fifty-two games in 132 days. They'd taken face-offs in The Hague, on the Iron Range and in Alabama.

In addition to Phil Verchota's loosened teeth in Minneapolis and Jack O'Callahan's swollen eye in Maine, in Birmingham one of the Carlson brothers, direct from the movie *Slapshot,* had gone after Mike Ramsey and opened a six-stitch gash under an eye.

They'd played the Canadian Olympic team three games in Calgary, and it had been a fiasco right away, twenty-seven penalties the first night, six players thumbed for fighting and four Canadian sticks broken over American limbs. Mark Pavelich had his forehead opened for him one night, his chin the next.

"Typical Junior 'A' style," Mark Johnson had observed. "Not too much hockey." Now Johnson, too, was hurt. A defenseman named Jay McFarlane, one of his old Badger teammates, had clobbered him; Johnson was hobbling around with a charley horse, unavailable.

Just ahead loomed another Willie Nelson special, Minneapolis to Fort Worth to Dallas to Milwaukee to Madison in seven days. But most fatiguing of all was the arithmetical paranoia, which was becoming epidemic.

Twenty hockey players could go to the Games. Twenty-three were still with the club, not to mention the optionals on Herbie's big yellow taxi. If you were Brooks' thirteenth wing or his seventh defenseman—or worse, if you thought you were but couldn't be sure—you saw unsettling omens everywhere.

Bobby Suter, the tough kid from the East Side, had somehow restored his busted ankle to working order in six weeks and was back in uniform. Mark Wells, after weeks of exile in Flint and Nova Scotia, was back, too. And every time the wings picked up the Minneapolis papers, they read how well Timmy Harrer was doing at the "U," how he just might be the sharpshooter Brooks could use.

So, composing mock rosters became the team pastime, everyone trying to slip into Herbie's persona. He would probably keep twelve forwards, four at each position.

Robbie McClanahan was a cinch for one left wing, and both Buzz Schneider and Phil Verchota looked solid there, too. And

Herbie had to keep his captain, didn't he? So Mike Eruzione was the fourth.

Mark Johnson, Neal Broten and Mark Pavelich seemed sure things at center. Would Brooks keep Wells as his fourth man there? Or move Eric Strobel back from right wing?

The right side was an open question. Steve Christoff, who'd scored more goals than anybody, was a certainty. If Strobel didn't play center, wouldn't Brooks want him at right wing just for his speed?

That left Dave Silk, John Harrington and Ralph Cox scrambling for two jobs. "I'm a better skater than those two guys," Harrington mused. "And I work harder. But they make better plays than I do. And Coxie is the best scorer by far."

No question about that. Nobody on the team, perhaps not even the Magic Man himself, had the touch that Ralph Cox did, an ineffable knack for finding unlikely openings around and through goalkeepers and threading pucks past.

If time was running out and you needed one on the board, Mike Eruzione swore by Coxie. He was the man you wanted taking the shot if you could only have one, the man you wanted pouncing on a rebound loose in front.

"He has a bad habit," Brooks would admit, wryly. "He scores goals."

No collegian in the land had scored more than Cox during the previous season, forty-two assorted sharply angled slappers, slot-poppers, 15-foot wristers, crease-sitters, screens, up top, down low, stick-side, glove-side, chinked off the post, whipped between the goalie's legs, over his shoulder, under his arm, past his outstretched skate, off his pads.

By the time he'd been graduated, Cox had piled up 127 goals in four years at New Hampshire, easily the school record. Nobody else had ever scored more than ninety-eight. He was All-East and All-America virtually by acclamation, and when UNH won the ECAC championship that year, Cox was voted Most Valuable Player.

He was a Bostonian (from Braintree, to be precise, a town on the South Shore) who'd bypassed the Boston schools to play in upcountry splendor at Durham.

For the city kid who'd had a bellyful of trolley tracks, street corners and urban hassle, UNH offered four years of Crosby, Stills and Nash–style funk, a hockey arena packed with certified screamers and just enough places to unwind over hot pizzas and pitchers of beer.

The school had played hockey since 1924, but until the late sixties, the level had been Division 2, its varsity a match for Bowdoin but a tune-up for Harvard.

All that changed with the arrival of a man named Charlie Holt who'd taught school, coached hockey, taken a few years off to work as a buyer for a tannery and finally wound up at Colby College.

By 1969 he was at Durham and UNH was Division 1, up there with Boston College and Boston University and Cornell and Harvard, making the post-season tournament their first year.

Throughout the seventies New Hampshire was a fixture among the East's top eight, the play-offs assumed now, the coaches able to go down to Boston to recruit and know they'd bring back an armful of All-Scholastics.

The city player who wanted out of the city, but not too far out, found New Hampshire a terrific option. You could drive there in just over an hour, breezing right up the Interstate, and dress down when you got there: work shirt, jeans, boots, parka. You could rent a farmhouse with four or five other hockey players, fill the icebox with beer and throw a roast in the oven for dinner. The air was clean and crisp, the snow squeaked beneath your step, the pace was laid-back.

But the hockey was inventive and challenging, the atmosphere a scaled-down version of what they had at Wisconsin. It was a deeply unsettling experience to play at Snively Arena, a drafty aircraft hangar of a building that was insulated with undergraduates but hardly soundproof.

The hubbub began the moment the blue jerseys appeared; the only way to stifle it was to get New Hampshire down by four or five goals, and that rarely happened.

UNH came at you a different way every time up the ice. They were always putting in new breakout patterns and power plays —things they'd seen the Czechs do, possibly. Look over at their bench and you saw Holt, the old history professor, with a fedora, wearing a sweater beneath his jacket, pointing, rearranging things.

"You needed a computer to figure out Charlie's practices," Cox would say. "He had four or five systems he could switch back and forth to."

Cox had thrived up there. He'd played for Archbishop Williams, a Catholic high school south of Boston that beat you with faceless waves of shock troops, one gold-helmeted line after another coming over the dasher, the forwards nearly indistinguishable from one another because all of them could skate.

Cox could skate, but the problem was, he didn't look as though he could.

He was a position player, Cox would explain, and he believed in conserving energy. From blue line to blue line, he felt he could stay with almost anyone, but Cox wasn't much for movement for its own sake. When his line was supposed to break out, Cox would be where he should be. All those goals hadn't come by serendipity.

The Bruins had drafted him after his sophomore year. The WHA's Winnipeg Jets had offered him a good contract, wanted him to leave school. Instead, Cox had played for Brooks on the 1979 U.S. World team and had wrecked his ankle playing the Poles.

Russian doctors told him it wasn't broken, but Cox knew better. He'd seen his toes come back to his shinbone. The Sports Festival was out of the question; Cox wrote Brooks telling him that he simply couldn't be ready by July, possibly not even by the time the Olympians left for Europe.

Brooks had promised Cox a spot among his twenty-six-man training team, and Cox had gone off to work with the Bruins at their fall camp, then joined the U.S. team in mid-October.

The ankle was fine; he was ready to go, but it was nearly a month before Cox got into a game, and he rarely played more than four in a row.

When he did play, Cox invariably performed well, usually getting a goal, sometimes more. "Herbie's got to put me on a regular line soon," Cox figured. But by Christmas he was still seeing spot duty; play one game, sit for three. It wasn't Cox's up-and-back skating that concerned Brooks, but his lateral movement. Now, whether because of the ankle or not, Cox seemed a step slow.

"Maybe it would be better for me if I played for a Bruins' farm team," Cox suggested to Brooks.

"No, play here," Brooks had told him. "You'll be playing more, you're right in there."

If I'm right in there, mused Cox, shouldn't I be playing almost every night? When he uses me six or seven games in a row, I score six or seven goals. What does he want from me?

That seemed to be Coxie's fate, teammates thought. He worked hard, didn't cause trouble and did what a forward is supposed to—score goals—better than anybody. Ralph's a fabulous guy to go have a beer with. Everybody likes him.

"The rap on Coxie," Bah Harrington concluded, "seems to be that no matter what he does, he can't do it."

But what he did scared both Silk and Harrington, who knew that if Brooks wanted the hockey equivalent of baseball's designated hitter—the man who does only one thing but does it superbly—he would choose Cox and one of them would probably go.

"We'd sit there in the locker room and look at each other," Harrington would say, "and think, 'Who's going, me or him?' "

You could trace the anxiety back to Joe Mullen's absence, actually. Had he been with the Olympians, the need for a Cox wouldn't have existed and the competition among the right wings might never have begun.

Brooks would probably keep six defensemen, and five seemed all but named—Bill Baker, Mike Ramsey, Ken Morrow,

Jack O'Callahan and Dave Christian. Brooks had already made
one tough cut in Les Auge who, at 26, had been the team's
oldest player. Auge had been an all-American at the "U," had
played on its first NCAA championship team and had been
Brooks' captain in 1975. He'd grown up in Brooks' neighborhood in St. Paul and gone to the same high school.

Emotion had tugged at Brooks to keep him; objective analysis
forced Brooks to cut him. One more man had to go. Would it
be Suter? Or Jack Hughes?

Hughes seemed to possess much of what Brooks wanted. He
was tall, strong and durable, with an instinctive passing sense
and a taste for cornerwork. Yet Brooks had been on him for
months about his skating, his mobility.

He'd see Hughes come out of his zone with head up, looking
to make the play. Then Brooks would watch something go awry
and shout at him: Hughes . . . Hughes . . . Hughes; then stop the
practice and read him out for lugging the puck when he should
have passed it.

"O'Callahan's smarter than you are," Brooks would tell
Hughes at one point. "You were both admitted to Harvard
. . . and O'Callahan didn't go."

You could see Jackie gritting his teeth when Herbie started
in, Mark Johnson said, see the Boston Irish temper start to rise.
Hughes had never been criticized that way. He'd been a fine
schoolboy defenseman from the day he made the varsity at
Malden Catholic, the dominant team in the dominant conference in Massachusetts in the mid-seventies.

His older brother George was the center on MC's first line,
the most gifted scorer in the state, headed for a fruitful career
at Harvard and a stint in the pros. Jack was the corresponding
defenseman, striding confidently out of his end, moving the
puck beautifully.

MC won the state title, both boys made All-Scholastic,
prepped at Choate, proceeded to Harvard. From the beginning, Jack played regularly for the varsity, and when his freshman season was over he'd made All-Ivy, been named the

ECAC's Rookie of the Year and been drafted in the seventh round by the Colorado Rockies.

By the end of his junior year, Hughes had already set Harvard records for most points and assists by a defenseman; but the squad had been playing poorly, missing the play-offs, and Hughes was restless, eager to get on to the next level.

The Olympics had always been something of a fantasy for him, so Hughes took off his senior year and tried out for the team. From the start, though, he felt his relationship with Brooks was spiky.

Hughes couldn't get used to the stare, the tight lips, the voice always correcting him. Sometimes he'd lie in bed, trying to fall asleep, and the voice would come back: "Hughes . . . Hughes . . . Hughes."

When the team returned to the States, Hughes thought of chucking it. It was obvious there was no spot on the team for him, that Brooks was going to be on his case all year. The Rockies would be happy to sign him; Hughes could report to their farm club in Fort Worth and get started on his professional career.

He'd called his agent in Boston, Bob Murray, and phoned his parents in Somerville, but they'd talked him out of it, urging him to stick it out, saying things might improve.

Now it was January, and he was still on the borderline and Brooks was still on him about his mobility.

Some nights, it would all come back, the original Jack Hughes, the scourge of the Catholic Conference, the East's Rookie of the Year. Other times his skating would be hitchy, his passes hesitant, his whole rhythm syncopated.

Several teammates had decided that Hughes' mind was all messed up. Jack takes everything personally. Now, with D-Day on the horizon, Hughes' confidence had sagged. "You've seen me play," Hughes would say to a Boston sports writer. "I can play, right?"

For a while, after Suter had broken the ankle, Hughes thought he'd probably make the squad. He'd played reasonably well at the Christmas tournament. Donnie Waddell had been sent back to Northern Michigan. Nobody else had been brought up. But now Suter was back, maybe not as mobile as he should be, but back nonetheless. Brooks had promised him he wouldn't lose ground.

So, Brooks might hold that final spot until the eleventh hour. Only the goalkeeping seemed set—Jim Craig backed by Steve Janaszak, with Bruce Horsch on call if either was hurt.

So things were volatile enough, even if Brooks weren't going to his taxi squad. But, suddenly, he was. He'd decided that Harrer deserved a look, maybe Aaron Broten, too. So Brooks asked Harrer to join the Olympic team in Milwaukee for the game against the International League All-Stars. Immediately, Dave Silk's blood chilled.

Harrer's a sniper, Silk thought. What if Herbie puts him with Magic? Magic makes everyone look good. What if he gets three or four goals? Why is Herbie bringing him in against these guys? Why not against Gorky Torpedo or Fort Worth?

Harrer was the only member of Brooks' 1979 Minnesota varsity who'd tried out for the Olympic team and not been chosen. Now he was having a marvelous season, leading the Gophers in scoring. He was an excellent skater with speed equal to Johnson's and McClanahan's, and only a tad less than Strobel's. But Harrer's trademark was his shot—hard, fast, dangerous. He was on his way to setting a major college-season goal-scoring record with fifty-three, and most of them were the kind you remembered. If Harrer had managed even a decent week at Colorado Springs, he'd have been on the club from the very beginning. Now, he'd have his chance.

In September, he might have been welcome, another comrade along for the great adventure. Now, noticed Janaszak, it was "Good to see you, when's your flight back?"

Harrer's presence in the dressing room unnerved every forward to whom Brooks had given a noncommital appraisal in December. That, of course, was part of Brooks' motive. Keep everybody jacked up, ward off complacency.

Even Jimmy Craig's game had been off. To spark him, Brooks took him aside. "Your curveball's hanging," Brooks began.

"What?"

"Hey, it's the seventh game of the World Series, the ninth inning. Guy's curveball's hanging, you gotta remove him. That's what you have a bullpen for."

"WHAT?"

"Janaszak hasn't played. I've gotta get him ready."

Craig blew his cork. "I'll show you, you son of a bitch."

Brooks nodded gravely. "I hope you do."

It seemed ludicrous. Craig had been Brooks' regular goaltender all year, playing 70 percent of the schedule. But Janaszak had been Brooks' starter at the "U" the year before, when the Gophers had won the National Championship. He had been voted the tournament's Most Valuable Player.

Janaszak could step in and play perfectly well if called upon, and Craig knew it. He'd been dubbed "The Man" at Hill-Murray, the private school in St. Paul whose varsity he'd been the backbone of for four years.

Janaszak had won ten letters there in hockey, football, golf and soccer, went to the "U" and gradually worked his way into prominence. At 5–8, he was short for a goalkeeper and had a reputation for letting in the cheap goal. More often, though, Janaszak kept the Gophers in games until their forwards got wheeling, challenging enemy shooters, playing best in the biggest games.

The year before, as Minnesota was making its late-season surge, Janaszak was indispensable, allowing only twenty-two goals over the final nine games, eight of which the Gophers won.

"This is it, guys," he informed teammates before their NCAA opener against New Hampshire at Detroit. "We didn't come here for a radio and a T-shirt." Then Janaszak went out and backstopped them to a second National title in three years.

He was an ideal back-up man, a proven player who'd work hard in practice, push the man in front of him, yet accept short rations of ice time.

From the beginning, Janaszak had guessed that would be his role. Shortly after the Sports Festival, he'd seen a press release that quoted Brooks as saying that if the team was going to do well at Lake Placid, it would have to have good goaltending— and that it had Jim Craig.

It's going to be a tough year, Janaszak told himself.

He would step in whenever Craig was hurt or needed a rest —a little more than a dozen times in five months—perform capably, then return to the bench, sip his tea, and root.

That was exactly what Brooks valued him for. Janaszak was bright (a chemical engineering major at the "U"), witty and popular. Mr. Debonair, Bah Harrington would think, seeing Janaszak crisply dressed and sporting his Fu Manchu mustache.

He bore his role with unfailing good humor, sitting in full gear at the end of the bench as participant/observer, ready with a good word for mates coming off the ice with burning lungs and watery knees. If Mark Johnson, Ken Morrow, Jack O'Callahan and Mike Eruzione each had their role, so did Steve Janaszak.

"You'll probably be at Lake Placid," Brooks had told him in December. "But there's no guarantee you'll play." Janaszak had accepted that, and willingly sharpened teammates' skates, boosted spirits and kept Craig on his toes.

Later Craig would thank him for it, saying publicly that Steve Janaszak had made him a better man. Now, with the Games coming up and Herbie talking mystically about ninth innings and seventh games, Janaszak was a disturbing shadow, always there, ready to go if Brooks glanced in his direction.

Craig had played well. But if his curveball hung on the eve of the Games, there were other options.

Nobody was safe, the message went. Not even the captain. Mike Eruzione had broken a hand in November and hadn't been playing to expectations. Now Brooks was calling him in too, and laying on an ultimatum.

There were four more exhibition games before the squad left for the Games. Brooks wanted to see some fire, or . . .

"You don't think I'd cut the captain?" he told Eruzione. "The way you're playing? You don't have this thing made. You're going to Lake Placid because you're good in one aspect. I won't embarrass you in front of the press. I'll just announce that Mike Eruzione has a lower back injury and can't play. You'll be right behind the bench with me. But you're not going to play."

He'd never do it, Eruzione told himself. But damn, he *might*. Shaken, he called the Eastern guys to his room and told them that his neck was on the block, that Herbie was bringing in Aaron Broten for a look. "If I play well," Eruzione concluded, "I make the team. If not, I'm an assistant coach."

It was outrageous, the Easterners agreed. After five months of sweat, tedium and crap, Herbie was yo-yoing his captain and bringing in a freshman Gopher. Eruzione was to call a team meeting and bear a message to Brooks. Enough is enough.

So the players convened before a game with Fort Worth on January 25 at the Met Center, and Eruzione laid it out to them. He was paranoid. The right wings, Silkie and Bah and Coxie, were paranoid and highly tense.

Why should Timmy Harrer make the team on the basis of some good college stats and a couple of games with the Olympians? He was a nice enough kid, Timmy, but it was too late. People were already making plans; parents were buying tickets and reserving rooms.

Even the Gophers, who'd played alongside Harrer and knew what he could contribute, agreed. "Silkie's been here all year," said Bill Baker.

The logic was compelling. All for one, one for all. Brooks would have to concede, scrap the taxi, end the suspense. So they confronted him . . . and Brooks exploded.

He was like the Wizard of Oz, Dave Silk thought, with thunder crackling and smoke soaring. We've tried our little coup and it hasn't worked, he thought. And now we're all going to lose our heads.

This whole thing has been done honestly and objectively, Brooks fumed. "It seems whenever we bring in a defenseman, everything's fine, nothing is said," Brooks said, looking at Eruzione. "Now it's a forward, some people are getting a little nervous."

"But we're a family now," Eruzione countered. "This shouldn't be happening." (We may be a family, one borderline candidate had thought, but some of us are adopted.) This, thought Brooks, is what I've been waiting to hear since last summer.

"You guys say you're family? Okay. You've declared yourselves. Out of this group will come the team."

That group, though, would include whoever was with it at the time. So Harrer and Broten stayed, and the arithmetical paranoia continued.

Meanwhile, there'd been some rumbling back at the "U," where Harrer was here one day, gone the next, then here again. He'd traveled with the Olympians to Milwaukee and Madison, then had joined the Gophers for a double date with Michigan. On Thursday he was with Herbie in Dallas, scoring a goal. The next morning he was on a plane bound for Lansing and two games at Michigan State. Then it was back on a plane for Warroad to rejoin the Olympians.

The shuttling was driving Brad Buetow crackers. How could he maintain any kind of cohesion with his two best forwards gone today, here tomorrow?

Brooks shrugged. "Brad has got to realize he's not the owner of the store," he said. "He's just the storekeeper. I'm still the boss over there." He simply had to be cold and callous toward the "U" at the moment, Brooks explained. No stone unturned. What if Harrer and Broten were precisely the ingredients he needed?

The rumblings might have stayed just that if not for a Sunday article that had appeared in the Minneapolis *Tribune* on January 6. Featuring a picture of Harrer flanked on one side by a photo of Buetow and on the other by one of Brooks, the column painted a picture of the two coaches struggling for Harrer's body and soul. Brooks was said to be torn between his dual roles as Olympic and Gopher coach. Kaminsky was portrayed by the reporter, John Gilbert, as working to influence Harrer toward the Olympic team. As the paper's primary hockey writer, Gilbert's opinion carried unusual weight at all levels of hockey in the state.

The effect was to put a spotlight on the decisions Brooks had to make and hold him back a bit. If Harrer was only marginally better than the other wings, Brooks reasoned, and if placing him on the team would trigger debate that might disturb the squad, then Brooks would lean toward passing.

Still, time was running down. Only four exhibition games remained—with one a mere twenty-minute scrimmage with the Canadian Olympic team between periods of the NHL All-Star Game in Detroit on Tuesday. Harrer was getting his passport, just in case. Brooks had to decide.

Kaminsky was in town, so the two men had a chance for their first face-to-face review since the pre-Christmas tournament in Lake Placid. On Saturday morning, they met over breakfast at Minneapolis' Leamington Hotel.

"I appreciate how you feel about your clients," Brooks told Kaminsky, "so I'll tell you how things stand now."

The team was beginning to taper off, Brooks said, like fighters before a title fight. He thought they were close to putting together the final roster.

Kaminsky nodded. Moving Christian back to defense had been a critical move, he told Brooks, because it provided more mobility back there. And most of the forward combinations looked solid.

"To a degree, yes," Brooks said. "But we still need that sharpshooter, that big gunner."

Kaminsky, who empathized with Cox's struggle to overcome his broken ankle, argued that he was the answer there.

"Yeah, he'd have to be a DH because his skating just costs us too much," Brooks said. "The question is, Can we afford a DH, afford to keep a guy whose skating just doesn't meet our standards?"

"If not him, who then?"

"What about Harrer? He's scored like crazy for the U."

"Well, how's he done with you?"

The Russian bench watches it slip away. From left: defenseman Aleksei Kasatanov, coach Viktor Tikhonov, defenseman Viacheslav Fetisov. (Associated Press)

Aleksandr Maltsev puts the Soviet Union up, 3–2: "He whipped the puck into the back of the cage with a clank that reverberated through the field house. You could hear it for what seemed endless minutes after." (Associated Press)

The goal that tied Sweden with 27 seconds on the clock: "Bill Baker saw the net ripple, saw Lindbergh asprawl, the red light on, the blue shirts going to the cage with their sticks up." (United Press International)

The final minutes of the Russian game: "Brooks walking up and back, up and back, saying the same thing: Play your game, play your game, play your game." (Associated Press)

A goal that came out of nowhere—Mark Johnson ties the Russians with eleven minutes to play. (United Press International)

After the buzzer: "Johnson, the first man in line, noticed something odd. Some of the Russians were smiling. 'They're excited for us,' he thought." (Associated Press)

U.S.A. 4, U.S.S.R. 3: "As the spectators whooped, snapped pictures, slapped hands and waved flags, the players melted into a white-jersey pudding." (Steven Sutton, Associated Press)

Do you believe in miracles?: "Mike Ramsey lay on his back, roaring with laughter and irony. And O'Callahan, arms up, open mouth showing all those missing Charlestown upper teeth, was on his knees, exulting over him." (Frank O'Brien, Boston Globe)

The medal ceremony: "C'mere," Eruzione called. "C'mere. Get up on the stage." (Royden Hobson)

Holding the bear at bay: "We'll do anything to win," Jack O'Callahan believed. "And they won't." From left, defenseman Ken Morrow (3), goalie Jim Craig (30), center Mark Johnson (10), defenseman Mike Ramsey (5). (Royden Hobson)

The gold-medal goal: "Deke him and beat him, McClanahan knew. So he waited for Valtonen to commit first, then slid the puck between his legs. U.S.A. 3, Finland 2." (Royden Hobson)

The red helmets congratulate Jim Craig: "Craig was the difference, a Horatio at the American bridge, holding off the Soviets until reinforcements arrived. He would stand up, then flop, challenge the Russians, then wait for them. They could not solve him." (Frank O'Brien, Boston Globe)

Mark Johnson's coup de grace against Finland: "4–2 now, and time to ice down a few dozen bottles of sparkling wine." (Boston Globe)

Herb Brooks as a member of the 1960 U.S. Olympic training team: "A fine forward, the fastest skater in the country." (Moss Photo Service)

Disbelief, euphoria, all that. Mike Eruzione's wrist shot stuns the Russians. From left, right wing John Harrington (28), Soviet forward Sergei Makharov (24), Eruzione, defenseman Bill Baker (6), goalie Vladimir Myshkin. (Royden Hobson)

The 1960 gold-medal game. Jack Kirrane, who left a Boston firehouse at age 31 to captain the U.S. team, blocks a Czech shot. Jack McCartan, the hero of the Games, tends goal in background. (Basgen-Photography)

The 1960 U.S. Olympic Hockey team gold medalists at Squaw Valley. Front row, left to right: Laurence J. Palmer, goalie, Wakefield, MA; John J. Kirrane, defense, Brookline, MA; William J. Cleary, Jr., forward, Cambridge, MA; Edwyn R. Owen, defense, St. Louis Park, MN; William D. Christian, forward, Warroad, MN; John W. McCartan, goalie, St. Paul, MN. Middle row: James H. Claypool, manager, Duluth, MN; Robert B. Cleary, forward, Westwood, MA; Robert P. McVey, forward, Hamden, CT; Rodney E. Paavola, defense, Hancock, MI; Roger A. Christian, forward, Warroad, MN; Eugene Grazia, forward, West Springfield, MA; Thomas M. Williams, forward, Duluth, MN; John P. Riley, Jr., coach, West Point, NY. Back row: John Mayasich, defense, Eveleth, MN; Paul Johnson, forward, West St. Paul, MN; Weldon H. Olson, forward, Marquette, MI; Richard Rodenhieser, forward, Malden, MA; Richard O. Meredith, forward, Minneapolis, MN; Ben Bertini, trainer, Lexington, MA. (USOC)

Billy Christian beats the Russians in 1960. Christian's son David played on the 1980 U.S. team. (USOC)

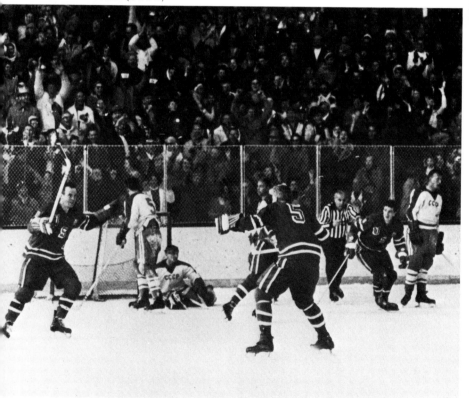

America's Children at the White House: "They'd dined at the President's table, been proclaimed magnificent Americans all...'It's over,' Dave Silk told Jack O'Callahan. 'It's over.'" (United Press International)

The 1980 United States Olympic Hockey Team, XIII Winter Olympics, Gold Medalist. Front row, left to right: Steve Janaszak, Bill Baker, Mark Johnson, Craig Patrick (assistant coach/assistant general manager), Mike Eruzione (captain), Herb Brooks (head coach), Buzz Schneider, Jack O'Callahan, Jim Craig. Middle row, left to right: Bob Suter, Rob McClanahan, Mark Wells, Bud Kessel (equipment manager), V. George Nagobads (physician), Gary Smith (trainer), Robert Fleming (chairman), Ralph Jasinski (general manager), Warren Strelow (goalkeeping coach), Bruce Horsch, Neal Broten, Mark Pavelich. Back row, left to right: Phil Verchota, Steve Christoff, Les Auge, Dave Delich, Jack Hughes, Ken Morrow, Mike Ramsey, Dave Christian, Ralph Cox, Dave Silk, John Harrington, Eric Strobel. (USOC)

Brooks pondered for a minute, "Not bad, but not overwhelming. It's not really his fault. We should have brought him up in November or early December. He would have had more games, he would have fit in easily. He wouldn't have had to shuttle back and forth."

"Well, do you think he's the answer?"

"I think he's our best shooter. He has the speed. I just wish he weren't so damn inconsistent."

So, two puzzled men did what puzzled men did for thousands of pre-computer years: they pulled out pencil and paper.

Kaminsky went first. "Okay, let's look at the first line. Johnson's obviously the center and he goes with McClanahan at left wing like hand in glove."

"Right. I guess our first problem is right wing. Let's leave it blank for now."

"Second line?"

"Well, Neal [Broten] is set at center, but after that it's tough. We could put his brother Aaron on the left side and move Christoff back to the right."

"You're sure you don't want to use Christoff at center?"

"No, he's definitely better as a winger."

"Do you think Aaron should actually be on the team? He's only worked out with the club, never played any games."

"I suppose you're right but the kid's just so damn talented, and plays great with his brother. They know each other's moves perfectly."

Brooks hesitated and Kaminsky jumped.

"But you realize to keep Aaron means Eruzione's off. Do you want that?"

"No, but I don't know if I told you this. Last week I scared the shit out of him, told him he'd be off the team and go to Placid as an assistant unless he started working again."

"I guess it worked. He had two goals last night and was really your best player."

"That's true," Brooks responded. "We've got to keep him."

"Is the third line set?"

Brooks chuckled. "Amazingly, that's the easy one. We'll keep the three Rangers together—Schneider, Pav and Harrington."

Kaminsky smiled. Harrington, too slow, too heavy-handed, too unheralded, had been a long shot all along and now he had made it. He'd always liked Harrington, who was the only free agent of the four (Harrington, Eruzione, Pavelich and Janaszak) on the club in whom the pros seemed to show any interest. The lawyer wrote "call" next to Harrington's name on his notes of the discussion.

"And the fourth?"

Brooks winced. "That's tough, but it depends on what we do elsewhere."

They started scratching out combinations on a napkin, constantly connecting the first and fourth units. For example, if you went: "McClanahan-Johnson-Christoff," then Christoff would have to be replaced on the second line.

"Well, how about Cox there?"

"No, too slow for Broten."

"How about Cox on the first line?"

"Maybe, but you really want speed there."

"So that knocks out Silk in that slot, too."

"I guess we go back to Strobel."

"But he's been so disappointing all fall."

"Except for the Lake Placid tourney—and remember he came up big in the NCAAs. Maybe he's a big-gamer?"

"I hope so, but maybe we should just put Harrer there," countered Brooks.

Kaminsky shifted in his seat. This was tough, really tough. They had gone over the Harrer situation many times; it *was* tempting to go with him.

"But are you sure he's the answer?" Kaminsky wondered.

"I'm not totally sure," Brooks said. "I wish Tim would have gotten a longer shot—a better chance to show everything."

"Well, let's say this. Unless you are sure of Harrer, and unless you put him on the first line, then we shouldn't make the radical change of putting him on the team and bouncing someone who's been with you all season."

"I'm going to think about it," Brooks decided, "but I'm sure you're right."

"Okay, what about the second line? Is it Broten and Christoff, for sure?"

"Yep, that's good."

"Do you put Aaron on the left?"

"That would mean no Eruzione. No, Michael's a good captain, a competitor. And we need his experience. He stays."

"We're down to the fourth and first again."

"Left wing on the fourth is fine. That's Verchota."

"Agreed."

"I think that means Strobel, Silk or Cox for the last two right wingers. I suppose the edge goes to Strobel on the first unit. Speed is so important, and we need what he has there."

"So, if he's there, the fourth line center is now open. Maybe you could move Silk there. He played center for BU quite a bit."

"I don't know," Brooks said. "David's been somewhat disappointing this year. What's he got, about eight or ten goals? He should have more, especially since he's supposed to be a scorer."

"Do you think Verchota, Silk and Cox would be too slow?"

"I'm afraid so, but I'm not totally comfortable with Silk in the middle. He hasn't played there in a while. But I think I prefer him to Cox on the wing. He's a better skater and a more all-around player."

"If you do that, who goes in the middle? Do you move Christian back there or what?"

Brooks smiled. "No, Christian has made us a different team. I suppose it's Wells. He's a center, he's quick and he's played well the last month."

Amazing, Kaminsky thought. Mark Wells makes the Olympic team despite spending much of the year in Flint and Halifax. And he'll get there because Tim Harrer didn't get much of a tryout, and because Eric Strobel's speed was needed on the wing and because Dave Christian had been moved to the blue line, and because Ralph Cox cracked his ankle. A chess piece in the right place at the right time. But he had earned it.

"Okay, let's review," Kaminsky suggested. "McClanahan, Johnson and Strobel on the first, Eruzione, Broten and Christoff next, then the three Iron Rangers and then Verchota, Wells and Silk. Cox is out, and the six defensemen remain Ramsey, Baker, O'Callahan, Christian, Morrow and Suter. That leaves Jack Hughes off. No additions from players who weren't with the team all fall like Harrer, Auge, Aaron Broten or Craig Homola."

"I think that's the way it looks," Brooks concluded, "but don't tell any of the players yet. I'll let them know in the next day or two."

"One last question. Do you like this club, this line-up?"

Brooks leaned forward. "Yes, I do," he whispered. "I know this sounds crazy, but if we have the perfect night, get hot goaltending and the crowd is behind us, we could beat the Russians; we could win it all."

The two men paid the check and went off to finish the day. Kaminsky drove out to the Met Center, where he met Christoff for lunch, and they went to the North Star–Los Angeles game that afternoon. Later, he drove out to the apartment complex where the players lived. He was anxious to give a very nervous Mark Wells some good news.

First, he called on Harrington and told him he would be on the team. Bah seemed to take it all in stride, but he was pleased. Wells, on the other hand, was both ecstatic and disbelieving.

"Are you sure he said all that?"

Remembering his promise not to tell, Kaminsky hedged slightly.

"Yes, he said all that, but it's not a hundred percent done. You know Herb. It's not official until he tells you himself."

"Oh."

"No, I'm not saying anything but good news," Kaminsky assured him. "I'm sure you've made it, but you just can't be absolutely sure until he tells you. Anyway, you've played well enough to earn it, haven't you?"

Wells brightened. "Yes, I have, and I'm going out and cele-brate."

First, Brooks had to tell Cox and Hughes that it was over for them, that after five months they wouldn't be going to Lake Placid after all.

There would be a civic luncheon for the Olympians at the Leamington before the team left for Warroad and a game there with the Lakers and then worked their way East. Brooks had to do it before the luncheon.

Soon, the phone rang in the apartment that Cox shared with Mike Eruzione. All the other Boston guys—Jack O'Callahan, Dave Silk, Jim Craig, Hughes—were there, hanging out, specu-lating.

"Ralph," Brooks said. "You're not coming with us. But would you please come to the banquet first and let me talk to you?"

He would explain it face to face, Brooks determined. One-on-one, lay it out, shake their hands. "And then," Brooks knew, "go into a closet and tear myself apart."

Now Cox was hanging up the phone, telling his mates that he wasn't going. Eruzione had known. As captain, he was privy to everything, but the last few days had been rough, what with Coxie talking about Lake Placid and how excited his family was. This is the toughest thing I've ever been through, Eruzione thought. Knowing Ralphie isn't going but not being able to tell him.

Hughes was upset. Ralphie got screwed, he decided.

Cox was stunned. I can't believe he's not taking me, he told himself. I haven't played that much, but still, I thought Herbie would take me. I've scored more goals than some of the people he's keeping.

Fifteen minutes later, the phone was ringing again. "Mike, do you know where Jack Hughes is?" Eruzione heard Brooks say.

"He's right here."

"Put him on."

Hughes was expecting it. It was destiny, almost. Maybe I wasn't supposed to make this team, he wondered.

Hughes got to the hotel before Cox and went to see Brooks,

to hear his regrets, to shake his hand. Brooks seemed disturbed, his voice unsteady, eyes filling up.

When Cox came by, Brooks looked as though he'd been crying—or was about to. When Brooks looked at him, he did see himself in 1960, getting the word from Jack Riley, choking back the disappointment and the anger. Cutting players always hurt, but this was worse.

"Hey, listen," Cox was telling him, "don't feel bad for me. I'm going to go on and play hockey. And you're going to go on and win the gold medal."

Now Brooks did feel himself about to cry. He shook hands, and Cox was gone. There was a plane to catch, a Bruins' farm club to join. Hughes was headed for Fort Worth, to join the same team he'd played against a few nights before.

Except for the Boston guys, nobody else knew that. "Let's go," Buzz Schneider told Cox downstairs.

"No," Cox replied. "I didn't make it. I got cut."

No official announcement was made. The Olympians merely looked up from their plates ("Hey, where's Jack and Ralphie?") and guessed what had happened.

It wasn't until the team arrived in Detroit for the one-period exhibition against the Canadians that Mark Wells got the word from Brooks himself. Detroit was his home town, and friends had been asking him, was he going? And Wells had no answer. Now he knew, and the U.S. Olympic team was complete. They would go on to Lake Placid, settle in, then take a chartered plane to Manhattan for a final exhibition against the Russians. The upper-case Russians.

9

THEM

A bunch of Toronto industrial workers were the first victims to return with chilling tales of Them. This was 1954, and they were what passed for the Canadian National hockey team, a band of semi-superannuated amateurs who played the game after supper going off to represent their country in the World Championships.

For years, their peers had been good enough to send anywhere the game was played seriously, because it was Canada's game. And because their senior amateurs, moonlighters or not, were still considered invincible.

This time they returned jabbering like the survivors in Japanese mutant movies who've seen something unspeakably awful. The Russians had sent a team to the Worlds for the first time, and they had beaten the Toronto industrial workers 7–2 and carried off the title.

For Canadians, it was something akin to being invaded and danced over by Aleuts. They had played the game for nearly a century, the Russians for eight years. Losing by five goals was unspeakable.

It was also, Canadians concluded, a fluke. They'd been tempting fate for years by blithely sending over their senior league champion to take on improving international fields. The scores had been growing closer. This time, it just happened they'd been caught short.

In 1955, Canada sent over the Pentincton Vees to restore order. The Russians were drubbed, 5–0, in the final and the title was regained. All it did, though, was set up the Canadians for an even greater fall at the 1956 Olympics at Cortina.

The Russians had been admitted late to the Olympic movement, not joining until after the Second World War. They'd been eligible to compete in the 1952 Games at Oslo; instead, they sent stone-faced observers who scribbled Cyrillic notes and took their impressions back to Moscow.

Later, in his book *Road to Olympus,* Anatoly Tarasov (the "father of Russian hockey") would thank the Canadians for inventing hockey. But now, he wrote, the Russians would improve upon it.

The 1954 Worlds had been their dress rehearsal. Two years later they showed up for the Olympics, confident and exuberant, shut out the Canadians and won the gold medal.

Nobody knew quite what to make of them. The Russians sat *en famille* at the dining table, devouring monstrous breakfasts and swilling fresh orange juice. They asked to trade a stick—one of their socialist-labor oddities—for three of your Northlands. They bummed cigarettes.

Then they came by the arena in fur coats and beaver-skin hats and rosy cheeks—and skated everyone into the ground. Their fans danced and passed out hammer-and-sickle badges and chanted *(Davay! Shaibu! Davay!)* as one. When Canada had been beaten, the Russian sports minister had sprinted and slid onto the ice, shouting, *"Molodtsi, molodtsi* (Well done, boys)" —and kissing the first Russian player he reached.

Then they vanished. They were mysteries, playing their game in seclusion, emerging once a year, saying humbly that they had come to learn and proceeding to give a tutorial of their own.

The Russians had an elite trade-union and military league that played mostly in Moscow, but game results were rarely seen in the West; the players were unknown. When they returned for the 1960 Games at Squaw Valley, they'd assumed mysterious proportions.

The Russians were not the best team there. The Canadians, led by captain Harry Sinden (later to coach Team Canada and the Boston Bruins), unbeaten in thirty exhibition games, were favored. When the United States, behind Jack McCartan's supernatural goaltending, defeated them 2–1, it was a superior upset.

Yet, for American jingoists it was still Creeping Red Menace time. The Red Army had descended upon Hungary, Sputnik was up, and John Kennedy was campaigning on a perceived missile gap. The Canadians were allies; the Russians, shadowy bogeymen. When the Americans beat them by a goal on national television, the Christian brothers opened a telegram from their Minnesota townsmen, who were reassured that "it takes a good Christian to beat a Commie."

Yet it had never happened again. The Christians had gone back in 1964 to Innsbruck, and the Russians won by four goals. In 1968 at Grenoble, the margin was double that.

From then on, the Americans and everybody else had reconciled themselves to playing for silver. By 1972 the Canadians, resigned to systemic inequities that wouldn't go away, had withdrawn their hockey team from the Games altogether.

There simply were not enough competent amateurs in the Dominion for a world-class team—NHL expansion had seen to that. The ambitious young forward from Peterborough or the defenseman from Edmonton had been prepared from his early teens for professional hockey. The Olympics were for the underequipped.

Not so in Moscow, where the Russians had developed their own version of the Toronto industrial worker. He was the trade-unionist who wasn't, a nominal hero of socialist labor who spent virtually all of his time on loan to the Dynamo hockey team or Wings of the Soviet, or another of the elite club squads.

Thus had the Russian hockey player come to dominate international hockey by the end of the sixties. His only superior played in the National Hockey League. By 1972 that had been recognized, and an eight-game challenge series had been arranged.

They would play in September, before the NHL season—four games in Canada, four in Moscow. The Russians would send their National select team, the same group of Mikhailovs, Vasilievs and Tretiaks that had won the gold medal at Sapporo seven months earlier.

The Canadians would send the cream of their professional league—the Phil Espositos, Brad Parks, Bobby Clarkes and Ken Drydens. It was an awesome amalgam, conceivably the finest hockey club ever assembled.

"I wouldn't mind playing the Russians," cracked Sinden, "with the players we won't dress." And once Canadian insiders glimpsed the Russians at practice in Montreal, their confidence turned to conviction. The Russians seemed to skate at half speed. Their shooting looked unimpressive, their goalkeeping worse. The Toronto Maple Leafs had had two men scout them, and the consensus was that maybe one Russian could play in the NHL.

"They won't win a game," predicted King Clancy, legendary doyen of the Leafs.

The team simply looked ragtag—ordinary red uniforms, primitive skates, cheap equipment. When Esposito poked the puck past the Russian goalie thirty seconds into the first game, every Canadian prejudice seemed justified. They can't play with us.

After six minutes, it was 2–0 and a rout seemed assured—until the Canadians realized that despite the score, the Russians had surely been holding their own. They were, in fact, magnificent skaters, heading instinctively for open ice, their passing uncanny, their confidence unmistakable. They were always circling, always weaving, cutting behind each other, picking up a puck dropped by another forward. When the Russians got near the goal, they'd pass up a shooting chance to pass, then pass again. When they finally did shoot, they used wrist and snap shots, no slappers. It was all very alien, but all very effective.

After one period, they had tied the score. After two, they led 4–2. In the final six minutes, with the Canadians hollow-eyed and panting, the Russians pumped in three more goals for the hell of it and left their hosts for dead, 7–3.

If 1954 had been a mutant movie, what was this? It was a bilingual debacle. WE LOST, mourned Montreal's *Sunday Express*. *"Le Canada humilié,"* concluded *Dimanche-Matin.*

In less than three hours, every assumption every Canadian ever had about his game and his team had been demolished. Team Canada had been thought to be in shape, well rested and uncommonly motivated.

"We're going to play this game for Canada," Sinden had told his players before the face-off. "We're going to play it for the people of the country, and for hockey and what it means to this country."

And they had been rubbed out cold in the Forum, the Vatican of hockey in the Western Hemisphere. "Christ," Sinden had said with a wince, "it hurts."

The Russians had arrived chanting their We're-here-to-learn mantra and had run a perfect reverse *pokazukha* number on their hosts. The concept of *pokazukha* goes back centuries in Russia, back to the Potemkin villages supposedly thrown up to deceive Catherine the Great on one of her trips through the countryside.

It was a concept of false fronts, of lengthy menus crammed with delicacies that weren't available, of model farms amid agricultural wastelands. If the Russians wanted to impress a foreign visitor, they did things *pokazukha,* "just for show."

This time they'd done it in reverse. The fake humility, the threadbare uniforms, the creaky skates had suckered the Canadians perfectly. The Russians had made them see precisely what the Canadians wanted to see.

The Russians were masters at keeping you off balance, bouncing you on your ear one night, losing to you the next, letting you think momentum had shifted in your favor—that you'd solved them—then tattooing you the third night.

By the time the series reached Vancouver for the fourth game, the last one in Canada, the Russians had managed a victory and a tie. When they grabbed an easy 2–0 lead out there, the spectators booed their own countrymen. When the U.S.S.R. prevailed 5–2, the series went to Moscow with the Soviets ahead 2–1–1.

But Canadians had endured winters as rugged as those in Russia and developed toughness and resiliency. They spotted the Russians game five, then made their comeback. Goalie Ken Dryden, twice a loser in Canada, used his legal mind, adapted his style to the intricate Russian passing game and held the fort for a tense 3–2 victory. Tony Esposito took over for game seven and brought off another one-goal Canadian victory.

So, it was 3–3–1 with everything riding on the finale.

After the first period, it was 2–2, but the Russians owned the next twenty minutes and took a 5–3 lead into the final period.

By all reasoning, Canada was finished. This was, after all, the ultimate road game, seven thousand miles from the Montreal Forum. Soviet goaltender Vladislav Tretiak had been awesome for 460 minutes, and Comrades Valery Kharlamov and Aleksandr Yakushev were the dominant forwards on the ice. Dryden had given up five goals already.

Yet Canada crawled back. Phil Esposito, the Canadian Yakushev, flipped in his second goal of the night with less than eighteen minutes to play. Dryden, who had actually played well despite the five goals, made a few big saves, and with seven minutes left, Yvan Cournoyer, his Montreal teammate, made it 5–5.

With less than a minute to play, the score was still tied. A draw would produce a 3–3–2 final result, but still enable the Soviets to claim an overall victory, since they had outscored Canada on a total-goals basis.

This game, however, was to be the triumph of the individual over the collective. With thirty-four seconds to go, Paul Henderson of the Toronto Maple Leafs, who'd scored the winning goals in games six and seven, found himself alone in front of the net. Every newspaper in Canada ran the photograph the next morning: Henderson in midair, stick up, teammates grabbing for him, Tretiak with his head down, beaten. By the slimmest of margins was Canadian honor saved—for the moment.

The timing was wrong, Canadian hockey people had decided. The format was wrong; all-star games proved nothing. So the next time, it would be the best Russian club team—the Central Red Army squad—against the best NHL clubs: the New York Rangers, Montreal Canadiens, Boston Bruins and Philadelphia Flyers. They would play in NHL rinks at midseason. No surprises, no excuses.

The Canadians had full scouting reports now; no more faceless Commies skating half-speed drills. They knew that Tretiak wasn't the gawky neophyte with a bad glove hand they'd first made him out to be. They also knew that the first line, Boris Mikhailov, Valery Kharlamov and Vladimir Petrov, was terrifying. Kharlamov was a quicksilver left wing, a jackrabbit freelancer with marvelous touch and guile, a man who could never be left untended, the world's most dangerous forward.

Mikhailov was the dynamo, the scorer who didn't mind the rough stuff along the boards, a right wing who could make plays like a center. And Petrov was the man in the middle, scoring or setting up goals with equal facility.

The Soviets were known factors now, their tendencies charted, digested and remembered. No reverse *pokazukha* this time.

Yet, the Red Army team came over and buried the Rangers on Thirty-third Street. They went up to the Forum on New Year's Eve, with the Canadiens at the beginning of their renaissance, and pulled off a tie. They skated away from the Bruins in Boston Garden. Only the Flyers defeated them and they had to mug the Russians to do it.

Later, Fred Shero, the Philadelphia coach, mused that that single game might have cost his team the Stanley Cup; it had taken them two weeks to prepare for one night.

In 1976, the Canadians made something of a comeback by winning the Canada Cup, an invitational tournament featuring National squads from Canada, Czechoslovakia, Sweden, Finland, the Soviet Union and the United States.

The Russians, in fact, placed third, but the result was misleading. They'd essentially "tanked" the tournament, deliberately sending over an inexperienced squad to give them international exposure, leaving half of their "A" team back in Moscow.

Most of those young players returned when the Russians and Canadians met again in the winter of 1979; this time, the NHL felt certain that this was the right format.

It was another all-star series, but all three games were in Madison Square Garden—home turf. And though the NHL squad had only been together for three practices, their confidence was considerable.

They knew the Russians by heart now, knew where they'd fallen short in other years. They made Mikhailov and Co. look dreadful in the opening game: bumped them off the puck, made them overskate the blue line, disrupted their swooping harmonies and won by two goals.

They ruled the Russians for much of the second game, too, going up 4–2 on just seven shots, making Tretiak look foolish. Then the evening had simply fallen apart. The Russians remained calm, their expressions unchanged, countered with two quick goals, then dominated in the final 20 minutes for a 5–4 victory.

The next night, they smothered whatever was left of Canadian self-esteem. It was 6–0, an unbelievable wipe-out, and in the NHL dressing room afterward, the only sounds were soft curses and choked-back sobs. Worst of all, Tretiak hadn't been in goal. A blond munchkin named Myshkin had shut out the NHL.

"We played as good as we could," said Bobby Clarke, who'd been the captain. "They are a better team."

That was the team—from Mikhailov to Myshkin—that the Olympians would play. In 1979 at the World Championships in Moscow, the Soviets had been at their peak, winning the title with ease, blasting the Czechs 11–1 and 6–1; the Canadians 9–2 and 5–2; the Swedes 9–3 and 11–3. The pride of the collectives swept to the title with an unblemished 10–0 record. These were indeed the upper-case Russians. The Americans had beaten their junior varsity in December. They'd belted one of their lesser-elite club teams, Gorky Torpedo, three out of four around the New Year. But none of that had mattered. The Russians had had four teams barnstorming North America during the holidays: (1) the Red Army squad, (2) a U.S.S.R. select group, (3) Gorky Torpedo and (4) their Lake Placid sacrificial lambs.

The team the U.S.A. would face in the final exhibition at New York would take the ice at Lake Placid for the Games.

That was exactly how Brooks was billing it, as one last exhibition game. Nothing cataclysmic. "We'll attack the Russians," he figured. "Throw everything we've got at them. But we can't be discouraged if we're blown out. It's the last game of spring training, and that's how we're treating it."

Yet it wasn't, and in his heart Brooks and every one of his players knew it. This would be the Izvestia game they never played—you could set the Lake Placid morning line by the result.

So they took a chartered plane down from Lake Placid on the Saturday morning before the Games, stepped off the bus in Manhattan and stood in awe of Madison Square Garden. Then, they spent the afternoon in awe of Them. Mark Johnson, who'd played against the Russians often enough to know how dangerous that reaction was, had been afraid of that.

"Don't ask for autographs," Johnson warned his mates before the game. "Or else it's gonna be 10–0."

After one period, it was 4–0. What are we doing out here? Neal Broten thought. Let's get serious.

Later, to take the pressure off the players, Brooks would tell the media that he should have let the Olympians play their game, let them be more aggressive and expressive. Instead, he'd given them a semi-conservative game plan, had sent them out in a limited forecheck mode, one man going in, the rest sitting back a bit, feeling the Russians out.

At last, trailing 6–0, the Americans loosened up and staged a last stand. Mike Eruzione rammed home a pass from Steve Christoff. At least they were on the scoreboard; the NHL hadn't managed that much. Phil Verchota snapped another past Tretiak early in the third period, so it was 6–2 and maybe it would be respectable.

Then Maltsev came racing down the right side and left them all, Brooks included, agape. He'd seen defenseman Dave Christian backing up, preparing to interpose himself between puck and goal. So Maltsev cut to the left at full speed, then did a 360-degree spin and flicked a backhand shot into the cage in one motion.

Christian ("Have you ever seen one like that?") stared, disbelieving. On the bench, Brooks shook his head in amazement. Nobody had ever scored a goal like that. Ever.

From there, the Russians added a few ornamental scrolls. Sergei Makharov came in on a breakaway for an eighth goal. Krutov finished off his hat trick with a burst of sprinter's speed. Then Balderis worked a give-and-go with defenseman Valery Vasiliev that so befuddled the official scorer that he gave the goal to Sergei Starikov. "I think the United States team has a very good future," Russian coach Viktor Tikhonov said straight-faced, with the final tally 10–3.

In the U.S.A. dressing room, black humor was the order of the day. "What do you think about that?" Brooks asked his troops, in approximately the same spirit Lord Cardigan might have used at Balaklava. "That was pretty good. That was fun to play them, huh?"

Press reaction was predictable, which was fine with Brooks, who'd been telling everyone that a bronze medal was the best the squad could expect.

The most fortunate among the players had been Mark Wells. He'd stayed back at the Olympic Village, nursing a strep throat. Months later, on the banquet circuit, he'd ask audiences a trivia question: Name the only man who'd never lost to the Russians.

Meanwhile, back at the front, McClanahan was peering at a swelling ankle, courtesy of a Russian shot. He'd been examining it in the dressing room late in the game when he heard the door open and saw Jack O'Callahan being helped in. Vasiliev had caved in his knee with a body check.

"Keep your heads up," Brooks told his people, then saw O'Callahan lying there half crying, looking shattered.

Seventy-two hours before the Games, O'Callahan thought. All that work down the drain. Back at Lake Placid, U.S.O.C. doctor Tony Daly gave him the bad news: "The knee's pretty loose. You'll probably need surgery, a cast, eight weeks in all."

Now Brooks had a problem. This was Sunday. The first game, against Sweden, was Tuesday. By Olympic rules, final rosters were due on Monday. If Brooks included O'Callahan's name and the knee was as bad as Daly thought, he'd wasted a spot. "What if we lose another defenseman?" Brooks mused. "We're down to four then."

Yet, O'Callahan had messed up knees before, and they'd always tightened up after a few days. What if Brooks sent him home and the knee came around after a week? O'Callahan would have blown a year's training, and the team would be without one of their most reliable competitors.

"Let's not panic," Brooks decided. "We'll wait a day." Meanwhile, he put in a call to Bob Murray in Boston and Kaminsky in New York, the agents for both O'Callahan and Jack Hughes.

"Better get Hughes ready," Brooks told them. "He'll probably be coming up here." It was Sunday morning, and Kaminsky tried to reach Hughes in Fort Worth where he'd been sent awaiting final word from Brooks. If the word was no, a contract had been worked out with Colorado, who held Hughes' rights.

Around noon, Kaminsky called Murray, who said he'd been in touch with Brooks, asking him to let O'Callahan get a second opinion. Brooks had agreed, and Murray told Kaminsky to hold off trying to get Hughes. Came Monday morning, and O'Callahan was able to walk, stiff-legged, around the village. He'd gotten an opinion from Dr. Richard Steadman, the man who'd put skier Phil Mahre back together after he'd broken a leg on Whiteface Mountain the previous winter.

"I think you can play," Steadman told O'Callahan. "But you might not be available for the first three or four games."

"Guess we've gotta roll dice," Brooks decided.

O'Callahan had always been good for the club. He'd done everything Brooks had asked of him. And it meant so damn much to him. So Brooks checked with the doctors once more, then went in to see O'Callahan.

"OCee, I'm going to stay with you."

At first, Brooks thought O'Callahan was going to hug him. Instead OCee thumped him in the chest with a grateful forearm, nearly knocking the wind out of him. "Thanks, Herb. Thanks."

"Looks like O'Callahan's going to play after all," Hughes heard by phone. He laughed to himself. "Well, that figures. That's the way the year's gone."

So Brooks filed his roster, the twenty gentlemen he was bringing to the dance, then had a word with them. This wasn't December any more. Dress rehearsal was over. Main Street was clogged with people, the field house would be full, the spotlights on. The Games were starting tomorrow, Brooks said, and you deserve to be here. It's a great opportunity, but you have a corresponding obligation. "And I'm not going to have anybody here who's just happy to be here. We're not here to watch the luge or climb up mountains."

His players glanced at each other. What, is he serious? What does he think *we* think we're here for? Brooks wound down his homily . . . then paused. "But whatever we do," he concluded, "we're going to have fun." Then Brooks walked out the door. The twenty gentlemen looked at one another. Fun. He did say "fun," didn't he? Someone started snickering. Then the whole room collapsed in laughter. That's Herbie.

10

QUADRATIC EQUATIONS

Usually, he made it a point never to watch an opponent practice. It was one of Jim Craig's little fetish/rituals, like not shaving before games, never staying for a full warm-up and affixing a four-leaf-clover decal to his stick.

But he'd gone down to have a look at the Swedes, and now Craig regretted it. "Oh, my God," he thought. "I can't stop any of those shots. We're going to play them tomorrow ... and we're gonna get killed."

Not that it would have been a novelty. No U.S. Olympic team had taken Sweden since 1960. The 1972 silver medalists had played them in the opener at Sapporo, lost by four goals and spent the rest of the Games scrambling to make up for it.

Nobody had seen the Swedes around Olympus since. Distressed by North American raids on their clubs during the NHL-WHA wars of the mid-seventies, they'd assessed their depleted talent pool and pulled their hockey team out of the 1976 Games. Now they were back, curiosities in blue and yellow.

Brooks had had a glimpse of them in Moscow in 1979, but the Swedes had been in the medal group and there'd been no direct head-to-head measure. They looked to be a veteran club with good technical skills. Their goalie, Pelle Lindbergh, had been drafted in the second round by the Philadelphia Flyers. Beyond that, Brooks knew only numbers. Fifteen, sixteen, eighteen, two and four looked very strong, he said. Otherwise they were a group of alert, pleasant faces in Sweden's official team book, their profiles listed cryptically beneath. Half a dozen of the players were 30 or older. One of them, a forward named Mats Aahlberg, had been on that Sapporo team.

He was like the rest of them, an accountant who played club hockey during the winter and joined the National team for the Worlds.

Unlike the Russians, the Swedish players actually *were* part-timers—students and engineers, clerks and soldiers whose livelihood did not depend upon bringing home a medal.

Although Brooks had always admired them, the rap on them, propagated mostly by NHL types, was that the Swedes had no guts, that you could intimidate them in the corners, that they wouldn't pay the price for a spot on the medal stand. "Look at the record," amateur historians advised. "Six times in fourth place."

And this time there'd been some squabbling back home between Sweden's top league and its national governing body. They'd thrown together something of an all-star team, had them practice six times, then sent them over.

Yet they dogged the Americans from the opening face-off. Ken Morrow or Mike Ramsey would go back into the U.S.A. zone to get the puck, and a Swedish forechecker would be on them at once, climbing up their backs.

After two shifts, Bill Baker found himself exhausted. "They're all over us," he thought. "Maybe we're not in good enough shape."

Or maybe anxiety had tightened muscles to the screaming point. There were twelve teams at Lake Placid, six to a group. Four would qualify for the medal round, and Brooks had calculated that the Americans would need two points out of their first two games (a victory being worth two, a tie one) to survive. Czechoslovakia was next up. Lose to the Swedes, and you'd have dug yourself into a hole before the opening ceremonies.

So, from the beginning, the Americans were overtense, missing connections, watching scoring chances slip away. Robbie

McClanahan came down on the first shift and put the puck over the crossbar. Steve Christoff watched a shot slide across the goalmouth. Nothing.

Then Eric Strobel came streaking down alone, deked too late and whipped a backhand high and wide. All of this in the first three minutes.

So it went. Seven minutes in, Buzz Schneider had a goal called back. Ten minutes in, Morrow broke in untouched, and Lindbergh blocked his shot. Morrow scooped up the rebound, went around behind the cage and tried to sweep the puck into the empty net. But Mats Waltin, the Swedish captain, was standing there and knocked it awry.

A minute later, the Swedes scored. They'd broken out, come down; and a defenseman, an insulation fitter named Sture Andersson, put the puck over Craig's shoulder.

The Swedes could operate this way all night, Brooks fretted. We're tentative, out of sync. They could wind up getting on a roll, wheeling and dealing. Then, ball game.

I've got to do something to shock the dressing room, Brooks told himself as the buzzer sounded to end the period. Get their minds off the Swedes.

Brooks had seen McClanahan go off early. Now, he was told, the Olympic committee's trainer (Brooks had also brought his own, Gary Smith, from the "U") had told McClanahan to take off his equipment, that he was done for the night. No need to turn a charley horse into something worse.

Annoyed, Brooks checked with Doc Nagobads. "Can Robbie hurt himself any more if he plays?" "No," Nagobads told him.

"Hmm," Brooks mused on the way to the dressing room. "Watch this," he told Craig Patrick.

McClanahan was sitting in his jock, half sobbing from frustration, an ice pack on his thigh. A Swede had picked him up coming down the left wing, stayed with him and slammed McClanahan into the boards. He'd felt the muscle knot and swell immediately and had hobbled off. Now he could barely move, and the implication devastated him. True to his nature,

McClanahan had wanted to play the Games in peak form and had arrived there in perfect condition, primed to go. One body check, he feared now, might have finished him in ten minutes.

Then Brooks came storming in, looked at McClanahan and went wild. "You gutless S.O.B.," he shouted. "Nobody's going belly-up now. Get your gear back on, you candyass." McClanahan, stunned, stared at him.

"He's lost it," John Harrington told Mike Eruzione. "Twenty minutes into the Olympic Games, and Herbie's lost it already."

McClanahan was on his feet now, yelling at Brooks. "You jerk, I'll show you. I'll show you." They were toe to toe. "Jesus," Bill Baker thought, "they're going to go at it."

But Jack O'Callahan, in street clothes, came up behind Brooks and grabbed him, trying to bust it up, to cool things out. Brooks left then, went into the hallway; but McClanahan, still furious, followed him.

"Listen, I'll go out there and give it a try," he told Brooks. "But don't you tell me if I can play or not. I'll tell you."

Inside the dressing room, players were agape, shaking their heads. "This is unreal," Dave Silk told himself. "Francis Ford Coppola is going to come out in a minute and say, 'Cut. Good.' "

It continued that way, Brooks and McClanahan jawing at each other in the hallway, as AHAUS people and security guards looked on, astounded.

Then they came back in and it was Brooks following McClanahan now, telling him that he was a goddam rich kid, that he'd had life easy up to now, that he was a big baby from North Oaks, that he'd better bite the bullet.

Finally Mark Johnson, who'd thought the first period had been weak but nothing to panic over, called over to the captain. "Mike, get him out of here."

So Brooks left, and on his way out, winked at Patrick. It was September again and they were back in Oslo, skating in the dark. Twenty guys who all hated Herbie. What's he picking on Robbie for? Robbie would go if he could.

So the Americans came out for the second period and the

tenseness had metamorphosed into adrenaline. Goddam Herbie. But as the minutes ticked down, nothing much changed.

Dave Christian hit the goalpost with a slapshot from the right point that made a clunk you could hear in the balcony. The Americans burst in, four-on-two on the power play, and Steve Christoff wasn't able to finish the play-off. Then Ken Morrow set up Buzz Schneider at the Swedish blue line for one of his labeled slappers and Lindbergh knocked it down.

Less than a minute left in the period, and it was still 1–0. Then Jim Craig turned away a routine shot; Mike Ramsey picked up the puck and got it to Johnson and Silk, who had broken free and left the Swedish defensemen trapped up ice.

For an instant, it looked as though they might entangle. Otherwise, there was nothing between Johnson, Silk and the Swedish goal. Bearing in, Silk pulled Lindbergh left with a feint, whipped a 10-foot wrist shot past him twenty-eight seconds before the buzzer, then did a solitary dance on his skate tops, stick aloft.

Okay, the Americans thought during the break. We're back. And rolling. Every time down now, it seemed they were getting off a good shot, something for Lindbergh to worry about. Three minutes into the second period, here came Silk again, pumped for another one—but Lindbergh stoned him. Then Magic Johnson leveled a shot that bounced off Lindbergh's leg pads, went behind him, dinged the post—then spun away. The Flyers were right, Brooks mused. This kid's a hell of a goalie.

Out came the Swedes, chasing the puck into the American corner, scuffling a bit, keeping it there. Harald Luckner, one of their 6-foot forwards, came up with it, looked across and saw his defenseman, Tommy Eriksson, standing directly in front of Jim Craig with no blue U.S.A. shirts anywhere near. All Eriksson had to do was redirect the passout past Craig and it was 2–1.

They're so patient, thought Bill Baker, who was gasping for breath between every shift. The Swedes would stay on you, all those alert and pleasant faces, a blue helmet always visible out of the corner of your eye. They would depend on Lindbergh to keep them out of trouble ("I wish the Flyers had signed him,"

Brooks would say). Then, when you got sloppy for four seconds in your end or left one of their people uncovered, the Swedes went right for the jugular. "Stay with it, stay with it, stay with it," Brooks had stressed. "They'll throw in the towel before you will. They'll crack." But there were few signs of that.

Fifteen minutes left now, with the Americans still dictating the tempo, still worrying Lindbergh—but still behind. Then Tomas Jonsson, Sweden's version of Mike Ramsey, their 19-year-old prima donna (and a second-round draft pick of the New York Islanders), was whistled off for tripping, and Brooks sent out his power play—with McClanahan on it.

McClanahan had gotten the muscle functioning a bit, had made a point of standing up between shifts to keep it flexed. Later, Brooks would say how gutsy McClanahan had been, but McClanahan said that it was bullshit; that he'd been worthless, just taking up space, skating in first gear.

Yet here he was at the edge of the crease, taking a pass from Baker and trying to jam it past Lindbergh. No go. As soon as the penalty expired, Eruzione and Eriksson shoved each other a bit and both went off. So it would be four-on-four for a while, a chance for some freewheeling pond hockey, and Brooks sent out a couple of his Coneheads, Mark Pavelich and Schneider, who knew how to improvise with some open space.

Sure enough, within twenty-five seconds they broke out two-on-one; and Schneider, home free, dropped the puck for Pavelich—who wasn't there.

So it went. Strobel came streaking down again, and the puck went whizzing over the crossbar again. Eriksson was whistled off again, this time for holding, and the American power play came up empty again. Less than six minutes left now, and here was Morrow crosschecking someone and going off for it.

Only two minutes of normalcy left. The Americans would be shorthanded for two. They'd play two even up. Then, if nothing had happened, Brooks would have to pull Craig, send on an extra man and hope for the best.

Morrow's penalty expired uneventfully; the Americans simply went aggressive, kept the Swedes from setting up. Three minutes left now, with the Americans trying to bust out and Craig trying to keep the puck moving—deflecting Swedish shots, pushing the puck to his defensemen. Nothing. Anywhere a glimpse of open ice might develop, there stood a blue helmet on patient sentry.

Two minutes, and Brooks sent out five forwards, hoping that Magic Johnson could create something. He was pacing behind the bench now in his camel's hair sport coat, head down—then up, to peer at the clock—then down again. One minute now, and time to go for it. Brooks made the signal to Craig, who came sprinting out of the goal and back to the bench as Dave Silk was going over the dasher.

Six American skaters on the ice—Magic and two of the Coneheads, Harrington and Schneider; plus Silk and two defensemen, Mike Ramsey and Bill Baker. Within nine seconds they got a face-off in the Swedish end and Brooks sent out Mark Pavelich for Harrington, to take the draw.

Pavelich came up with the puck and flung it back to Ramsey at the left point, who wound up and fired—and watched a Swedish defenseman smother it, blocking the puck back to him.

Ramsey thought of winding up again, then noticed Baker, who was already doubling back to guard against a Swedish breakout but was all alone. Thirty-five seconds. Here you go, Willie, Ramsey thought, moving the puck over to him.

Baker lofted it along the right boards, into the traffic behind Lindbergh.

Schneider, with the good Range grinding instincts, scrambled and scuffled behind the net, held off a Swede who was clutching him and somehow got the puck over to Pavelich at the left face-off circle. Thirty seconds.

Pavelich whirled, saw Baker untended on the other side, at the top of the right face-off circle and threw the puck over to him. And Lindbergh, who'd been looking to his right, trying to make sense of the scramble, now looked straight ahead and saw Baker turning, wheeling and winding up.

Just get it on net, on the fly, Baker told himself; then blasted the puck about a foot off the ice. At least there'll be a rebound, he figured.

Instead, he saw the net ripple, saw Lindbergh drop asprawl, the red light go on, the blue shirts go to the cage with their sticks up. Craig, on the bench with his head down, gasping for air, saw nothing. Brooks had seen Pavelich grab the puck, had seen Baker wind up. "And then," he said, "everybody was standing up in front of me."

There were twenty-seven seconds left to play. The Swedes, spooked, played them out in a haze, and it was done. The Americans danced at center ice.

"We were lucky," Brooks conceded. "We jockeyed guys around, we had the goalie out."

That was the point, Bengt Ohlson, the gloomy Swedish coach, would say. It was a typical North American goal: The North Americans were always most dangerous in the final minute. "They never give up," Ohlson concluded.

Give up? Hell, the Games hadn't been officially opened yet. They'd set the master schedule before the hockey federation had decided to increase the number of teams, so half a dozen matches had to be played the day before the Olympic flame was lighted.

To march into the stadium in your cowboy hats, sheepskin jackets and jeans with your backs already to the wall might have been unsettling. Actually, to Brooks, marching anywhere in any cowboy hat was unsettling. "Even when I was a little kid growing up on the East Side of St. Paul, I never wore a cowboy hat," Brooks muttered the next day. "I can't believe I'm wearing one now."

He'd told Olympic officials he'd lost his—so they'd issued him another one, so large he'd had to stuff paper into it. Then he'd marched contentedly with his team, who'd been half a minute from Tap City, and had survived. You didn't have to win to not lose.

Brooks had wanted two points out of the first two games, so

the team was on target. Now came the Czechs, the same Czechs who'd ripped Norway 11–0, scoring all the goals in the final 35 minutes, pouring it on long after the Norwegians had bagged it.

That was the difference between the Russians and the Czechs, Phil Verchota thought. The Russians might beat you 11–0 but the pacing would have been consistent, the goals scored mechanically. The Russians merely kept scoring, kept skating, until time ran out. If the opportunities were there for 11 goals, then they scored 11. Nothing personal.

But the Czechs seemed to relish running it up on you, wouldn't think twice about pumping in eight in the third period, their eyes seeming to light up when they saw you on one knee, white flag at the ready.

The Czechs had beaten the Russians for the World championship in 1972, then done it again in 1976. The Czechs had been peaking then, playing beautifully inventive hockey, using breakout patterns and power play alignments never seen elsewhere.

They'd gone to Innsbruck for the 1976 Games and had the Russians on the ropes, up 3–1 in the third, and should have beaten them, but lost by a goal.

The Russians had always had trouble with the Czechs, and the political tensions merely made their meetings more bitter. So it was not surprising that after the Americans had beaten the Russians at Squaw Valley in 1960 and were trailing Czechoslovakia by a goal in the final game, Sologubov, the Soviet captain, had come by the U.S. dressing room and urged them to take oxygen for the final period.

It was a lovely, selfless thing to do, some people thought; then they remembered that a Czech victory would give them the mythical European championship over the Russians. Of course.

They'd had a brutal match in 1969, and though the Russians wound up with the World Championship, the Czechs had won their meeting—then dropped to their knees and put their ears to the ice. Just to make sure that the Soviets back in Moscow hadn't turned off the petroleum pipeline.

By the mid-seventies, the Czechs had all but caught the Russians, could skate with them equally more nights than not, relying on a big-play offense, shooting forwards up ice for long passes and resultant breakaways. However, by 1980, the whispers were that they were aging, their star fading a bit. The Russians had beaten them horribly in Moscow during the 1979 Worlds. The Americans had tied them. But almost all their big names were still there—Milan Novy, considered the finest forward in the 1976 Canada Cup, Jiri Bubla, the big defenseman, and the three brilliant Stastny brothers.

"Don't be in awe of them," Brooks told his players in the dressing room as a capacity crowd was beginning to elbow its way into the field house above.

"Yeah, I know they average twenty-eight years of age," Brooks admitted. "Eight or ten of them played in the 1976 Games. So what?"

That was precisely the point, Brooks said. You're young. With youth comes hunger, and when you're hungry, things happen.

"You're the youngest team here," Brooks continued. "Use it to your advantage. Use your youth, your enthusiasm, your skating ability."

In a sense, the Czech game had always been the most critical to American medal-hopes. No U.S. team had ever lost to the Czechs and won an Olympic medal. And no U.S. team had ever beaten them and failed to win one. In 1960, it had been the gold medal game, and the Americans had won it on uncut adrenaline, banging home the six goals in the final twenty minutes. In 1972, they'd taken heavy thumpings from the Swedes and Russians, but had taken home the silver because Lefty Curran, the goalie, had played out of his mind against the Czechs and because the Americans had stormed the Czech goal all night.

Now they'd survived the Swedes. Beat the Czechs, tend to their knitting against the sub-Europeans and the medal round —and at least a bronze—would be there.

"Go up to the tiger," Brooks concluded, reaching into his

collected works, "spit in his eye . . . and then shoot him."

So the Americans clomped out of the room, up the runway
—and it was Williams Arena on a Friday night in February with
UMD in town, Dane County Coliseum with the Gophers and
the Badgers, the Beanpot final with B.C. and B.U.

They'd performed before polite applause against Sweden two
nights earlier, half of the seats unfilled. Now, Bah Harrington,
noticed, the place was bonkers, flags waving everywhere he
looked, every chair occupied.

The Czechs were circling, blue helmets, red from shoulder to
skate top, white lions rampant on their jersey front, names
crammed with consonants and accent marks on the back. Dvo-
rak. Kadlek. Novak. Kralik. The Stastny brothers, all three of
them, sturdy forwards who looked as though they should be
playing for the Prague Packers. Wild and crazy guys.

So the Americans came out supercharged, ready to wheel.
Jack O'Callahan's knee had tightened up already, and he was in
uniform, his mere presence on the bench spurring on his comrades.

"Hope we're not too pumped," Jim Craig fretted, preparing
his goal crease for a night of heavy going. "If everybody's racing
around running people, we'll be dead. I'll be looking at two-
on-ones all night."

That was how the Czechs were, Brooks knew. Quick and
crafty counterpunchers that found ways to work off your current. So the plan was to muck them up a bit, stick-check the
Czechs to distraction, crowd the neutral zone, play the body,
use the youth. And don't play them the way Norway did, working out of the shell, hoping merely to control the damage. That
strategy made for 15–1 carousels, a red jersey swooping around
every two minutes.

So the Americans went out to rock and roll—but within forty-
five seconds here was Bill Baker, the man who'd chilled the
Swedes, groping on all fours, fighting for breath. He'd been hit
in the throat with a shot. Two minutes later, the Czechs were
hugging each other. Jaroslav Pouzar, one of their forwards, had

been sitting on Craig's doorstep untended when the puck came out to him from the left corner. A 10-foot wrist shot to Craig's stick side was automatic. A minute later, they were back again, three-on-one, Craig's eyes darting back and forth, caught in a shell game—but the Czechs blew the chance.

Already, the tempo was fast-forward, the American wings cruising, picking up red jerseys, moving with them, then slamming them into the boards. In two more minutes, the U.S.A. had tied the game on its trademark adrenal burst—a Mike Eruzione breakaway.

Neal Broten had won a draw just outside the Czech blue line, fought his way across and slipped the puck to his accelerating captain.

Eruzione was off balance, the angle wasn't the best, but he'd whipped a shot that glanced off goalie Jiri Kralik's leg and went past his glove.

Seeing the red light flick on energized Eruzione, who sprinted back to the bench and began yelling to his mates ("C'mon, c'mon") from the bench.

The Coneheads were on the ice now, and Harrington and Mark Pavelich were suddenly back at UMD, free-forming it. Within seconds Pavelich sent Harrington in all alone, but Kralik batted away his bid. Next rush up, they went at it a different way. Buzz Schneider flipped a backhander at Kralik, who knocked the puck out in front. Pavelich, gliding past the goalmouth, simply poked it past. U.S.A., 2–1, with the whole team on the ice, whooping.

This was the game Brooks had taught them to play. "Controlled enthusiasm," Schneider called it. Quick young legs. Eyes alert, shifting. Boisterous work in the corners. Disciplined patterns. Puck control. With Craig, unshaven, the clover decals on mask and stick, standing cool and tall behind them.

"Maybe they're as afraid of us as we are of them," Bobby Suter guessed. "They've heard about us—a young team, all that speed—but they've never seen us."

The team the Czechs had waxed, 5–0, at Innsbruck never

skated like this one. Didn't hit the way this one did, either, clocking you from the opening face-off. Here was Kenny Morrow with a scowl on his face, pushing around Anton Stastny. Here was Baker, breathing easy now, lining up Frantisek Kaberle and knocking him ass-over-teakettle into the Czech bench.

Sometimes, they were careless. Sloppy clearing and coverage soon gave Marian Stastny an easy goal with Craig out of the net after a rebound. So it was 2–2 when the first period was done, but there was little doubt about who was in command.

"Hey, this should be 4–2," Eruzione told his people in the dressing room. So they promptly went out and made it so.

Not five minutes into the second period, the Coneheads came over the dasher and up the ice, Pavelich skittering up the right side ("I'll get it there, Buzzy") and laying in a long pass from the boards to Schneider in the slot which was so perfect that Schneider merely had to tip it past Kralik.

Now the Americans had the lead again and were dictating. Ten minutes passed, and here came the Magic Man out of the corner, taking a pass from Robbie McClanahan and diddy-bopping from left to right, changing from forehand to backhand and flipping the puck through traffic and past Kralik. Four–two, with Roadrunner Hour yet ahead.

The final twenty minutes were everything the Olympians had daydreamed about on all those bus rides in December, and while lacing up skates in Omaha and Glens Falls. "Every time we come across their line," marveled Phil Verchota, "we either score a goal or get a great chance."

He had come down the ice with Mark Wells and Dave Christian three minutes into the final period, saw Christian break across the blue line and be tripped by a Czech defenseman, skated into a flailing cluster in front and watched the red light flash. Somehow, Verchota, along for the ride, had gotten his stick on the puck and pushed it past Kralik.

A minute later, the Coneheads did their Night at the Improv number again, with Harrington rushing the length of the rink, going into the corner and one-handing a pass to Schneider, standing unmarked in front, for an easy goal between Kralik's legs.

Prague, Schneider thought. Fifteen to one. All we saw that night was the backs of their jerseys. Doesn't feel like that tonight. Now it was Yanks 6, Czechs 2, and more giddiness in store. With less than ten minutes to play, here came Johnson, dancing and dealing, splitting the defense and laying a centering pass on McClanahan's stick. A Czech stick took McClanahan's legs out from under him. So, on his face, the puck sliding away, McClanahan casually took a swipe at it and poked it past Kralik for a seventh one.

Suddenly the Czechs had turned old overnight, confused and desperately leg-tired. They had tried to blitz the American kids, and the kids had outskated them. They had tried to roughhouse with them and the kids had mugged them. Their goalie had fallen apart, letting pucks go off his pads, under his glove, through his legs. In one night they'd gone from almost certain silver medalists to tired old Socialists in the Trade Union League.

So, as the clock ticked down and the "U.S.A., U.S.A." chant filled the building, the Czechs turned it into Saturday night in Saginaw. The Magic Man, who'd eluded them all night, was the first target. A defenseman named Jan Neliba took a running charge at Johnson with less than three minutes to play, crumpling him with a forearm and temporarily dislocating his shoulder. "Four years of work," Johnson thought, gritting his teeth. "Am I through now?"

Brooks, pacing behind the bench, went insane. Unbelievable cheap shot. "We'll bury the goddam stick right in your throat," he shouted at Neliba. "You're gonna eat that goddam Koho, (Number) Three. You're gonna eat it."

As Neliba skated away, with Johnson still writhing on the ice, the Americans began calling after him ("Hey, Three, stay on the ice"), daring him to skate the next shift. Steve Christoff had words with Peter Stastny and went after him.

Then, after Johnson had been helped off the ice and play resumed, Anton Stastny rammed Eruzione into the wingboards from behind. Eruzione, furious, turned around and confronted Stastny, and saw the third brother, Marian, coming up to offer support. "You shut up," Eruzione told him, ready to deal with the whole family.

Then he nodded, smirked, looked up at the scoreboard and pointed. It was the old Boston Arena put-down. "Up *there*, sucker," the expression said. "Seven–three."

The kids owned this building now. The crowd, waving the flags and chanting, was theirs. The game was theirs. A spot in the medal round, too, God forbid anything unusual.

They'd done what Herbie had told them, spat in the tiger's eye and drilled him cold. "Everything we've been working toward for sixty games," Eruzione said, "you saw tonight."

In two hours they'd become instant celebrities, their backgrounds, idiosyncrasies and breakfast preferences matters of national concern.

"Does your roommate snore?" a media type asked Craig.

"Does he *what?*"

"Do you have a girl friend?"

"Did you ever drink a beer?"

Where's Charlestown? What's the Iron Range? What does Eruzione mean in Italian?

As soon as possible, Brooks and Kaminsky slipped out into the snowy night. A week before the Games, everyone in Lake Placid had been in a panic about the lack of snow. Today it wouldn't stop. Brushing flakes off their faces, they trudged to Ruth's Diner, a 1920s-era outpost that Kaminsky fondly recalled from 1970 when he had delightedly watched Cornell cap an undefeated 29–0 season with an NCAA crown.

Over bacon and eggs and butter-soaked white toast, they saluted each other with huge glasses of cold milk. But Brooks worried about the instant celebrity. He wanted to keep it under control, at least until the Games were over. So he'd announce that the U.S. players would not be going to the customary post-

game press conferences in the high school auditorium next
door.

He knew the routine—the captain, the goalie and the game's
leading scorer up there on stage before 600 note pads and tape
recorders. That meant Eruzione, Craig, and, probably, the
Magic Man every day for two weeks dominating the headlines
willy-nilly. Never a Morrow, a Wells, a Verchota.

The Olympians had gotten here as a family, treated equally,
at least by Brooks. Press conferences weren't good for family
life. If we start extracting guys from the locker room, Brooks
figured, it'll destroy our main asset, our comradeship. It'll kill us.
So he simply never mentioned the press conferences to the
players and went himself to handle the questions.

You want all the credit, a New York *Daily News* columnist
told him. You dirty bastard, Brooks thought. Okay, he decided,
I'm not coming back. Craig Patrick will go in my place as long
as we win. When we lose, I'll go in and face the music.

It wasn't as though he'd excluded the press. All they had to
do was walk out of the high school and up a flight of steps and
the whole team would be straggling out of the field house en
route to the shuttle bus. Everybody would be available.

The spotlight would be more evenly diffused that way, the
players more anonymous in their team parkas and ski hats, a
Bobby Suter as likely to be quoted as a Bill Baker. Then they
could go back to the Olympic Village, to the disco and the game
room and the trailer/dorms and be away from the vortex and
the growing Boys of Winter hype.

The more they were profiled, photographed, fussed over, the
less likely the players would be inclined to take the sub-
Europeans seriously. Blow a game to a Rumania, and the whole
sixty minutes with the Czechs would slide down the sewer.

That was why Brooks was terrified by the idea of Norway. He
told Kaminsky that this was exactly the kind of trap he had to
avoid: "You know, win the big one and then overconfidently
blow one against a team you should wire." After the Oslo Skate
back in September and all his talk about setting the tempo then

and the 9–0 blowout the next night, how was Brooks going to get his people to take them seriously now?

The Norwegians had turned up in Lake Placid looking every bit as plodding and awkward as predicted. They were delighted to be running in such fast company, but were wary of being *really* embarrassed—as in 19–2.

So Norway had become Team Armadillo and had given a new meaning to the concept of passive resistance. "We try to defend in our own zone," one of their coaches explained, "and keep the score down."

They would send one forward into your zone to do recon work and keep everybody else back to defend the homeland. If you grew careless and left the puck lying in the middle of the ice, the Norwegians would come in and try to score. Otherwise, it was hockey a la Gandhi.

They'd played Czechoslovakia in their first game, and for twenty-five minutes it was the siege of Leningrad revisited. Norway ventured exactly three shots, buttoned up tight and took the shelling. When the Czechs finally broke through, they'd poured in eleven goals, more goals than Norway had shots.

Unbowed, Norway had hunkered down against the West Germans two days later, and actually took the lead after six minutes. Shaken, the Germans scored a goal a minute for the next five minutes until the Norwegians hoisted the white flag. Keeping the score down that day had meant 10–4.

How could you motivate anybody to take these people seriously? Brooks wondered. None of the Olympians had been born in 1952, which was the only time the U.S. had ever played Norway in the Games.

The Olympics had been in Oslo that year, and the Americans had beaten Norway narrowly in the opening game. They'd been booed all the way to the medal stand for their rough play. But nobody under the age of fifty remembered that.

This Norwegian team belonged somewhere in a Division 2 college league; in fact, when they'd come to the States for a few

tune-ups, Norway had played Division 2 teams—and been
tuned instead. Everybody had seen the scores. Now the Americans would be playing them in the old Olympic Arena next door
to the new field house, which held maybe one-eighth as many
people. Face-off would be at 1:00 on a Saturday afternoon.

Terrific, Brooks thought. All the ingredients were present for
a dreadful two hours.

"You guys aren't good enough to beat Norway," he told his
team in the dressing room. Smirks. Nods. Diverted eyes. Right,
Herbie. So he fished out an old Brooksism and served it up: "You
guys aren't talented enough to win on talent alone."

There was not an ounce of juice in the room, no spark in the
eyes. "Remember these guys?" someone yelled. "We had to
skate all night." Nods. Halfhearted vows of retribution.

So they went out and watched the Norwegians skating
around, and any force-fed inspiration quickly melted away. The
whole story was written diagonally on the red New York Rangers–style jerseys: NORGE. No U.S. hockey team had ever lost to
a refrigerator.

They're just terrible, Dave Silk thought. There's no way we're
going to lose.

So the puck was dropped, and within five minutes it was a
fiasco. Players going off for roughing, hooking, elbowing, high
sticks at the rate of one a minute. No grace, no rhythm. Then
an Oslo plumber named Oeivind Loesaamoen took a slapshot,
the rebound came out to an Oslo taxi driver named Geir Myhre,
and Norwegian sticks were up, Norwegian voices shouting in
delighted surprise.

"Here we go," Bill Baker thought. The Americans had come
out flatter than a fourteenth-century globe, and in a matter of
four or five shifts, were skating as if their kneecaps were on
backward.

The Norwegians were rank tyros—salesmen and doctors and
repro technicians—but they were surprisingly sturdy, one of
the biggest clubs at the Games, and they had a knack for getting
in your way.

You would break out and come blowing into the Norwegian zone, and things would begin going wrong, your patterns would become bollixed, out of sync. The Americans never seemed to get an open shot on the goal; the firing lanes were clogged with Norges. If the puck did get through, the goaltender—Jim Martinsen—would knock it down somehow and jump on it.

When the buzzer sounded, with the refrigerators leading 1–0, the Americans trudged into the dressing room, sat down and cursed. If we lose to Norway, Mike Ramsey told himself, we'll remember it for the rest of our lives.

It was the Oslo Skate all over again, and Herbies ad infinitum loomed. They had to loosen up, get back into their game, quit glaring at each other.

"Why don't we all say something nice about each other," Dave Silk suggested. So they did. "Michael, your hair looks wonderful . . ." "Mark, you have lovely eyes . . ."

Finally, the giggles stopped. "How can we be joking?" someone said. "Down one–nothing to these guys?"

They'd been anticipating a light comedy: two goals and an assist for anybody who could skate three strides forward. "Let's just win the damn game," one Olympian advised.

So they went back out, and in forty-one seconds Mike Eruzione willed the puck into the Norwegian net. The Americans had gone on the power play almost as soon as they'd gotten back on the ice. The puck fell at Marthinsen's feet, and Eruzione simply jabbed and poked at it until it slid across the line.

"He'll be a catalyst," Harvard coach Billy Cleary had told Brooks, and it was true. Eruzione had provided the spark that ultimately shocked the Czechs. Now he'd done it again.

Four minutes later, Johnson took a pass from Dave Christian, busted down the middle and slapped home a 20-footer. The shoulder was still sore as hell (Olympus does not dispense painkillers), but Johnson had spent a day icing it and wrapping it and icing it again, and now it was serviceable. Or at least good enough to wind up with.

So it was 2–1 now, the danger past, but the rhythms still off.

Baker was terribly frustrated. "I can't seem to do anything right," he told himself.

Everybody wanted to bust it open now, to be done with it, to be elsewhere. Brooks was disgusted. One guy would get the puck and go kamikaze, one-on-four, trying to blow the goddam armadillo apart.

This, Jack O'Callahan thought, is like B.U. playing Merrimack. They're looking for the big upset. And we just want it to be over.

So Mark Pavelich and Silk administered the knockout blow. Pavelich going behind the Norwegian net, zipping a pass to Silk in front; and it was bang-bang-goal. "The longer you let a team like that hang in," Silk reasoned, "the more they start smelling an upset."

Seven or eight hours later, it ended 5–1, but nobody on the American side was happy about it. The fine edge honed by the Sweden and Czechoslovakia games had been stripped away in one afternoon, and there were two more problem games ahead with Rumania and West Germany.

Anybody could get the arterial blood flowing for the Czechs. The great teams were those that found some compelling reason to take marginal opponents seriously, that could always get to a consistent level. You never saw the Russians life-and-death with turkeys; it was always 6–0 after one. Euthanasia City.

So Brooks gave everybody Sunday off and decided to talk to a few people. Except for Eruzione, who'd been the starter motor for the last two games, the second line had been unproductive—Neal Broten and Steve Christoff shadows of themselves.

The third and fourth lines had been carrying the team. The Coneheads, jokers in December, had beaten the Czechs virtually alone. And the Mark Wells–Phil Verchota–Dave Silk combination had been remarkably responsive. You didn't lose much with them out there.

But the first line, which should have been the centerpiece, had been struggling. Injury accounted for much of that. By the time Robbie McClanahan's thigh unknotted, Mark Johnson's shoulder was done in. And Eric Strobel had been a loose wire for three games, his shooting everywhere but on net.

"You're not playing," Brooks told him. "You're lackadaisical."

Strobel shrugged and looked at Craig Patrick. "What am I supposed to do? You want me to score goals? Play defense? What do you want me to do? I need a niche."

The niche, Brooks decided, would be as right wing with Eruzione and Broten. Christoff would move up to the first line with Johnson and McClanahan. The other lines would stand pat. Everything turned on the first-line right wing, just as it had when Brooks and Kaminsky had scribbled combinations on a napkin at the Leamington Hotel.

The other problem was more elusive—goal differential. If a tie-breaker was needed to determine advancement to the medal round or to award a medal itself, goals allowed would be subtracted from goals scored. So it was to your advantage to bury people, just as the Russians did. The hell with sportsmanship and Baron de Coubertin's credo about taking part being more important than winning.

By nature, an American eased up when the score got to 5–1, satisfied that the point had been proven. You gained nothing by humiliating opponents, particularly if you had to play them again later.

Yet the Americans had seen what the Czechs did to Norway; Sweden had rocked Rumania 8–0. Better if they'd been able to work up a fine gut-level hatred of those Oslo plumbers and done them up in double digits.

There was at least one more chance for that. Rumania seemed the sort of crew that skated just well enough to remain upright. Ion Tiriac, the brooding, shaggy-haired tennis pro, had once doubled as a defenseman for the national team. Involved in a sprightly go with a couple of Russian forwards, Tiriac was said to have snapped his stick over a knee, brandished the jagged end and said, "Hokay, who *iss* first? Better to make your mother weep than make my mother weep."

The Rumanians had never won an Olympic medal of any denomination, and their sole mission seemed to be defeating somebody, anybody. The West Germans had accidentally obliged them in their very first try, by letting the Rumanian captain, a man with a name like a Romany dessert wine (Doru Tureanu), score three goals in nine minutes.

That much achieved, the Rumanians had taken shreddings from the Swedes and Czechs with good grace and now seemed to be looking forward to some sort of showdown with the Norwegians—conceivably for the championship of sub-Europe.

They would be the last, best chumps the Americans would play, and Brooks made that clear to his players in the dressing room. "Playing in these Games is a great opportunity," he said. "And being in the position of controlling your own destiny is a miracle opportunity. Don't blow it by losing to Rumania. If you do, you'll carry the memory of the blown opportunity to your graves. To your graves."

He'd thought of starting Steve Janaszak in goal as a nice thank-you bouquet for service above and beyond the call. Then Brooks thought about goal differential, about controlling one's destiny and about the implications of disrupting Jimmy Craig's rhythm; and he decided to let things be.

He sent the Coneheads out for the face-off—Who better to get something going? Valerian Netedu, the Rumanian goalkeeper, sensing the bad karma, carefully heaped a barrier of ice shavings around either post and braced himself for the onslaught. It came quickly.

Three minutes in, Eric Strobel came jitterbugging down, collected a centering pass from Mike Eruzione—and missed the chance, leaving the puck lying in the crease. Maybe, Strobel wondered, it just isn't meant for me to score goals.

Or for anybody that night. The Norwegian game had offered one sort of frustration; speed bumps and semi-barriers and interposed sticks and torsos, never an open shot. But the Rumanians were conceding everything, leaving Netedu standing there like an arcade duck, daring you to hit the bull's-eye—and letting you blow it yourself.

Dave Christian hit the post. Eleven seconds later Mark John-son breezed in alone—and couldn't cash. A minute passed, and Steve Christoff missed an open net on the power play.

Then Mike Eruzione, after drawing Netedu forty-five feet out of the cage and stranding him there, faked around him, broke for the vacant cage and somehow slid to his knees in the corner without getting off a shot. Now Christoff, taking a perfect centering pass from Robbie McClanahan, jammed the puck into Netedu's pads.

Eight minutes; six labeled scoring chances; no goals. The Americans were skating back to the bench, sitting down hard, banging their sticks against the floor and cursing.

Craig, who had little to do at his end, was shaking his head. "It's gotten so you can't tease guys any more when they come back after missing a chance," he would say.

Finally, a Rumanian defenseman named Ellod Gergely Antal fell down at the U.S. blue line, and the Coneheads broke out for a little light pinball; three-on-one, Pavelich to Harrington to Pavelich to Schneider, who tapped the puck casually into the open left side of the cage. Twelve minutes, one goal.

Within four minutes, the Americans had themselves another. Strobel, defying whatever had been messing with his mind and/or stick for a week, got hold of a rebound and whipped it high into the cage.

So the primary matter at hand—the iron imperative *not* to lose to Rumania—seemed to be settled when the U.S. went off for intermission. But the anxious eyes and tight lips in the dressing room said that it wasn't nearly good enough. Eight good scoring chances had gone *pfft*—Phil Verchota had seen two vanish on him in the last six minutes. By any reasonable standard, the score should have been 6–0 by then, maybe more.

The Americans had leveled twenty shots on Netedu in twenty minutes. In the next twenty, they laid on sixteen more and scored twice more. But Tureanu, no dessert wine he, got one back for the Rumanians with a fluky power-play goal. The puck had bounced crazily off the back boards and Tureanu had swatted at it, a nine-iron shot, and knocked it past a startled Craig.

With five minutes left in the evening, it was still only 5–2; the sons of Ion Tiriac were being decidedly uncooperative. As every early-rising milkman in the Carpathians was switching off his black-and-white set, Neal Broten walked in for a sixth goal, then McClanahan chipped in a seventh.

The Americans should have been rumpling each other's hair when it was done. Instead, they left the field house mumbling about the Swedes, who'd waxed compliant Norway 7–1 earlier in the day.

It was the goal differential. The Swedes and Americans had tied. If they both reached the medal round, the tie would count in the standings. If they ended up tied, there, too, goal differential would decide the medals. At the moment, the Swedes, who'd run up heavier numbers on the sub-Europeans, had a four-goal edge.

"When we came up here, people thought if we got through the first four games unbeaten, it would be unbelievable," Craig was saying. "And now, it's not good enough. Beating somebody seven–two in the Olympics is not good enough."

Baron de Coubertin would be spinning two meters under Mount Olympus if he knew what the hockey federation had done to his credo. Not only was taking part not good enough any more, even winning didn't quite make it.

It was the Olympics according to General Curtis LeMay. You had to make the rubble bounce. The Canadian goalie let in a bad one the other night, Craig mused. Now it's probably going to haunt him for the rest of his life.

Crazy. Used to be a player's best friend was his Koho. Now it was his Texas Instruments pocket calculator. The easiest thing, the Americans knew, was to have Czechoslovakia dump Sweden, which was what usually happened. That way, the Czechs would qualify, and the U.S., having bounced the Czechs, thus would have the advantage in the medal round.

They would also play the Russians—certain winners of the

other group—on Sunday afternoon instead of Friday night.

"The Czechs better get going, that's all I have to say," Craig concluded. "You look at them practice and you think they can beat anybody. I think we caught them asleep. I sure as hell *hope* we caught them asleep. I just hope every pipe goes in on the Swedish goal tomorrow."

Unless, of course, the United States happened to lose to the West Germans. Then, the Czechs would qualify, and the second spot in the medal round would come down to, yes, goal differential between the United States and Sweden.

They talked about all of the algebraic possibilities before the West German game. "And all we decided," Jack O'Callahan said, "was that they were confusing."

At least one variable had been eliminated by face-off time. The Swedes, with Lindbergh starring as Lefty Curran, had stoned the Czechs for the first time in three years. They'd gone up 3–0 late in the second period and Lindbergh had helped them hang on, knocking down 41 Czech shots.

So for the first time since 1960, the Czechs would not win a medal. And unless the Americans croaked the West Germans by seven goals, the Swedes would have an edge in goal differential, would win the group, and would force the United States to play the Russians first.

Used to be it had been easy. Even the 1964 and 1968 U.S. teams, the unmedalworthies, had beaten the Germans by seven or eight goals. But that had changed in Innsbruck in 1976.

The Americans had gone into the final game virtually assured of the bronze medal. They'd beaten the Finns and Poles, both seeded ahead of them; only the West Germans were ranked lower. And it had turned into dust for them.

The difference had been the giant Kuehnhackl, standing 6–6, who had played them for Lilliputians, scoring one goal and setting up the other three. It had ended 4–1, and the Americans, enraged, had stomped, swearing, into their dressing room and flung equipment around.

The team had met again in Moscow at the 1979 Worlds, and

the West Germans had handled them twice, easily. Now they
had absolutely nothing to gain—or lose—by playing the United
States. Depending on the Germans' mood, that could make for
either a pleasant two hours—or a nightmarish *déjà vu.*

For one thing, the Germans did not play like Europeans;
weren't particularly fond of weaving and drop passes and 10-
foot wrist shots. They were a gang of semishaven bullyboys with
unruly hair and unruly attitudes who played you pretty much
like an NHL team, taking the body with abandon and unloading
blasters at your goalie.

Yet they had lost to Rumania, for godsake; the Czechs, who
hadn't done much else, had drilled eleven goals through them.
"You're going to beat yourselves if you lose to these guys,"
Brooks told the Americans.

"Seven goals," the players told each other. "Gotta win by
seven." So they went out into the field-house vortex, every seat
filled, the crowd noise and expectations something out of the
chariot race in *Ben-Hur.* And from the beginning of warm-ups,
it was Kafkahockey.

Mike Eruzione cruised in on Craig, flipped up a high one, hit
him on the neck—and knocked him cuckoo. When Craig came
to, he saw a dozen faces around him, peering in with curiosity
and alarm. Brooks motioned to Steve Janaszak and sent him out
to loosen up.

Finally Craig shook off the cobwebs, donned mask, glove and
stick again; and went back in for the face-off of what was supposed to be a turkey shoot. Instead, after twenty minutes, it was
the Americans who'd become the gobblers.

The game was less than two minutes old when a German
forward named Horst-Peter Kretschmer (known as "Wacki" to
his intimates), who had the best slapper in the *Bundesliga,*
decided to launch a what-the-hell mortar shot at Craig from
outside the U.S. blue line, seventy feet from the goal.

"It's off the net," Craig told himself—then watched, amazed,
as the puck went under his arm.

Then, with fifteen seconds left in the period, a defenseman

named Udo Kiessling got the puck at the point from a face-off and fired it past Craig from fifty-five feet away.

"What the hell," Phil Verchota asked as the Americans filed into the dressing room for intermission, "is going on?"

Just those Innsbruck Blues again. The Americans had dominated West Germany, had been walking in on goaltender Sigmund Suttner almost on demand.

Bah Harrington had gone in by himself, then had tripped and fallen. There'd been a few nice chances on a power play, but nothing had come of them. Neal Broten had strolled almost to the German goalmouth, and put the puck wide. Bill Baker had come barreling in, had the puck knocked off his stick; then he watched it slide past an open net. Then Eric Strobel slipped a pass across a yawning goalmouth to Eruzione, and Eruzione hadn't had the angle to punch it home.

So here it was 2–0 for the Germans, which meant that the United States was trailing by the equivalent of 9–0. It was a mystery. Maybe something was wrong with Craig. He'd had the flu for a week and was operating with a load of penicillin. "I'm not going to let myself be sick," he'd told himself. "I'll be sick after the Games."

Or maybe Rizzo's pregame shot still had Craig on Queer Street, his reflexes just off by enough to let in a couple of screamers. "Nope," Craig would say, "I blew the first one. And I just didn't see the second one."

Yet the problem remained. Not just the seven-goal problem, but a more essential problem. "Let's just go out," Mike Eruzione said, disgusted, "and win the goddam game."

Even that much was beginning to seem a challenge. Time and tide had done in the Norwegians and the Rumanians. But seven minutes into the second period, the Germans still led, 2–0. Only the Swedes had kept the Americans scoreless that long.

At last, Dave Christian and Robbie McClanahan broke loose and came down two-on-one on Suttner. McClanahan cruised in the final 40 feet, determined that the shot would be perfect, that there be no more missed connections, and flicked a back-hander into the net.

But Suttner gave them nothing more until the final two minutes of the period, and only when Broten managed to knock home a rebound off a German stick.

Not until the first five minutes of the third period were the Americans able to get the knockout. McClanahan, the charley horse no more than a painful memory now, cakewalked in for another goal. Then Verchota tipped in a Christian slapshot. So it was 4–2, which was good, but possibly not good enough.

By now, nobody was in the mood for solving quadratic equations. "We'll just keep winning," Jack O'Callahan declared, "and let 'em figure it out afterwards."

Craig nodded. "All I know is, when this thing's over, if I have some kind of medal hanging around my neck, I'll be happy. If I don't, I'll be very disappointed."

11

ONLY AMERICANS

For two weeks, life had not been unlike being 50 miles at sea on an oil rig or at an Antarctic naval base. The Olympians needed only to leave their trailer-dorms and walk a few hundred feet to find video games that never stopped; beefsteaks on demand; every movie from *On the Waterfront* to *Star Wars;* discos; Dionne Warwick singing her heart out for them.

"Fantastic," Michael Eruzione had called it all, after one day inside the Olympic Village that the Russians had labeled "inhumane" because of its planned future use as a federal prison. (It was a desecration, the Soviets complained, of the Olympic spirit.) "What more can you ask for?" Eruzione wanted to know.

The atmosphere was a bit stark, what with all these cream of mustard modules that had been built as prison cells. The only other hint of color, besides the national flags someone had grouped in a semicircle, was God's own Adirondack blue sky above. There never had been enough snow and ice to build the sculptures the organizers had planned.

But there was a lovely sense of escape, of sybaritic isolation —particularly for the Americans. There hadn't been enough cells for everybody, so the Americans were assigned to rows of stretch-trailers which they actually found preferable.

You could while away an hour or two, having a cold one with Rizzo and Buzzie, and never read a newspaper, hear a radio, watch TV or meet anybody from Dubuque.

Every forty-eight hours the Americans would climb aboard a shuttle bus, move along the several miles of two-lane blacktop into Lake Placid, play their game—and contentedly return to Antarctica.

It was a fine sort of voluntary quarantine. No press conferences, no madding crowds, no turbulence. "We get all the attention we want," Mike Ramsey said, "just by walking out the door."

If they wanted to go out and watch Eric Heiden win his morning gold medal, see the figure skaters or observe the night run of the luge, the hockey players simply pulled on their generic red-white-and-blue parkas—which gave them the same camouflage as anybody else—and went semi-cognito.

So they had no idea of what had been building back in The World, no hint of the America's Children hysteria awaiting them. The Red Army had been in Afghanistan for nearly two months. Jimmy Carter was pushing a boycott of the Summer Games in Moscow. The hostages were still playthings of the Ayatollah. Inflation was roaring along, unemployment up, Carter a lame duck nine months before the election.

The national mood was malaise; the citizenry was gloomy, frustrated, angry, helpless. Suddenly, twenty unknown kids, playing a game maybe 20 percent of the populace knew much about, were finding themselves billed as America's Team, screw the Dallas Cowboys. They were one day from facing the Russians now, and found themselves carrying the load for the President, the State Department, the Pentagon, the hostages, General Motors, Dow Jones, the *Saturday Evening Post* and the Four Freedoms. When you think about it, Jim Craig mused, we're a bunch of kids playing against a whole country.

It unsettled them. We're here to play a hockey game, Eruzione kept telling people who wanted it to be something else. Our political feelings don't matter.

There was enough baggage to carry as it was. The Russians were the world's best team. They'd owned the Olympic gold medal since 1964, had crunched the NHL's best only a year earlier, had beaten the Americans by seven goals in an exhibition they had no reason to want to win and had outscored their opponents in these Games by 51–11.

"Maybe we shouldn't show up," Brooks suggested puckishly, thinking of goal differentials. "The rules say we lose only 1–0. Then we go into the second game down only a goal. What do you think? Would they kick us out of the tournament for that?"

What the hell. The Olympians bore the Russians no ill will.

The Americans would see them in the game room, monopolizing the Phantom II game, Mig pilots in search of Yank jets, whooping when they scored a direct hit.

Mike Ramsey found himself sitting next to Boris Mikhailov in the movie theater and was fascinated to have Stan Laurel as a seatmate, then astonished to hear Mikhailov speak English ("Excuse me") as he was leaving.

Tretiak seemed to know English well. He and Buzz Schneider, old rivals from World championships past, got on well together, and sometimes Tretiak would come over to chat if he spotted Schneider in the cafeteria.

After the Americans had whomped the Czechs, Tretiak had come up to Schneider and given him a hug. "He's a nice guy," Schneider told people. "Classy."

Still, the Russians were walking enigmas, their personalities guessed at—conclusions reached by observation and deduction. Valery Kharlamov seemed to be their most nearly blithe spirit, as close to a wild man as the system had turned out. There were tales of him tearing around Moscow streets in a well-appointed Volga, a Bolshevik Belmondo.

Vladimir Petrov, his linemate of a dozen years, seemed bright and friendly, willing to offer up *znachki,* a few hundred words of cracked English, smiles, the big handshake. Helmut Balderis, the mercurial Latvian forward, was said (inaccurately) to be unhappy, thinking of defecting. One of the brothers Golikov, maybe it was Vladimir, had steel teeth.

Only Doc Nagobads, who'd been the U.S. National team physician for well over a decade, knew the Russians well. He was a Latvian immigrant who understood the language and could chat easily with Balderis, Zhluktov, Vasiliev, Tretiak and several others.

They were all supposed to have learned some English in school; but mostly, you got a nod of recognition, the suggestion of a grin, a friendly vibe or two.

Not that the Americans were much more communicative. Beyond *da, nyet, vodka* and *pizda* (a particularly vile word for a certain female organ), none of them could speak Russian.

So their contacts, for two weeks, had been perfunctory. Sometimes the Americans would watch a period or so of a Russian game from the stands, then go downstairs to dress for their own.

For the first week, there hadn't been much to watch. The Russians had blown away the Japanese (16–0), the Dutch (17–4) and the Poles (8–1) pretty much the same way they'd handled the Americans at Madison Square Garden.

A textbook goal, three touch passes and a 15-foot wrist shot up high. Two linemates tapping a third's helmet in brief salute. Two minutes later, another goal.

Then they played the Finns a game that brought everybody's head up abruptly. Finland had started slowly at Lake Placid, losing to Poland, but had come on to handle the Japanese and upset Canada in a sloppily played game. Now, late in the second period, they were leading the Russians 1–0. In the press center, where the hockey game flickered on every other television screen, eyebrows were cocked, amused but skeptical, at each typing table.

But when all but five minutes had ticked down and the Finns still led, 2–1, the skeptics began sprinting for the field house. And it had vanished. The Finns had gone into a defensive shell and scrunched down, playing for the tie that would almost surely get them into the medal round. The Soviets had come storming in, and within a minute and nineteen seconds had scored three goals; Krutov, Maltsev, Mikhailov. Ball game, 4–2.

"Interesting," the reaction had been. "But so what? The Russians have been beating up on the Finns for a hundred years in some form or other. So they drowsed for fifty-five minutes, then flicked on the automatic."

But then the Russians played Canada two days later and did the same thing, sleepwalking from the face-off. And the Canadians burned them, firing one goal past Tretiak in the first ninety-five seconds; and two more in the first three minutes of the second period.

Now, less than a minute remained in the second period, and the Canadians came down on a clean break with a fantastic chance to make it 4–1, to put the Russians down on one knee, ready for the TKO.

But they missed. The Russians came cruising back down and scored, thirteen seconds before the buzzer. When they returned, Mikhailov and Golikov put them ahead in barely two minutes.

Canada made one last stand, tying the game briefly, but Mikhailov, the long face expressionless, soon put them away. So it ended 6–4; and coach Viktor Tikhonov, enormously relieved, kissed each Russian player on the cheek as he came off the ice.

They're not into it, Brooks realized. For some reason, the Russians are off their game. They're ready to slit their own throats. All we have to do is hand them the knife.

That was his theme to the Americans the next morning. "What do they have left?" Brooks told them. Half a dozen of the Russians were playing in their third Olympic Games and already had two gold medals gathering dust in Moscow apartments. How many times can they win it? How many times do they *want* to win it?

The time is now, Brooks stressed, and most of the Americans had begun to believe it. There had been stretches during the Madison Square Garden debacle when they'd stayed with the Russians. The score might have been 6–1, the issue beyond doubt, yet the Russians generally played at the same level, regardless of the scoreboard.

So maybe it meant something. Maybe if the Russians came out sleepwalking again, assuming they could mash down the accelerator at will, and the Americans came at them the same way they'd swarmed the Czechs . . .

We've got to score early, Jack O'Callahan figured. We've got to get the good goaltending. Get the breaks. And play out of our minds. But then they can put Krutov out there and it's over—and he didn't even play against the NHL.

They could never, ever beat the Russians in anything like a best-of-seven series. No delusions there. But one time, one night, one shot? Why not?

"Maybe it's history in the making," Craig was telling people. "We might all be making history. You never know."

He had watched the Russians play Finland and Canada, and found himself rooting for them, wanting the aura of invincibility intact. Something was at work here, pushing Jimmy Craig and his mates toward some sort of time-and-place crossroads.

They all began feeling it when they arrived Friday afternoon and saw the dressing-room walls plastered with hundreds of telegrams imploring them to do everything from "Go for the gold" to "Save us from the cancer of communism."

Outside, where $67.20 center-ice tickets were being scalped for $300 and up, the mood was anxious, expectant, even a bit hostile. It was a year's worth of pent-up frustrations about the general nature of things—the economy, Iran, a national indirection—touched off now by the arrival of one hockey team with Cyrillic tongues and steel teeth.

They'd been targets ever since they stepped off the jet in Washington and baggage handlers had refused to touch their luggage. In Wellesley, an affluent Boston suburb where the Russian figure skaters were training at a local college, the weekly newspaper ran an unpleasant editorial—and students picketed the rink.

They arrived in Lake Placid deeply unsettled. The Russians had been treated badly in New York, Tretiak told Nagobads. They'd expected to be pelted with eggs and tomatoes when they marched in the opening ceremonies. Instead, the Russians had been applauded. Now, they weren't sure what to think.

Newsweek called the meeting a "morality play on ice." Brooks, addressing his players one last time, called it predestination. No Brooksisms this time; he'd prepared note cards.

This time they were words that captured much of that American amalgam of arrogance, bravado, success and predestination.

"You were born to be a player," Brooks told them. "You were meant to be here. This moment is yours. You were meant to be here at this time."

It was literally midnight in Moscow when the players took the ice, and when Muscovites switched on their black-and-white *televizors,* they saw a field house full of American flags and chanting spectators that wanted the Bear stuffed and mounted. The Russian players were booed thoroughly the moment they stepped on the ice. The Americans, anonymities except to mothers, lovers and college hockey buffs until two weeks ago, came out now as Daniel Boone, Alvin York, John Glenn.

Brooks used a different metaphor—David and Goliath. I just hope, he mused, we remember to bring our slingshots. Not to mention a new plan of attack.

Two weeks later, Goliath had been shown to be at least a bit vulnerable. But the Finns and Canadians had proven, again, that you could not play tentatively against him—not even for a minute. Goliath picked up instinctively on caution and fear, and it made him go for the kill.

So Brooks dictated the plan he realized he should've gone with the first time: Stay calm, maintain possession, and forecheck like hell.

The pressure would be entirely on the Russians. They'd come to Lake Placid as "mortal locks," to use the Las Vegas term, to win an unprecedented fifth consecutive gold medal. They'd toyed with the American kids and virtually named the result in Manhattan. So, what had changed?

The Americans had home cooking, youth, hunger and the

spirit of rowdy adventurism going for them. "If Tikhonov loses," Brooks figured, "he goes to Siberia. If we lose, I go to Payne Avenue in St. Paul, which is where I'm heading anyway."

"It was simply a matter," Mark Johnson said, "of going for it." So they did. In the first seven minutes, the Americans came storming in for four good scoring chances, three of them close enough to the goal to see Tretiak's facial expression. Two skidded wide; Tretiak kicked out the third and smothered the fourth.

Nothing new there. Yet the mood was different. Ken Morrow and Mike Ramsey caught Kharlamov in a vise and flipped him like a sack of flour. Craig, who'd told himself he'd be satisfied to limit the Russians to three goals a period, was playing as though he'd only allow them three all night.

No more Ice Follies. No more standing back and watching Maltsev do his 360-degree turns or applauding as Balderis changed gears. The American faces were deadly serious now; Buzzy Schneider looked as though he were playing for his life on every shift.

Then they looked up and saw the red light on, and four blank-faced Russians patting Krutov's helmet. Aleksei Kasatanov, one of their defensemen, had taken a routine slapshot from the right point; and Krutov had routinely tipped it past Craig, nine minutes in.

O'Callahan shook his head. We can play out of our minds, and they can put Krutov out there . . .

All without the slightest change of expression.

"They're so unemotional," marveled Mike Eruzione. "They play the same at the 19:58 mark as they do the first minute."

The Russians would make a mistake, let a Johnson have a bit too much breathing room in front, and Tikhonov, in his baggy brown suit and pomaded hair, would shout at them as they came off. They'd listen, their faces masks, go back out; and next time, Johnson would be wearing three red jerseys.

There'd been too much freedom for the U.S.A. forwards those first few minutes. Now, a rawboned Russian defenseman was always stationed 10 feet from the goal; one of their forwards cruised warily in from the blue line. Nobody else was going to see the whites of Tretiak's eyes.

Enter Schneider, who'd seen a few Soviet early-warning defenses in his time. Mark Pavelich spotted him breaking down the left side and got him the puck, flung it all the way across the rink. Schneider had always liked that extra 15 feet or so of width that international rinks offered. Now, his expression fierce, he unloaded a wicked slapshot from a severe angle that flew past Tretiak and into the upper far corner. It was 1975 again, the World Championships, and Schneider was still drilling holes through Tretiak.

Six minutes left in the period now, with the Russians jolted awake and suddenly all over Craig. Sergei Makharov launched a bomb that Craig managed to kick out. Thirty seconds later he was back, his linemates working a drop pass followed by a give-and-go, a bit of sleight of hand, a Russian version of three-card monte.

Aleksandr Golikov took the shot, Craig left a rebound and Makharov casually put it away. More helmet tapping ("We do this all the time," the nonexpressions said), greeted by booing from the crowd, which sensed that normalcy was returning.

The atmosphere had settled down quickly after the warm pregame greeting. During a commercial break, Dryden and Al Michaels, broadcasting for ABC, remarked that the crowd was too quiet, no factor, useless.

There was none of the bug-eyed mania of Williams Arena, of Boston Garden, of Dane County Coliseum; none of the steady roar that began with the opening face-off, rose whenever a friendly jersey touched the puck, and exploded at a goal.

This was a World Series crowd, made up not so much of impassioned fans as $67.20 high-rollers who knew it was the place to be. There was a limit to their willingness to check civility at the door.

Perhaps the curious starting time—5:30 P.M.—had something to do with the somnolence. By any measure, a U.S.–U.S.S.R.

match in any sport cried out for Friday night prime time. That was ABC's argument to the International Olympic Committee and the International Ice Hockey Federation. Nobody watched television at 5:30 on a Friday afternoon. They were either eating dinner or still caught in traffic.

Yet the schedule went unchanged. The master plan had the Red Group champion playing the Blue Group runner-up at 5:30 Friday. Period. Had the Americans beaten Sweden and won the Blue Group, they would have played the second game, at 8:30, against the Finns. That hadn't happened, so 5:30 it was.

Two minutes left now, with Craig seeing heavy duty in the American end. Aleksandr Skvortsov tried a rebound in close. Craig denied him. Then Boris Mikhailov, from the slot. Squelched.

Finally, with the clock showing less than a minute to play in the period, Eruzione and Neal Broten broke out, two-on-one, but found themselves with no angle; and the puck wound up lying in the Russian crease, just out of reach.

Ten seconds now, with the puck back in the American end. Morrow came out and dropped it for Dave Christian at the U.S.A. blue line, figuring Christian would dump it in Tretiak's general direction and waste the last few moments.

So Christian took a sure-why-not slapper from the red line that seemed to bounce harmlessly off the meat of Tretiak's pads. On the bench, Broten—seeing three seconds on the clock and Mark Johnson at the Soviet blue line—turned and headed for the dressing room.

Then he heard a roar, saw zeroes on the clock and the red light on. Johnson, frustrated because his line hadn't been playing well, because they'd barely been seeing the puck, had just decided to go for it. He'd seen the puck bounce out, sensed the two Russian defensemen relaxing, knew time was running out, but thought there might just be time to whip in a rebound. So Johnson burst between the two Russians, Vasili Pervukhin and Zinetulla Biljaletdinov. Had he been bigger, their somewhat lazy shoulder checks would have caught him. Instead, Johnson squirted past and suddenly was in the clear. He glided for a stride, picked up the loose puck and now was in control. All alone in front, he was Mark Johnson, the greatest goal-scorer in collegiate history. It mattered not that it was Tretiak. He was still a goalie, and this was Mark Johnson's moment.

He swept wide to his left, creating a large gap behind the goalie. A quick flick of the wrist; a flailing of Tretiak's stick hand; rippling net cords. Goal or no goal? *Goal,* the referee, a Finn named Kaisla was nodding. The buzzer had not sounded. Besides, the red light wouldn't function if the green light signaling the end of a period had come on. So it was 2–2 now, with Kaisla calling for both teams to come back for the final second and a meaningless face-off.

The Russians, already in the dressing room, reaching for their intermission tea, decided it was ridiculous, and sent out Mikhailov and Krutov and, finally, Makharov to stand there and take the draw.

Meanwhile, Eruzione noticed something, and skated over to Brooks. "Myshkin's in the net," he said. "Does that mean Tretiak can't come back?"

Tretiak had let in a couple of bad goals in the Canadian game. Now the Americans had stung him twice. Some people were saying he'd hurt his glove hand, that he just wasn't up to form.

Later, word was that he'd been nervous, spooked by Schneider's goal and the bad memories it dredged up—and undone completely by Johnson's. Schneider's was a long slapper; no goalie looks good allowing one. Still, it had been a powerful shot, deceptive, tricky to handle. Tretiak had no chance on Johnson's goal, but the rebound that produced it shouldn't have happened. It was an uncharacteristic display of humanity by both goalie and defensemen.

Yet, when the Russians came out for the second period, Tretiak was on the bench. Vladimir Myshkin, the short, blond 23-year-old, was roughing up his crease.

"Well," figured Ken Morrow, "they're not losing a whole lot with Myshkin." The Russians had plucked him out of obscurity to play in the decisive game against the NHL All-Stars the year before, and Myshkin had shut them out.

They were always coming up with amazing new faces and plugging them in. A Vasiliev would start showing his age a bit, and here would come a Fetisov. A Petrov would begin winding down, and up would pop Helmut Balderis, *Eliktritchka*, the Electric Train, flying by like the Riga Express.

It was crazy, Dave Silk thought. As the game went on and he kept skating out to line up across from Mikhailov, he'd think, Great, it's Mikhailov—because it meant he wouldn't have to face Krutov. What am I thinking of? Silk wondered. I'm looking forward to playing Mikhailov?

So Tretiak was done, but for the next twenty minutes it didn't mean a damn. The Americans were barely making it out of their zone, as it was. Johnson's goal had been an aberration; otherwise, the Russians had dominated the last half dozen minutes of the first period. Now, they merely picked up where they'd left off.

With fifty-eight seconds gone, Harrington was sent off; it took the Russians little more than a minute to score. Yuri Lebedev, after being knocked off his skates, scooted down and checked Broten at the red line. The puck skittered over to Krutov on the right side; in one motion he chipped it to Maltsev, charging hard, at center ice.

Maltsev caught the puck square in the gut, then artfully dropped it to his feet without breaking stride and burst over the blue line, past Christian, into the clear.

This time, Maltsev needed no 360-degree swivels. One quick fake took Craig down and out. Then Maltsev whipped the puck into the back of the cage with a clank that reverberated through the field house for what seemed endless moments after. The crowd made no sound.

So the Russians had the lead again and had the Americans in leg irons. For eight minutes the U.S.A. didn't get a shot on net. Then Harrington came down on a breakaway—and put the puck wide to the right. Two minutes later, with the Americans shorthanded again, Johnson managed to shake free with

Schneider and swooped down on Myshkin. No use.

After that, the Russians conceded nothing. They peppered Craig thoroughly for the final six minutes, testing him with combinations—Mikhailov slapping, then Petrov flicking at the rebound in close. They used long-range mortars from their defensemen, knowing that the Germans had found them useful. They thwacked Craig in the mask with a stick and brought him to his knees.

Craig was the difference, a Horatio at the American bridge, holding off the Soviets until reinforcements arrived. He would stand up, then flop, challenge the Russians, then wait for them. They could not solve him; with anyone lesser in the cage, the count might well have been six or seven to two.

But when the second period was done and the Russians had outshot the U.S.A. 30–10, it was still only 3–2. Maybe, Mike Ramsey thought, we can pull this off.

Much had changed in two weeks. After forty minutes at Madison Square Garden, the score had been 6–1. Now we're down one, Harrington thought. That's progress.

"Okay," Brooks told them in the dressing room, "you've got plenty of time. Look at the third period as four five-minute segments. You don't have to tie it in the first one or even the second. Just stay with your system. Play your game."

Your game. They did have a game now, a style, a method of attack, just as the Russians did. It had mystified the Czechs all night long, and now it had the Americans stride-for-stride with the Russians for two-thirds of a hockey game.

They had been outshot, but they had controlled the puck as well as any Western team ever had against the Soviets—with the possible exception of the Canadiens in their 3–3 New Year's Eve tie with the Red Army club in 1975.

They had often shot wide, either out of nerves or by cutting the margin too thin, but they were in the game. The U.S.A. defense had played well, thumping the Russians hard and frequently, giving them one shot on a rush, clearing out loose pucks quickly.

So the Americans went out and kept the pace humming:

three minutes, five minutes, six minutes. Then Krutov was sent off for high-sticking Broten and the U.S.A. was on the power play.

For a minute and a half, the Russians held them off. Thirty seconds left now, with Brooks' hand up, fingers wiggling, signaling his forwards to change up.

One more rush, Johnson figured, and came past the Russian bench where Tikhonov was shouting to his players. Silk had the puck now, coming down the left side, looking for Johnson, seeing Vasiliev (who'd done in O'Callahan in New York) lining him up for a hip check.

Sergei Starikov, Vasiliev's partner, was in between the two Americans, looking to knock away any centering pass.

Silk had made his reputation from moments like these. He'd been a fourth-line wing for four games, but had been playing well. His goal against Sweden had been one of the biggest of the Games; when Strobel went cold and the Christoff shift produced no magic, Brooks had shifted Silk to the first line.

Now Silk flipped the puck across, looked over to see whether Johnson had gotten it—and found himself dumped by Vasiliev.

But the red light was on; the Americans were jumping around (as Mike Ramsey would put it) like a bunch of yard apes. The puck had bounced off one of Starikov's skates and onto Johnson's stick not five feet from the goal. Pure ice cream for the Magic Man, an automatic wrist shot right between Myshkin's legs.

Starikov, frustrated, bashed his stick on the ice.

"That was a goal," Ken Dryden shouted, "that came out of nowhere."

Eleven minutes and twenty-one seconds remained now, with the Mark Wells line on the ice. A month before, Wells had been in limbo somewhere between Flint, Halifax and Olympus. He'd made the team as fourth-line center, as filler to be used whenever Brooks figured the Johnsons and Brotens needed a breather. Brooks had intended giving the bulk of the ice time to the first two lines, but when all four played well, he shifted plans and went to an even rotation. Now, Brooks had Wells out against the best forwards in the world, the Mikhailov line.

We're mucking 'em up, Wells thought. Phil Verchota was all over Kharlamov, Eric Strobel step for step with Mikhailov. And Wells was skating Petrov to a frazzle. We've got more speed than they do, he concluded.

Brooks had been implying that for days. So, you were watching these guys play Team Canada since you were bantams? That means, if you're 21 years old now, they're getting old.

The Wells line was off, the Coneheads on, with Baker and Christian back on defense. Brooks was pacing the bench, glancing up at the clock, blowing exhaust out his mouth. Now Christian was passing the puck across to Schneider, who leveled a long slapper at Myshkin, then lifted his stick and signaled to his bench.

He was short-shifting himself, looking for relief. Over vaulted Eruzione, ("I'll go, I'll go") the eager BU freshman again. The puck had gone behind the Russian cage, where Harrington and Pervukhin were scuffling for it. The Russian tried to pass it up the boards to Makharov, who, sensing danger, moved across from center ice.

But it bounced over, somehow, to Pavelich, who was hit, lifted, mashed, just as he whacked the puck toward the slot.

And here came Eruzione: dashing across from the bench, turning, wheeling, and snapping a 25-foot wrist shot through the perfect screen—Pervukhin, down on one knee—past Myshkin's stick into the net.

Disbelief, euphoria, all that. Eruzione went screaming and dancing, stick over his head, into a corner. Everybody else in a white jersey followed, mobbing him. U.S.A. 4, U.S.S.R. 3— with exactly ten minutes to play.

Now, the Americans felt certain, would come the Russian late surge. The Finns had tweaked the Bear's nose. The Canadians had had him tied up and dancing as though the game were a gypsy carnival. And it had come to nothing.

Hell, the Americans had the Russians tied up at the 1975

Worlds with that much time to play, and had lost by several goals. "They can still score," Brooks kept saying as the clock ticked down. "They can still score plenty."

Damn, Mike Ramsey thought, Why couldn't we have scored with nineteen seconds left?

Ken Morrow peered up at the scoreboard and set his jaw. These, he assured himself, are going to be the longest ten minutes of my life.

Within seconds, the Russians were back on them, zeroing in on Craig. Krutov chinked the post, then Maltsev came loose, appeared suddenly in front—and missed the rebound. Vladimir Golikov boomed one off Craig's pads. Eight minutes left now, with the crowd wild and the Americans alternately panting or pacing behind their bench, staring up at the clock, hoping for some bizarre kind of time compression.

I don't want to go out there and make the mistake that costs us the game, Robbie McClanahan thought. But if I'm not out there, the clock won't move.

So McClanahan went out, shift after shift, and put his body on the line. All of them did, the full kamikaze. Fetisov would wind up at the point, and three Americans would throw themselves in front of him, happy to take the shot off the leg, in the chest. Delighted to absorb a bone bruise or worse if it meant mucking him up, spoiling the bid, buying time.

"We'll do anything to win," Jack O'Callahan believed. "And they won't."

O'Callahan had already given one knee to these people. Now he was diving giddily, risking the other. Mark Johnson was going full tilt into corners, the hell with the shoulder.

Seven minutes left now, the charm still holding. In the U.S.A. cage, Craig made a vow to himself: no slop goals. "If we're gonna lose," he told himself, "because I've seen 'em come back thousands of times, goddam it, it's gonna be a good goal. I don't want to have people telling me I couldn't play in the big games. I don't want them asking me, Were you nervous, Were you nervous?"

Craig was scared as hell. Everybody was. This was precisely the time when the Russians broke your heart without breaking a sweat, when some faceless wonder slipped into your zone and put it by you without a trace of emotion.

But it didn't have to happen, Brooks believed. When the Russians delivered the knockout blow in the final few minutes, it came because they knew it would and you knew it would. What if you didn't happen to buy the scenario? It was like something from *The Twilight Zone*. If you believed it would happen, it would. If not, maybe it never would.

"Play your game," Brooks reminded his people. "Stay with the forechecking. Keep possession. Rock 'em. And maintain the poise, just like they do."

Six and a half minutes left. Morrow, seeing Fetisov winding up, dove in front of him and smothered another slapper. Then he rose, glanced at the clock—6:26—and skated off for a brief rest, the Greek god. If anything happens, he told himself, I want to be out there. I'm not losing it on the bench.

Six minutes now, and something curious was happening. The Russians were shouting at each other, Phil Verchota noticed. They were always yelling instructions, but they were usually corrective, telling a man to pick up a wing or move to an open spot. The tone was sharply different this time, anxious and angry.

The Americans were still skating with them, worrying the Russian defensemen, hurrying them into mistakes, forcing them to retreat and regroup. "They smashed the Russians' attack not before their eyes," Anatoly Tarasov would say afterward, "but behind their backs."

Every time a fresh set of Russian attackers looked up, they saw grim young American faces staring back and staying with them. I'm sticking with Mikhailov, Eric Strobel had decided. I'm hanging on to him. I'm not letting him get started.

The Russians wove, and the Americans wove with them. They doubled back into their zone, and the Americans homed in on them, buzzing and bumping. They broke out and saw that

four Americans were waiting, somehow, on their blue line sending out strong Restricted Entry vibes. Petrov saw that, boomed
a desperate long slapper and turned away to change up.

Maybe the Russians had taken their best shot back in the
second period, when they'd outshot the U.S.A. 12–2 and reaped
one goal for their trouble. Five minutes remained now, and the
U.S.S.R. had been held scoreless for the last thirty-three.

Nobody sat on the U.S.A. bench now. Brooks walked up and
back, up and back, saying the same thing: Play your game, play
your game, play your game.

Three minutes now, with the Mikhailov line on, Tikhonov
putting everything on the shoulders of his old boys. And Brooks
countering with eager young legs, Wells and Verchota and Strobel, completely unafraid to use his fourth line.

Doc Nagobads was standing by Brooks with a stop watch,
marking the seconds ("Herb thirty-five, Herb forty"), Brooks
running his lines through a revolving door. Finally, Petrov,
after looking up between draws and seeing Johnson, then Pavelich, then Broten looking at him on the same shift, glanced
across at Nagobads. "What's going on?" Petrov growled in Russian.

"Ask your coach," Nagobads shrugged. But Tikhonov was
waving his hand, motioning for Petrov to stay on the ice. They
had done that for a decade, going instinctively to the Mikhailov
line whenever the Russians were in a tight spot.

"This has got to be his last year," Johnson would think at the
Worlds each year, seeing a Kharlamov or a Petrov skate out.
"How old are these guys? Sixty?" But the clock had run down
on all of them now.

They would start down on a rush, see the access lanes
blocked, dump the puck in and bag it. Russian teams didn't play
hockey that way. Or never used to.

Less than a minute to play now, with the Johnson line on the
ice, Jimmy Craig keeping the puck moving, the clock ticking,
wanting no face-offs, no chance for the Russians to settle down
or for the Americans to realize the magnitude of what was
about to happen.

Tikhonov was keeping Mikhailov, Petrov and Kharlamov on the ice, going for broke, hoping that savvy would compensate for fatigue, that one of the American kids would suddenly clutch, leave an opening, let a Russian forward in for the tying goal.

"Watch their goalie," Brooks told Gary Smith, his trainer, knowing that any second now Tikhonov would be motioning to Myshkin and sending out a sixth skater—Krutov maybe, or Balderis.

Forty seconds now, and it wasn't happening. You've never got them beaten, Mark Johnson kept telling himself, until there are three zeroes on the clock.

So the Americans kept their legs pumping, draped themselves over every red jersey and waited for the moment when they knew they'd have to play five-on-six.

But only thirty seconds remained now and Myshkin stood unmoving in the Russian cage. I can't believe it, Brooks thought.

They were going to play the final seconds out, leaving Myshkin put. Petrov had made one last bid, having flicked a final backhander at Craig at the 50-second mark, and Craig had turned it aside. The Russians were skating confused now, taking random shots or not shooting at all.

The Mikhailov line, on the line for several minutes—much longer than the normal shift—looked desperately leg-tired. Herbie's words came back: You're afraid of Stan Laurel? Mikhailov was an old man now, struggling to keep up with the Magic Man.

Twenty seconds, and everybody on the American bench sensed what was happening, what had been happening for the last six minutes. "We're going to win," Strobel realized.

The puck was in the right corner. Morrow flipped it around the end boards toward Johnson, who got it to Ramsey in the other corner. With fifteen seconds, Pervukhin went for it, and Ramsey flattened him with one last check. McClanahan had the puck now, then Johnson. Twelve seconds.

Once more into the right corner, to Morrow. Ten seconds,

nine . . . eight . . . seven . . . the crowd counting down. A quick pass for Silk, but Johnson picked it up. A backhand over the blue line. Three . . . two . . . one. . . .

"Do you believe in miracles?" Al Michaels asked a nation. "Yes." he exulted as the horn sounded.

And then everybody was on the ice—except for Brooks. When the buzzer went off, the poker face and taut lips had burst into a combination of amazement and euphoria. He threw a haymaker at the air—then vanished down the ramp. This was the players' moment.

In the American end of the rink, as the spectators hallooed, snapped pictures, slapped hands and waved flags, the players melted into a white-jersey pudding. Five players buried Craig. Strobel embraced Bah Harrington who still had his stick in the air. Mike Ramsey lay on his back, roaring with laughter and irony. And O'Callahan, arms up, open mouth showing all those missing Charlestown upper teeth, was on his knees, exulting over him.

Meanwhile, as American sticks and gloves began tumbling back down out of the rafters, twenty Meritorious Masters of Sport stood at their blue line, chins hooked over their sticks, and watched.

The Russians had lost an Olympic game before (the last one in 1968), but not since 1960 had they lost the Games. And unless the Finns managed to bring down the U.S.A. in the Sunday finale, that was going to happen.

So the Russians waited patiently, sportsmen to the last, for the American ecstasy to be spent, for the white jerseys to pick themselves up, regain some sort of manic composure and line up for the traditional handshake.

When they did, Johnson, the first man in line, noticed something odd. Some of the Russian players were smiling. Vasiliev was, for sure, and the rest of them seemed to be somewhere between bemusement and curiosity.

They're excited for us, Johnson thought. They're used to winning, getting their gold medal, having their vodka and going on.

This is a new experience for them. But they're smiling. If you're going to lose, you should lose like this. It's a classy way to lose.

Maybe they're relieved, Eruzione thought. Maybe after twelve years, they can finally go back to Moscow with the pressure off. And maybe I can go home Sunday and say I was on the best team in the world.

The ritual done, the red jerseys skated off silently; Tikhonov shutting the gate behind them, to shower, dress, and go to the bus, heads down.

The Americans stayed on the ice, hugging in pairs, shaking exuberant fists at countrymen who were still standing, cheering, clinging to the moment. Off to the side, finally, Dave Silk, Eruzione, O'Callahan and Craig came together in a cluster. "Just like B.U.," Eruzione proclaimed.

"Sometimes," O'Callahan decided, "you gotta get regional."

Ten thousand spectators felt delicious. Absolutely delicious. Fans screeched, hollered and hugged. Parents went bonkers. Brooks' brother, David, went storming through one state trooper after another in an uncontrolled dash to the locker room.

Around the country (it was about 8:15 in the East and 5:15 on the Coast), celebrations began. Drivers drove off the road and honked in exultation. Impromptu parties and celebrations sprang up everywhere. Cheers rocked airliners when captains announced the score, and glasses were hoisted in the nation's taverns. High school basketball, a Friday-night tradition, yielded the spotlight for this one evening.

After a while, the players straggled off the ice, down the runway and into the dressing room, dazed. Brooks wasn't there. He'd told someone he had to visit the men's room, then stayed there, not wanting to intrude on the moment. Presently, the phone rang. It was Jimmy Carter, wanting Brooks to know his players had made the American people proud.

Most of them were still sitting, slumped, eyes glazed, unbelieving. Nobody was ever a goal up on the Russians when the buzzer sounded. They half expected a knock on the door, a security man telling them it was time, that there were another twenty minutes to go.

But nobody came. Eventually, somebody began singing "God Bless America"—until the Olympians realized they didn't know the words. So twenty of America's favorite sons began *humming* "God Bless America."

Enter Brooks, tears welling up in his eyes. Bob Fleming, chairman of the U.S. Olympic Hockey Committee, looked at him and grinned. "You might be human after all," Fleming told him.

It was incredible, Brooks kept thinking. We beat them at their own game with a system we put in six months ago and with a bunch of kids.

Down the hall, Mark Johnson and Eric Strobel were sitting in the doping room with cold bottles of beer, the chosen U.S. guinea pigs for the urinalysis. Across from them—Johnson blinked—were Boris Mikhailov and Valery Kharlamov.

As a teenager, Johnson had a Madison sporting goods store make up Russian jerseys with their names on the back. When they played their Sunday pickup games, Johnson had been Petrov, his father Kharlamov.

These are my heroes, Johnson thought. In 1975, I flew over with my mom to watch them play. I played against them in 1978. Now I've beaten them.

Mikhailov looked terminally weary now. He and Kharlamov weren't saying much to each other; there wasn't much to say. "Nice game," Mikhailov told Johnson. It's sort of sad, Johnson thought. I've grown up with these guys since 1974. Last time I'll see them.

Johnson wanted to get back to the dressing room now, to share in the hilarity and the chaos, but his plumbing simply wouldn't function. He'd stood behind the bench for the final ten minutes, unable to sit, the adrenaline sluicing through every vein. Now, an hour later, everything was knotted up or shut down.

"You were the greatest player in the world tonight," said

Kaminsky, who'd wandered by to offer congratulations. "No one else could have done it. Two goals against the Russians." "I can't believe it," Johnson kept saying. "I cannot believe it."

Outside, once the players actually got around to showering, dressing and stuffing gear into bags and ambling out there, more hilarity loomed, more chaos. "Michael," Mrs. Eruzione chided him. "You're gonna give me a heart attack."

More than three dozen parents and relatives had been going through this for two weeks now, living elbow to elbow at a rented place they called Hostage House, sharing meals and anxieties, going down to the field house to sweat out another sixty minutes, then going back to Hostage House to begin worrying all over again.

"Tonight," Jack O'Callahan's father was saying, "Billy Christian became Dave Christian's father."

The fathers were celebrities in their own right, pursued by scriveners from Los Angeles and Dallas, Minneapolis and Chicago, Boston and New York. Eugene Eruzione was pressed for his philosophies, questioned about Boston Harbor. "I was on C.B.S. this morning," Jack O'Callahan, Sr. said. "I might just begin doing this for a living. Forget Edison."

Their sons were national heroes now, overnight sensations. "Surprise?" Mike Eruzione said. "It isn't a surprise. We're beyond being surprised now. We're the surprise. They're the best team in the world, you know. Wait a minute. No, they're not. Maybe we are."

Nobody on this side of the Atlantic was arguing that point. Eruzione's wrist shot, and the ten minutes that followed it, brought the country to a standstill.

In Warroad, Eveleth, Winthrop, Madison, Minneapolis, Detroit and a dozen other American addresses, friends and neighbors pummeled each other and dashed off to Western Union. Newspapers everywhere began setting headline type usually reserved for wars and acts of God. WE WON! And somewhere in the Mediterranean, the U.S. aircraft carrier *Nimitz* flashed the news by signal light to a nearby Soviet intelligence vessel. Later, as two Soviet patrol planes were being intercepted by American fighters near the aircraft carrier *Coral Sea* in the Indian Ocean, the Russian pilots switched their radio to the international frequency and said, in English, "Congratulations."

Not everyone got word immediately. ABC, which taped the game for prime-time broadcast that night, warned viewers who wanted to be kept in suspense before they flashed the result.

And in the Olympic Village, still an Antarctic-like sanctum, almost nobody knew until he watched the ABC tape. So Neal Broten and Steve Christoff, anonymous in their U.S.A. parkas, slipped into the relaxation area and watched everybody watching.

Back on Main Street, the mood was a curious mix of elation and defiance and unabashed jingoism. With one blow, America's kids had stuffed it to the Russian hockey team, the Red Army in Kabul, the Iranian captors, the American economy and anything else that might have been out of control at the moment.

Within hours, you could buy a T-shirt that showed a cross-eyed bear being beaned by an American slapper.

No doubt, the Bear was stunned. Later that night, back at the Village, Bill Baker noticed Helmut Balderis and two other Russians strolling slowly along the fence that encircled the complex, heads down, just walking. Tikhonov was said to have gone to his room and wept, but Doc Nagobads said he doubted it. Tikhonov was simply too much of a steel-face for that.

If there was a common Russian mood, it was puzzlement. Their players had gone into the dressing room after two periods up a goal and already celebrating—Valeri Vasiliev told Nagobads the next day. Nobody, certainly no amateur team, had ever stayed with the Russians in the final twenty minutes.

"Then we came out," Vasiliev told Nagobads, "and, my God, your boys are going like crazy. We came back to our bench, grabbing our heads and saying, 'Horror, horror, horror.'"

Vasiliev was still mystified. "Doc, we've known each other for many years. What was your secret?"

"Vasily, if I tell you, and you tell the doping committee, I'll be in trouble," Nagobads replied.

"Doping? Come on."

"Fountain of youth," Nagobads said with a shrug.

It was the conditioning, all those Herbies paying off. What Brooks had wrought was a club that could stay on the ice until midnight if that was what it took.

Balderis had joined them now, surprised that Vasiliev hadn't seen it. "They were using three lines against one of ours," Balderis told him. "That's what happened."

Later, Tarasov, the man Brooks had idolized since his playing days, would write an essay on Lake Placid as he'd seen it.

Man for man, he felt, the Russians had a superior team. The difference, the trump card, had been Herb Brooks. Brooks' constant search for the new, his fanatic love of the game, his confidence and coolness in running the bench and his superb scouting and tactics—all of them had combined to undo the Russians.

The Americans, Tarasov wrote, skated beautifully, forced the Russian defensemen into mistakes and disrupted their forwards. Unimaginative Russian coaching—and overconfidence —had done the rest.

Back at the field house for off-day practice, Brooks was worried about the same thing. Eighteen hours earlier his players had been hyperventilating college kids tilting at windmills. Now, they'd saved the world from Godless Communism.

The telegram count had doubled overnight, covering two walls now. Billy Cleary had come in beforehand and told them that the 1960 team was nothing compared to them. Security men were wandering in and asking for souvenirs. The President had called. They were familiar faces in every American barroom and parlor.

So Brooks came in before the workout, saw them signing

sticks, scribbling autographs; and he went bonkers. What was this crap?

"You're not good enough for all this attention," he told them. "You're too young to win this thing. You haven't got the talent." Et cetera, et cetera.

"Okay, Herbie," twenty expressions told him. "Sure."

But Brooks was worried. Despite the victory over Russia, the U.S. still could wind up empty-handed. If you did the arithmetic and ran yourself through the possibilities, you could actually put together a scenario that had the United States placing fourth, out of the medals entirely.

After Friday night, it stood like this:

Final Four Semifinalists

	W	L	T	Points	Goals For	Goals Against
U.S.A.	1	0	1	3	6	5
U.S.S.R.	1	1	0	2	7	7
Sweden	0	0	2	2	5	5
Finland	0	1	1	1	5	7

Includes games against semifinalists in preliminary round.

The Swedes and Finns had tied 3–3 the day before. If the Finns beat the Americans by at least two goals, and the Russians and Swedes played to a tie, then the Russians would win the gold medal. All four teams would have three points. Since they would have the worst goal differential, the Americans would be nowhere. But a tie with Finland would guarantee the United States a medal, probably the silver, and in this game a victory would guarantee the gold.

The Finns had never won an Olympic medal and had only defeated the United States once, in 1964, and then by a single goal. But they'd handled Canada, and had the Russians on the ropes with five minutes left.

They were gritty players, hard to dislodge, with considerable talent, speed and good goaltending. The Finns seemed comfortable in games where the difference was never more than a goal either way. The Americans had won their 1976 meeting 5–4; the gap between the two countries seemed to be narrowing with each quadrennium.

So Brooks was determined to arouse his players one last time. Before their last workout, he blew the whistle and called them together at center ice.

"You're too young," he told them again. "You can't win this."

Midway through the practice, he blew the whistle again. "You're too young." And again afterwards. "Too young," Brooks said to a bunch of now sullen faces. "Too damn young."

When they stomped off to the dressing room, Brooks felt pleased with himself. "Good," he decided. "I've got 'em mad at me again."

Back in the Village, Mike Ramsey was sitting around with Steve Janaszak, Neal Broten and Dave Christian. In September, Ramsey had vowed to Christian that if they ever won the gold medal, he'd take off every stitch of equipment he was wearing and fling it into the stands. Now, that moment was sixty minutes away.

What happens if we blow it now, they mused, after coming all this way?

Don't blow it. That was Brooks' homily to them the next morning, as they were dressing for the finale. They'd been together for nearly six months now, had played seventy games; and astonished themselves and the world with their achievements. One game, one last effort remained.

"This is our last sixty minutes," Brooks said. "Our last will be our best."

So they went out into the vortex for the final time. Every seat was filled with a screaming countryman determined to push the U.S.A. over the top. It was 11:15 A.M. in the East, 8:15 on the West Coast. As in 1960, an entire nation was up early for this one. No hesitancy, no quiet now. The $67.20 swells were hockey fans—just like Gallery Gods in Boston Garden, rowdies in the greens at Madison Square Garden; as loud as the loudest Wisconsin band member. The Finns seemed to take all of this in—the flags, the chanting, the Americans two meters off the ground—without their pulses quickening a single beat.

Steadiness was their game. Grind for ten minutes, maybe score a goal, assume the goalkeeper would do his job, grind for ten minutes more. Maybe they'd beat you, maybe they wouldn't. It wasn't their full-time job anyway.

Although he marveled at their technical skills, the Finns were different from the Swedes, Brooks had noticed. Maybe because they'd never won medals, because their tradition told them they were destined for fifth place or worse.

Poland had beaten them, and they'd taken it as part of life. The Russians had zapped them, busted apart the dream, and it seemed normal to the Finns. There was something self-consciously Darwinian about it, or at least Calvinist. You got what you deserved, and more often than not it was an hour's sweat for little reward.

So they went out against the Americans, who'd begun to believe in predestination ("Herb," Jack McCartan, the goalie/-hero of the 1960 Games told Brooks minutes before the face-off, "it is meant to be"), and put the U.S. through a grinder for twenty minutes.

Their captain, a forward named Jukka Porvari, had tormented the Russians all game long, scoring both goals. You saw him literally every other shift, legs driving, black mustache bristling. Now, less than ten minutes in, he was blasting a 50-foot slapshot past Jim Craig, putting Finland ahead.

No novelty there, Craig figured. The Americans had conceded the first goal to everybody they'd played except Rumania. It was their own perverse way to jump-start themselves, to get the juice flowing. Besides, the Germans had also scored on long slappers.

But when the period was done, the score was still 1–0; and Jorma Valtonen, a 33-year-old who'd been tending goal for Finland in international matches for a decade, had brushed off fourteen American shots. Some of his saves had been disturbingly spectacular. Once, Steve Christoff had whipped a sure goal over him, and Valtonen, on his knees, falling back, gloved it. "Oh, no," Brooks groaned, as Christoff stared, disbelieving.

Plenty of time. No anxiety in the American room. Just play your game. Somebody would get it moving—and five minutes in, here was Christoff, scooping up the puck (after Neal Broten had spooked a Finnish defenseman into giving it away), back-handing it through Valtonen's legs. Tied up.

The U.S.A. was rolling toward the medal stand—until Buzz Schneider was sent off a minute or so later for slashing. Thirty seconds later, the Finns slipped one of their centers, Mikko Leinonen, past Mark Johnson and had a defenseman named Hannu Haapalainen thread him a pass for an easy tip-in.

They were exactly like the Swedes in that regard, at least. Skate and wait, then put one up on the board the moment you gave them the chance.

Two periods gone now, and Brooks was giving them The Last Word. "Twenty minutes, gentlemen," he told them. "If it's not twenty, you'll never live it down. This will haunt you the rest of your lives."

Nothing more needed. Every Olympian thought the same thing. We win this one, Mark Johnson thought, and nobody catches us. That's all we need to know.

Twenty years before, another bunch of Americans had sat in a room at Squaw Valley, winded and trailing by a goal. They'd been offered oxygen; they used, instead, adrenaline—and scored six unanswered goals for their gold medal.

Billy Christian had set up the goal that tied the score that day and loosed the deluge. Now his son, David, broke out of the U.S. zone, fed Phil Verchota breaking down the left side and watched him beat Valtonen with a crisp 15-footer. Tied again, less than three minutes in. The Americans were in charge now —decisively.

Six minutes gone now, and Christian was at the point, back-handing a shot that ended up behind the goal for Johnson to pick up and push out to Robbie McClanahan. *Deke him and beat him,* McClanahan knew. So he waited for Valtonen to commit first, then slid the puck between his legs. U.S.A. 3, Finland 2, with fourteen minutes to kill.

So why should they make it easy? The Americans had dangled everybody for 59:33 before they nailed the Swedes. They'd given the Czechs first poke. They'd let Norway lead them for a period, spotted the Germans two goals, trailed the Russians three times before throwing them over.

Why not play mind games with themselves, Herbie, the Finns and a couple hundred million of their fellow citizens? So, precisely forty-three seconds after McClanahan had supposedly put his teammates out of danger, they began taking cheap penalties, daring the Finns to do something painful with their power play.

First man off was Broten; two minutes for hooking. Six seconds after he returned, off went Christian for tripping. Finally, Verchota vanished, for roughing, a questionable call. The Americans' poise seemed shaken. Four minutes and fifteen seconds from the gold medal.

Enough, decided Christoff, and suddenly he was "Rif," pissed-off Gopher nonpareil, whomping some poor Finn against the boards, commandeering the puck and getting it to the Magic Man for one final bit of prestidigitation.

The shot, a fine open chance on Valtonen, was there; but the puck was jiggly, wouldn't sit. So Johnson moved the puck around, walked in and whipped a backhand at him.

Valtonen went splay-legged and batted the puck down. Two burly defensemen, Haapalainen and Lasse Litma, sandwiched Johnson, seemingly foreclosing the rebound. But a flick of Johnson's stick, and the red light blazed. Four–two now, 3:35 showing, and time to ice down a few dozen bottles of sparkling wine.

The Finns were bagging it. They seem depressed, Broten thought. They're not playing as well as I thought they would.

Two minutes were left; the American bench was starting to get rowdy, watching the action for a moment—just to make sure things were still under control—then whooping and congratulating each other.

A minute left, with the Coneheads coming on. McClanahan, returning exuberant to the bench, rapped Broten playfully on the helmet with his stick. Broten, energized, yelped and got McClanahan in a fraternal headlock. Thirty seconds, with Schneider almost knocking in a rebound, the U.S. in total control, the bench—and the country—in bedlam.

Everybody had his stick over the dasher now, thumping it against the boards. The crowd, which simply would not hear of anything less than pure gold, was roaring.

Ten seconds now, with Broten and Bah Harrington slapping hands, preparing for the great vault onto the ice and a few hours of Bacchanalia.

Then the buzzer, with everybody on the ice, but the tone subtly different from Friday night. Then, the ecstasy had come of shock, of a world turned upside down in fourteen days. This time, it was a whoosh of relief, achievement, emancipation.

No more games. No more mortal duels between one way of life and another. No more strange European faces and stranger European names. No more Herbies. No more Herbie.

Brooks had shaken hands quickly, then done his disappearing act again. It would have been completely out of character for him to run, skidding and slipping, across the ice, to embrace his players. Craig Patrick could do that, because Patrick had been one of them.

If I did that, Brooks knew, they'd say, hey, where were you for eight months? At least they can respect me for being consistent.

Again, the moment belonged to the players; and now they belonged to the country. Somebody handed McClanahan an American flag. Then some kid came, careening, across the ice and gave a huge, filthy American flag to Jimmy Craig, who decided he had to wear it.

So they spent a free-form twenty minutes out there, all taboos lifted, no tomorrow to be concerned with. Johnson and Bobby Suter, Americans but still Badgers, embraced. Schneider and Eruzione, Americans but also refugees from the "I," hugged, too. Eric Strobel handed Harrington a beer, and Harrington washed his face with it.

Amid all of them was Craig, still holding the flag and his stick, the mask off now, showing the ritually unshaven face and an anxious expression. "Where's my father?" he kept asking. His family, and his father, had inspired him for two weeks, driving down each day from Montreal. Now, all Craig could see were thousands of exuberant faces, all the same. One of them had to be his father.

They had to leave the ice, finally. The Russians and Swedes had to play for the silver medal in an hour. The dressing room was stocked with champagne and beer; and Walter Mondale, the Vice President, was getting Jimmy Carter on the phone again.

"Where are the players from Minnesota?" Mondale wondered aloud. Forty eyes rolled simultaneously. Hey, Fritz, don't get regional.

"We have no players from Minnesota, Mr. Vice President," Brooks informed him. "We have only Americans."

Brooks was summoned to the phone. Carter wanted to remind him what a terrific thing his boys had done for America.

But the line was dead. "Yes, sir, Mr. President," Brooks deadpanned. "I'll come right down tomorrow and register for the draft."

Now Carter was on the line. "You told me last night you had one more game to win," he told Brooks.

"Mr. President, I lie a lot," Brooks replied. "I didn't know if we were going to do it. It was a great win for everybody in sport and the American people in general. From the things we had to overcome, to the different beliefs, ways of life. It just proves our life is the proper way to continue."

"We were working on Iran and economics," Carter told him, "but nobody could do business because we were watching the T.V."

"Well, the other two are more important," Brooks said. "But we are all looking forward to seeing you tomorrow."

Carter wanted to talk to Eruzione now. Then to Craig, to get some sort of a luncheon order. He wanted the whole bunch of them to come down tomorrow and see him.

"Two lobsters, sir," Craig told him. "Oysters. You know, the kind of sea food we get at home, sir."

There was a press conference with the whole team, still in uniform, unwinding up on the high school auditorium stage, and the players would dictate the format. Brooks had violated one Olympic rule by bringing no players out after the first game. Now, he violated another. He brought everybody.

"What's the one word you all would use to describe this victory?" they were asked.

Eruzione, as captain, took the microphone. "I guess we're all a bunch of big Doolies now. Phil Verchota will explain what a big Doolie is."

Terrific, Verchota thought. Put me right on the spot. "As for what a big Doolie is, I don't know," Verchota said. "I won a gold medal today, so I'm a big Doolie. It's just a big wheel, a big gun. That's about it."

Cheers, halloos, general approbation from his mates.

"This press conference," Eruzione told himself. "This is us." None of the usual false "humble," attributing it all to luck, thanking Coach Brooks. The Olympians lounged about in Roman-banquet fashion, cavalierly disregarding Brooks, answering what they chose, ignoring what they deemed impertinent.

"Gong that question," a player would say if somebody from Sioux City happened to ask what all this meant to the people of America. And it was done, brushed aside for good.

Now, shuffle-trotting down the corridor along the far wall ("Hi, guys") was OCee himself, brandishing a bottle of Japanese beer, fresh from the doping room.

He and Harrington had been the day's chosen few. "Seventeen and twenty-eight," someone had said. "Let's go." So they'd sat there for twenty minutes, drained six beers apiece; then came to the auditorium to enrich the national archives.

"I'm from Charlestown," O'Callahan informed the self-styled

elite of the nation's sporting press. "In the shadow of Bunker
Hill. The Americans won at Bunker Hill, the Americans won at
Lake Placid."

"But the Americans didn't win at Bunker Hill," someone
protested.

"Hey, I don't wanna hear that," O'Callahan countered.
"What do you think there's a monument there for? I can see it
from my house."

Was there a Brooksism that might be relevant to all this?
Harrington, as curator, stepped to the mike. "Well, ah, you
know, we were damned if we did and damned if we didn't. Fool
me once, shame on you. Fool me twice, shame on me. Well, ah,
you know, we looked like a monkey screwing a football out
there for two periods and blah, blah, blah. But we walked up to
the tiger, we spit in his eye and we shot him. Then we went to
the well again and the water was colder, the water was deeper.
What else can I say? Well, ah, for lack of a better phrase, that
just about wraps it up."

There was champagne to bathe in back in the dressing room
and a medal ceremony to dress for. The Americans would have
three hours to while away during the Russia–Sweden game;
three hours of idle reminiscence—champagne streaming down
their faces; three hours of saying, "Unbelievable, unbelievable"
to each other; three hours before they went out to be fussed
over by Lord Killanin.

They'd been reasonably grim Games by most standards. The
Taiwanese had been excluded; Carter had been talking about
a Summer Games boycott; the bus system had broken down,
spectators left freezing in the dark. The Europeans had bitched
about living in a prison, Killanin had dropped somebody's
medal in a snowbank, the locals had jacked up prices, everybody had grown snappish. But they would always be remembered for one fine moment and twenty college kids who'd gone
for it.

When they came out for the medals shortly after 4:30 in the
afternoon, they'd been goofing and giggling and swilling out of

random bottles for nearly three hours. "They came out drunk as lords," one sports writer observed, "to meet the Lord himself."

It was hard to tell precisely where the spirits left off and bug-eyed emotion began. Nobody cared. Killanin seemed amused as one American after another swaggered up to receive his medal and variously stared at it, kissed it or chewed on it to determine authenticity.

Craig was the first man up. Then Harrington, who promptly thrust both hands into the air. Then Dave Silk and Mike Ramsey, each throwing a fist high overhead. Then O'Callahan, bouncing up and down and grinning a great gap-toothed grin at Killanin. "Jackie," his father would groan afterward, "how many times have I told you? When you go up to accept an award, always put in your teeth."

One by one they came up, savored their moment in the spotlight, and left to roam the ice, accept the accolades, seek out an old buddy for a celebratory Two Musketeers–salute, a little horseplay, or a full Yogi Berra-jumps-into-Don-Larsen's-arms-after-his-World-Series-no-hitter number.

Meanwhile the Russians, who'd waxed the Swedes 9–2 just moments before and collected a novelty, their first silver medal, stood by amused. The Swedes, delighted to have a medal of any denomination, were still in uniform, dripping sweat, their hair tousled, almost as pleased as the Americans.

Finally, they called Boris Mikhailov, Mats Waltin and Eruzione, the three captains, up to the stand for the anthems. Eruzione, his team behind him in their blue sweats, put his hand over his heart, watched the flag go up and sang the "Star Spangled Banner." No prompting needed.

Then he turned and motioned to the whole crew, Terriers, Gophers, Badgers, Bulldogs, Falcons and Sioux. "C'mere," Eruzione called. "C'mere. Get up on the stage."

So they all crowded up there, hip to hip, shoulder to shoulder, index fingers pointed to the roof, chanting U-S-A, U-S-A. The Arena had remained filled; this was star-spangled frosting. Then

Eruzione led them in a victory parade around the ice. Had it been the Stanley Cup, he would have skated around, trophy held high over his head. Instead, they walked around and displayed their medals to their countrymen.

"We're twenty guys playing on the Olympic team," Eruzione would explain later. "We're not from Boston or Minnesota. We live today in the Olympic Village. Our home is in a Burnsville apartment, where most of us still owe some money."

Somebody else would settle up that account. There were matters of state to attend to in the morning, a President to see. "Get in early," Brooks told his people. "I'm not taking a bunch of tipsy hockey players to see the President of the United States."

So they stayed out all night, just wandering and loafing, nothing rowdy. Most of them got back to the Olympic Village as dawn was breaking over the Adirondacks. Bill Baker glanced at a clock—five minutes to six—shrugged, and went off to take a quick shower and cram his gear into a bag.

Mark Wells had gotten in at a decent hour—somewhere around four—and heard a female screaming for help. He came upon a drunken Russian athlete mugging an American girl, "trying to get into her private life."

The Russian took one look at Wells in his U.S.A. jacket and fled. Wells shook his head. Maybe they were all supermen now. They'd won the gold medal, saved the world. The President had asked about their menu preferences. NHL clubs were suddenly panting to get their names on contracts.

A couple of hours later, they were at Andrews Air Force Base. Carter had sent an Air Force jet to bring the entire U.S. Olympic Squad, hockey players, skiers, speedskaters, lugers, the works, to the capital. It wasn't until they noticed the traffic blockade, the faces crowded together, flags waving, that the Olympians began to realize the enormity of it. If it's like this here, Mark Johnson wondered, what's it going to be like elsewhere?

Back in Lake Placid the mania had been contained, a small

pocket of giddiness that could be sampled or avoided at will. There was always the trailer to go back to, another practice to prepare for, another game ahead.

Now they'd dined at the President's table, been proclaimed magnificent Americans all. Guess it's time to get back on the bus, Jim Craig thought. There had to be another town up ahead, another bunch of Flint Generals waiting to take their heads off.

Instead, everybody was shaking hands, see you sometime, I've gotta catch a plane for Chicago, for Atlanta, for Winnipeg. Got a contract to sign, a team to join.

Now Brooks was hugging Craig ("Jimmy, you did everything I ever asked of you"), patting backs, shaking hands, wrapping it up. Players were standing around, conversations trailing off amid awkward leavetakings.

"It's over, Jack," Dave Silk told O'Callahan. "It's over." And then, Silk began to cry.

EPILOGUE

When their Chief Executive was done with them, the Olympians came home, severally, to victory celebrations worthy of Cincinnatus. Two weeks earlier, Mary Harrington's Virginia school board had docked her a week's pay when she went to Lake Placid to root for her son. Now the city council bought a large photograph of John Harrington and hung it in the Miners Memorial Building.

The good people of Warroad painted Dave Christian's name on the side of a building along Route 11, visible from North Dakota and points west. Back in Boston, Mike Eruzione was borne home in a gold Rolls-Royce and summoned back to Boston University with his three fellow Terriers for gold watches and a few words of inspiration for the varsity. "By the end of the week everyone was saying my name right," Eruzione marveled. "All my life I've never had that happen."

Thousands of well-wishers crowded into the Twin Cities Air Force Reserve terminal to greet Herb Brooks and his dozen Minnesotans, who spent the next day being fed, photographed and motorcaded on both sides of the Mississippi. Brooks' old St. Paul bartender told him he could have a free beer every day for the rest of his life. "I asked him if I could bunch them up every so often," Brooks said. "He said no."

For a week, it was giddy and chaotic for all of them—dozens of calls from grateful strangers across the country, marriage proposals from un-known maidens ("I told them to send pictures," said Eruzione), fawning politicians, endless luncheons, interviews, endorsement offers. Later, when Walter Mondale moved into North Oaks, he was informed that he was only the second most famous resident. Robbie McClanahan took precedence.

After a quick, overwhelming brush with unchecked adulation, though, several Olympians were looking for an escape hatch. Mark Pavelich grabbed rod and reel and headed for an uncharted lake. Eric Strobel breezed off Air Force One, saw the hordes and decided to skip the rest. "I want," he told a waiting friend, "to get the hell out of here."

None of them ever got the time to decompress. Ideally, the players would have liked to hang out at the Olympic Village for a few days and unwind as the crowd melted away. Then, they'd have wanted a raucous breakup dinner somewhere in the "We're-outta-heah-Donnah" tradition; cold beers and hard rolls within easy reach. Then, a debriefing. "It would have been great to get in a room with Herb," Harrington would declare, "and say, 'Okay, why?' "

There had never been time for that. The Olympians were a hot commodity now, their NHL clubs eager to sign them and cash in on the gold-medal aura. It was dizziest for Jim Craig, who quickly came to realize that a couple hundred million people now knew his face. Everyone had seen him with the American flag around his neck, searching anxiously for his father. Coca-Cola paid him $35,000 for the privilege of showing them together in an advertisement. The Atlanta Flames, dying at the box office, fetched him south within days and ran him through a gauntlet of promotional appearances. Then they plugged him into their goal and expected performances worthy of Olympus.

"I saw Jimmy three weeks later," Ken Morrow would recall, "and his eyes were half-closed. I felt sorry for him. He didn't look as though he'd had more than three hours' sleep."

Not that Morrow's transition had been much more leisurely. From Washington, he'd gone to his wife's house for three days to let the adrenaline settle. By Friday he'd signed with the New York Islanders. By Saturday he was playing in his first professional game. Three months later, Morrow's name was on the Stanley Cup, where it has been reinscribed every year since.

Of the nine Olympians who had college eligibility remaining to them, only Neal Broten returned to school. His brother Aaron was still at the "U," and Broten wanted to play alongside him for at least one season. (Later Broten joined the Minnesota North Stars and set NHL records for most goals and points by an American.)

Everybody else who wanted to signed a professional contract and went off to seek his fortune. Steve Christoff joined the North Stars and set a play-off mark that spring for most goals by a rookie. Dave Christian went off to Winnipeg, Mark Johnson to Pittsburgh, Mike Ramsey to Buffalo, Jack O'Callahan to Chicago.

Some of them made a rapid and firm mark with the parent club; others began the climb in the minor leagues. Once there, the Olympians immediately discovered themselves to be marked men, targets for marginal players who resented their celebrity.

After two and a half games with Rochester, Harrington found himself with a broken jaw, a fractured nose, four loosened front teeth, a concussion and half a dozen stitches in his chin.

Mark Wells had guessed that sort of thing might happen, so he'd decided not to join a pro club until the fall. I've been labeled before, he told himself. But this time I'm really labeled. Somebody's going to want to put me in a hospital or kill me. So I'm going to let the thing cool off, and then go.

Several of the players had opted for the European leagues—Phil Verchota signed on with Jokerit in Finland's elite circuit, and the Coneheads went Swiss (Pavelich, soon joined by Harrington, played for Lugano; Buzz Schneider chose Bern). But they quickly realized they were expected to be supermen; the gold medal was viewed as a mystical talisman.

Schneider would be pulling off his gear after a solid game—maybe a goal and a couple of assists—and would notice team officials wearing disappointed expressions. You're a gold medalist, the presumption went. Why aren't you playing like one?

They expect you to stickhandle past everybody and score a goal on every rush, Schneider thought.

Thus did the euphoria of Lake Placid recede. Brooks had been touted as a coaching genius, a stylistic pioneer; yet, NHL interest was limited to an offer from the moribund Colorado Rockies. So he signed a two-year contract to oversee a semi-pro Swiss club in Davos, then found that he might as well be speaking in Mandarin. His new players worked day jobs; they had little patience for demanding workouts or weaving squiggles on a blackboard. "Hey, Herbie," one of them told Brooks. "We're not out to beat the Russians."

It was the fall of 1980 now, and reality had set in. "It's a great memory," Harrington decided, "but life goes on." Strobel had broken an ankle and spent time in Baltimore, which he'd dubbed "Nam." Now he was out of hockey and back in Minneapolis.

Before he'd broken *his* ankle, the Los Angeles Kings had been interested in Bobby Suter. "After that," Suter said, "it was, 'Who are you?' "
So Suter opened a sporting-goods store in Madison, before he had put
in one year in the club. That proved to be enough, and then it was back
to Madison.

Eruzione, to the surprise of some, retired a week after the Games. He'd
played three years in the International League, where each day's preoc-
cupation was whose stick you'd have to duck that night.

Eruzione knew that the Rangers or Hartford might have signed him, let
him skate wing for a few weeks, then shipped him to the AHL. Those
memories, he had plenty of in advance. The memory he wanted was one
goal against the Russians, then the flag going up and him glancing down
at Boris Mikhailov. "I don't want to be remembered as a struggling hockey
player," Eruzione would say. "I'm going out on top."

He had gone to Lake Placid expecting little, so everything that spun off
from those two weeks he would consider gravy. He happily took a job
doing color commentary for Madison Square Garden Cable Television.
Named technical adviser to the ABC Televison film *Miracle on Ice,* he was
able to use that position and his frequent travels to maintain a quasi-post-
Olympic captaincy for the team. He hopscotched the country giving up-up
speeches to businessmen, watching their eyes fill and their chests swell
when he ran the highlight film.

His shelf life as Yankee Doodle Dandy, Eruzione knew, could be brief,
so he would savor it. When it was done, he would do what he would have
done if the team had come up empty: go back to Winthrop, marry Donna,
get a coaching job, buy a house, have some kids. "Even if I become a
bum," Eruzione reasoned, "I can still go into a bar with that gold medal
and tell stories."

Yet, the celebrity, as Jim Craig found out, cut both ways.

He could never again be anonymous, and gradually Craig came to
realize that. When a car he was driving collided with another on a wet
spring night on Cape Cod in 1982, and a woman died, the incident made
nationwide news.

Ultimately, Craig was acquitted of all charges and a civil suit was settled
out of court. When he came to the National team again that fall, he had
had a bellyful of "celebrity" ("If anybody wants to change places . . .").
Craig was 25 now, and wanted simply to get on with life and a career.

His Olympic teammates kept tabs on him and on each other through
paragraph-long reports in their local newspapers and agate type in *The*

Hockey News. They had gotten together at Mark Johnson's wedding during the summer after the Games and again at a reunion of the 1960 and 1980 U.S. teams at the U.S. Hockey Hall of Fame in Eveleth. After that, their meetings were haphazard—lunch in Minneapolis if the North Stars happened to be playing the Sabres, a quick beer or two after a game in Manhattan.

Serendipity brought a bunch of them together in New York, where Brooks was hired in 1981 to coach the Rangers. Fred Shero had resigned, and Craig Patrick, who'd become the club's general manager, told Brooks the job was his if he could settle accounts with his employers in Switzerland.

Silk was already in New York. Before long, a mini-colony of Olympians had sprouted, collected one by one by Brooks and Patrick. They signed Pavelich, who'd grown weary of Switzerland, and whom no NHL club had bothered to draft; and Pavelich quickly became the Rangers' most artful center and their leading scorer in 1982–83. McClanahan, who'd played for five major- and minor-league clubs in two years, arrived on Thirty-third Street and blossomed. Bill Baker, having bounced from Montreal to Colorado to St. Louis, was gathered in too. And up in a Garden television booth, barbered and blazered and commenting on their play, was Eruzione.

Everybody else had scattered. Johnson was traded from Pittsburgh to Minnesota, then to Hartford, where he bloomed with a 31-goal season in 1982–83. Steve Christoff hurt a shoulder and was sent from Minnesota to Calgary. In the summer of 1983, after an injury-laden season, the North Stars reacquired the speedy forward but shipped him to Los Angeles four months later.

They'd entered adulthood. Steve Janaszak married an interpreter from Lake Placid named Jackie Minichello. Others wed too: Broten, O'Callahan, Eruzione, Johnson, Christoff, Harrington. Their gold medals were encased in Lucite (Dave Christian's was placed next to his father's on the family coffee table) or stashed away. Life went on.

Life on the other side of the ocean had also returned to pre-Placid normalcy. Predictions that the Soviet team would be trucked off en masse to a Siberian salt mine were slightly off the mark.

The initial shock and disgruntlement ("They played like old men," one Muscovite *babushka* grumbled the following morning) gave way to a philosophical shrug ("These things happen sometimes," Helmut Balderis would tell Doc Nagobads) and some official examination. Viktor Tikhonov and his assistant laid it all out in an interview in *Sovietskaya Rossiya,* the Central Committee's mouthpiece.

Years of ragtag equipment and too few indoor rinks had taken their toll, the two coaches charged. How could Soviet youth be expected to develop into world-class players given such handicaps? Worse, too many of the world-class players they did have had grown lazy, "parasitic," unwilling to play for the elite Moscow teams where the regimen was more demanding. How long could they depend upon the Mikhailovs and Vasilievs?

But as in the West, the players had a different viewpoint. Tretiak, for one, told ABC Sports that he laid the blame for the loss to the U.S.A. at Tikhonov's feet. "We had the team to win the game. But the coach took me to the bench. And I think he made a mistake [because] . . . when I'm in the net . . . the guys believe in me and calm themselves."

Before the next quadrennium had reached its midpoint, Mikhailov and Petrov retired, and death claimed Kharlamov, their fast-life comrade. He and his wife were tooling around the rain-slicked Moscow streets in their sports car and something went wrong; the report from *Tass* was sketchy, but it was stated that she was driving.

Yet, there were replacements for all of them in the system. A new blank face moved up, claimed his red helmet and slipped in as the appropriate cog in the dynamo. The Russians turned up at the 1981 World Championships and beat everyone hollow. That fall, they came back to Montreal and blitzed the Canadians 8–1 for the Canada Cup. In 1983, with another world title in their pocket and another yet ahead, the Soviets sent another select team over to bop as many individual NHL clubs as they could in nine days. When they were done, Philadelphia captain Bobby Clarke said, no, he just didn't see the point in playing those people any longer.

The team and the system and the society had a stability, a rigidity to it that kept the odds prohibitively on their side. Several of the Soviet players had been drafted by NHL clubs on a chance, just in case the world turned upside down one day and a Tretiak might find himself an unattached tourist. It was fantasy; no Russian hockey player had ever defected. Czechs did that.

In fact, two of the three Stastny brothers did defect in August of 1980. Moments after a game with the Russians in Innsbruck, Anton and Peter bade Marian (who followed later) farewell, stepped into a red Mercedes and outraced the Czech secret service to Vienna—where they boarded a plane for Montreal, soon signed a contract with the Quebec Nordiques and began taking French lessons. "We want to be good in French," Anton would say. "We plan to be here a long time."

The NHL was also a powerful lure for others who did not need to step into getaway cars. By 1983, no fewer than nine members of the Czech team were under NHL contracts—the rest of them with their government's blessing. So was a quarter of the Finnish national team, including the captain, Tapio Levo, and six members of Sweden's bronze medal side, led by goaltender Pelle Lindbergh and defenseman Jonsson, now a New York Islander mainstay.

But the Russians remained too consistent, too stable, too talented for most professional clubs. The odds against any amateur team ever beating them again were prohibitive. "But that time," Jack O'Callahan would muse, "that moment . . ."

APPENDIX

OLYMPIC HOCKEY MEDALISTS

Year	Site	Gold	Silver	Bronze	U.S. Finish
1920	Antwerp	Canada	UNITED STATES	Czechoslovakia	
1924	Chamonix	Canada	UNITED STATES	Great Britain	
1928	St. Moritz	Canada	Sweden	Switzerland	DNC*
1932	Lake Placid	Canada	UNITED STATES	Germany	
1936	Garmisch	Great Britain	Canada	UNITED STATES	
1940	NOT HELD				
1944	NOT HELD				
1948	St. Moritz	Canada	Czechoslovakia	Switzerland	4th
1952	Oslo	Canada	UNITED STATES	Sweden	
1956	Cortina	Soviet Union	UNITED STATES	Sweden	
1960	Squaw Valley	UNITED STATES	Canada	Soviet Union	
1964	Innsbruck	Soviet Union	Sweden	Czechoslovakia	5th
1968	Grenoble	Soviet Union	Czechoslovakia	Canada	6th
1972	Sapporo	Soviet Union	UNITED STATES	Czechoslovakia	
1976	Innsbruck	Soviet Union	Czechoslovakia	West Germany	4th
1980	Lake Placid	UNITED STATES	Soviet Union	Sweden	

*Did not compete.

WORLD HOCKEY CHAMPIONSHIPS

	Champion	Second	U.S. Finish
1930	Canada	Germany	DNC
1931	Canada	UNITED STATES	
1933	UNITED STATES	Canada	
1934	Canada	UNITED STATES	
1935	Canada	Switzerland	DNC
1937	Canada	Great Britain	DNC
1938	Canada	Great Britain	8th
1939	Canada	UNITED STATES	
1940–46	NOT HELD		
1947	Czechoslovakia	Sweden	5th
1949	Czechoslovakia	Canada	3rd
1950	Canada	UNITED STATES	
1951	Canada	Sweden	5th
1953	Sweden	Germany	DNC
1954	Soviet Union	Canada	DNC
1955	Canada	Soviet Union	4th
1957	Sweden	Soviet Union	DNC
1958	Canada	Soviet Union	5th
1959	Canada	Soviet Union	4th
1961	Canada	Czechoslovakia	7th
1962	Sweden	Canada	3rd
1963	Soviet Union	Sweden	8th
1965	Soviet Union	Czechoslovakia	6th
1966	Soviet Union	Czechoslovakia	6th
1967	Soviet Union	Sweden	5th
1969	Soviet Union	Sweden	6th
1970	Soviet Union	Sweden	B Group (1st)
1971	Soviet Union	Czechoslovakia	6th
1972	Czechoslovakia	Soviet Union	B Group (2nd)
1973	Soviet Union	Sweden	B Group (2nd)
1974	Soviet Union	Czechoslovakia	B Group (1st)
1975	Soviet Union	Czechoslovakia	6th
1976	Czechoslovakia	Soviet Union	4th
1977	Soviet Union	Sweden	6th
1978	Soviet Union	Czechoslovakia	6th
1979	Soviet Union	Czechoslovakia	7th
1981	Soviet Union	Sweden	5th
1982	Soviet Union	Czechoslovakia	8th
1983	Soviet Union	Czechoslovakia	B Group (1st)

1980 OLYMPICS, U.S. SUMMARIES

U.S.A. vs. SWEDEN, FEBRUARY 12, OLYMPIC FIELD HOUSE

Final Score

U.S.A.	0	1	1	2
Sweden	1	0	1	2

FIRST PERIOD
Swe: Sture Andersson (Lars Molin, Per Lundqvist), 11:04

SECOND PERIOD
U.S.A.: Dave Silk (Mike Ramsey, Mark Johnson), 19:32

THIRD PERIOD
Swe: Thomas Eriksson (Harald Luckner), 4:45
U.S.A.: Bill Baker (Mark Pavelich, Buzz Schneider), 19:33

SHOTS ON GOAL

U.S.A.	7	12	10	29
Sweden	16	11	9	36

Goaltenders: Jim Craig, Pelle Lindbergh

U.S.A. vs. CZECHOSLOVAKIA, FEBRUARY 14, OLYMPIC FIELD HOUSE

Final Score

U.S.A.	2	2	3	7
Czechoslovakia	2	0	1	3

FIRST PERIOD
Cze: Jaroslav Pouzar (Frantisek Kaberle, Milan Novy), 2:23
U.S.A.: Mike Eruzione (Neal Broten), 4:39
U.S.A.: Mark Pavelich (Buzz Schneider, John Harrington), 5:45
Cze: Marian Stastny (Peter Stastny), 12:07

SECOND PERIOD
U.S.A.: Buzz Schneider (Mark Pavelich), 4:33
U.S.A.: Mark Johnson (Rob McClanahan), 15:28

THIRD PERIOD
U.S.A.: Phil Verchota (Dave Christian), 2:59
U.S.A.: Buzz Schneider (John Harrington), 3:59
Cze: Jiri Novak (Vincent Lukac), 5:36
U.S.A.: Rob McClanahan (Mark Johnson), 10:54

SHOTS ON GOAL

U.S.A.	11	5	11	27
Czechoslovakia	13	6	12	31

Goaltenders: Jim Craig, Jiri Kralik

U.S.A. vs. NORWAY, FEBRUARY 16, OLYMPIC ARENA

Final Score

U.S.A.	0	3	2	5
Norway	1	0	0	1

FIRST PERIOD

Nor: Geir Myhre (Oeivind Loesaamoen), 4:19

SECOND PERIOD

U.S.A.: Mike Eruzione (unassisted), :41
U.S.A.: Mark Johnson (Dave Christian, Rob McClanahan), 4:51
U.S.A.: Dave Silk (Mark Pavelich, Ken Morrow), 13:31

THIRD PERIOD

U.S.A.: Mark Wells (Dave Silk, Phil Verchota), 4:28
U.S.A.: Ken Morrow (Rob McClanahan, Eric Strobel), 11:29

SHOTS ON GOAL

U.S.A.	16	16	11	43
Norway	9	7	6	22

Goaltenders: Jim Craig, Jim Martinsen

U.S.A. vs. RUMANIA, FEBRUARY 18, OLYMPIC FIELD HOUSE

Final Score

U.S.A.	2	2	3	7
Rumania	0	1	1	2

FIRST PERIOD

U.S.A.: Buzz Schneider (Mark Pavelich, John Harrington), 12:03
U.S.A.: Eric Strobel (Buzz Schneider, Mike Ramsey), 15:52

SECOND PERIOD

U.S.A.: Mark Wells (Phil Verchota, Ken Morrow), 9:34
Rum: Doru Tureanu (Constantin Vasile Nistor), 13:40
U.S.A.: Buzz Schneider (John Harrington), 17:05

THIRD PERIOD
U.S.A.: Steve Christoff (Jack O'Callahan), 8:14
Rum: Alexandru Halauca (Doru Iosif Morosan), 12:48
U.S.A.: Neal Broten (Mike Eruzione), 16:12
U.S.A.: Rob McClanahan (Mark Johnson), 18:09

SHOTS ON GOAL

U.S.A.	20	16	15	51
Rumania	9	9	3	21

Goaltenders: Jim Craig, Valerian Netedu

U.S.A. vs. WEST GERMANY, FEBRUARY 20, OLYMPIC FIELD HOUSE

Final Score

U.S.A.	0	2	2	4
West Germany	2	0	0	2

FIRST PERIOD
WGer: Horst-Peter Kretschmer (unassisted), 1:50
WGer: Udo Kiessling (Ernst Hofner, Horst-Peter Kretschmer), 19:45

SECOND PERIOD
U.S.A.: Rob McClanahan (Mark Johnson, Dave Christian), 7:40
U.S.A.: Neal Broten (Eric Strobel, Mike Eruzione), 18:31

THIRD PERIOD
U.S.A.: Rob McClanahan (Mark Johnson, Dave Christian), 1:17
U.S.A.: Phil Verchota (Dave Christian, Mark Wells), 4:17

SHOTS ON GOAL

U.S.A.	14	9	9	32
West Germany	7	6	13	26

Goaltenders: Jim Craig, Sigmund Suttner

U.S.A. vs. SOVIET UNION, FEBRUARY 22, OLYMPIC FIELD HOUSE

Final Score

U.S.A.	2	0	2	4
Soviet Union	2	1	0	3

FIRST PERIOD

U.S.S.R.: Vladimir Krutov (Aleksei Kasatanov), 9:12
U.S.A.: Buzz Schneider (Mark Pavelich), 14:03
U.S.S.R.: Sergei Makharov (Aleksandro Golikov), 17:34
U.S.A.: Mark Johnson (Dave Christian, Dave Silk), 19:59

SECOND PERIOD

U.S.S.R.: Aleksandr Maltsev (Vladimir Krutov), 2:18

THIRD PERIOD

U.S.A.: Mark Johnson (Dave Silk), 8:39
U.S.A.: Mike Eruzione (Mark Pavelich, John Harrington), 10:00

SHOTS ON GOAL

U.S.A.	8	2	6	16
U.S.S.R.	18	12	9	39

Goaltenders: Jim Craig, Vladislav Tretiak, Vladimir Myshkin(1)

U.S.A. vs. FINLAND, FEBRUARY 24, OLYMPIC FIELD HOUSE

Final Score

U.S.A.	0	1	3	4
Finland	1	1	0	2

FIRST PERIOD

Fin: Jukka Porvari (Mikko Leinonen, Lasse Litma), 9:20

SECOND PERIOD

U.S.A.: Steve Christoff (unassisted), 4:39
Fin: Mikko Leinonen (Hannu Haapalainen, Markku Kiimalainen), 6:30

THIRD PERIOD

U.S.A.: Phil Verchota (Dave Christian), 2:25
U.S.A.: Rob McClanahan (Mark Johnson, Dave Christian), 6:05
U.S.A.: Mark Johnson (Steve Christoff), 16:25

SHOTS ON GOAL

U.S.A.	14	8	7	29
Finland	7	6	10	23

Goaltenders: Jim Craig, Jorma Valtonen

1980 OLYMPIC HOCKEY RESULTS

Preliminary Round

Red Group	**Blue Group**
Feb. 12 Canada 10, Holland 1	United States 2, Sweden 2
Poland 5, Finland 4	Rumania 6, West Germany 4
Soviet Union 16, Japan 0	Czechoslovakia 11, Norway 0
Feb. 14 Soviet Union 17, Holland 4	Sweden 8, Rumania 0
Canada 5, Poland 1	West Germany 10, Norway 4
Finland 6, Japan 3	United States 7, Czechoslovakia 3
Feb. 16 Soviet Union 8, Poland 1	United States 5, Norway 1
Japan 3, Holland 3	Sweden 5, West Germany 2
Finland 4, Canada 3	Czechoslovakia 7, Rumania 2
Feb. 18 Canada 6, Japan 0	United States 7, Rumania 2
Soviet Union 4, Finland 2	Sweden 7, Norway 1
Holland 5, Poland 3	Czechoslovakia 11, West Germany 3
Feb. 20 Soviet Union 6, Canada 4	United States 4, West Germany 2
Finland 10, Holland 3	Sweden 4, Czechoslovakia 2
Poland 5, Japan 1	Norway 3, Rumania 3

Final Preliminary Standings

Red Group	W	L	T	Pts.	GF	GA	**Blue Group**	W	L	T	Pts.	GF	GA
Soviet Union	5	0	0	10	51	11	Sweden	4	0	1	9	26	7
Finland	3	2	0	6	26	18	United States	4	0	1	9	25	10
Canada	3	2	0	6	28	12	Czechoslovakia	3	2	0	6	34	16
Poland	2	3	0	4	15	23	Rumania	1	3	1	3	13	29
Holland	1	3	1	3	16	43	West Germany	1	4	0	2	21	30
Japan	0	4	1	1	7	36	Norway	0	4	1	1	9	36

Medal Round

Feb. 22	United States 4, Soviet Union 3
	Sweden 3, Finland 3
	Czechoslovakia 6, Canada 1 (5th-place consolation game)
Feb. 24	United States 4, Finland 2
	Soviet Union 9, Sweden 2

Final Medal Standings

	W	L	T	Pts.*	GF	GA
United States (Gold)	2	0	1	5	10	7
Soviet Union (Silver)	2	1	0	4	16	8
Sweden (Bronze)	0	1	2	2	7	14
Finland	0	2	1	1	7	11

*Includes preliminary game against medal round opponent from own division.

RESULTS OF UNITED STATES IN OLYMPIC GAMES

1920	Antwerp	U.S.A. 29	Switzerland 0
	Silver	Canada 2	U.S.A. 0
		U.S.A. 16	Czechoslovakia 0
		U.S.A. 7	Sweden 0
1924	Chamonix	U.S.A. 19	Belgium 0
	Silver	U.S.A. 22	France 0
		U.S.A. 11	England 0
		U.S.A. 20	Sweden 0
		Canada 6	U.S.A. 1
1928	St. Moritz		
	DID NOT COMPETE		
1932	Lake Placid	U.S.A. 4	Poland 1
	Silver	Canada 2	U.S.A. 1
		U.S.A. 7	Germany 0
		U.S.A. 5	Poland 0
		U.S.A. 8	Germany 0
		U.S.A. 2	Canada 2
1936	Garmisch	U.S.A. 2	Czechoslovakia 0
	Bronze	U.S.A. 0	Great Britain 0
		Canada 1	U.S.A. 0
1940 and 1944	NOT HELD		
1948	St. Moritz	Switzerland 5	U.S.A. 4
	Fourth	U.S.A. 23	Poland 4
		U.S.A. 31	Italy 1
		U.S.A. 5	Sweden 2
		Canada 12	U.S.A. 3
		U.S.A. 13	Austria 2
		U.S.A. 4	Great Britain 3
		Czechoslovakia 4	U.S.A. 3

RESULTS OF UNITED STATES IN OLYMPIC GAMES (cont.)

1952	Oslo	U.S.A. 3	Norway 2
	Silver	U.S.A. 8	Germany 2
		U.S.A. 8	Finland 2
		U.S.A. 8	Switzerland 2
		Sweden 4	U.S.A. 2
		U.S.A. 5	Poland 3
		U.S.A. 6	Czechoslovakia 3
		U.S.A. 3	Canada 3
1956	Cortina	U.S.A. 7	Germany 2
	Silver	U.S.A. 4	Canada 1
		U.S.A. 6	Sweden 1
		Soviet Union 4	U.S.A. 0
		U.S.A. 9	Czechoslovakia 4
1960	Squaw Valley	U.S.A. 6	Sweden 3
	Gold	U.S.A. 9	Germany 1
		U.S.A. 2	Canada 1
		U.S.A. 3	Soviet Union 2
		U.S.A. 9	Czechoslovakia 4
1964	Innsbruck	Soviet Union 5	U.S.A. 1
	Fifth	U.S.A. 8	Germany 0
		Sweden 7	U.S.A. 4
		Canada 8	U.S.A. 6
		Czechoslovakia 7	U.S.A. 1
		Finland 3	U.S.A. 2
		U.S.A. 7	Switzerland 3
1968	Grenoble	Czechoslovakia 5	U.S.A. 1
	Sixth	Sweden 4	U.S.A. 3
		Soviet Union 10	U.S.A. 2
		Canada 3	U.S.A. 2
		U.S.A. 8	West Germany 1
		U.S.A. 6	East Germany 4
1972	Sapporo	Sweden 5	U.S.A. 1
	Silver	U.S.A. 5	Czechoslovakia 1
		Soviet Union 7	U.S.A. 2
		U.S.A. 6	Poland 1
1976	Innsbruck	Soviet Union 6	U.S.A. 2
	Fourth	U.S.A. 5	Finland 4
		Czechoslovakia 5	U.S.A. 0
		U.S.A. 7	Poland 2
		West Germany 4	U.S.A. 1
1980	Lake Placid	U.S.A. 2	Sweden 2
	Gold	U.S.A. 7	Czechoslovakia 3
		U.S.A. 5	Norway 1
		U.S.A. 7	Rumania 2
		U.S.A. 4	West Germany 2
		U.S.A. 4	Soviet Union 3
		U.S.A. 4	Finland 2

U.S. OLYMPIC HOCKEY COACHES

1920	Ray Schooley	1960	Jack Riley
1924	William Haddock	1964	Eddie Jeremiah
1932	Alfred Winsor	1968	Murray Williamson
1936	Albert Prettyman	1972	Murray Williamson
1948	John Garrison	1976	Bob Johnson
1952	Connie Pleban	1980	Herb Brooks
1956	John Mariucci	1984	Lou Vairo

1980 U.S. ROSTER

GOALIES

30	Jim Craig	6–1	190	22	North Easton, MA	Boston University
1	Steve Janaszak	5–8	160	23	White Bear Lake, MN	Minnesota

DEFENSEMEN

6	Bill Baker	6–1	195	23	Grand Rapids, MN	Minnesota
23	Dave Christian	5–11	170	20	Warroad, MN	North Dakota
3	Ken Morrow	6–4	210	23	Davison, MI	Bowling Green
17	Jack O'Callahan	6–1	185	22	Charlestown, MA	Boston University
5	Mike Ramsey	6–3	190	19	Minneapolis, MN	Minnesota
20	Bob Suter	5–9	178	22	Madison, WI	Wisconsin

CENTERS

9	Neal Broten	5–9	155	20	Roseau, MN	Minnesota
10	Mark Johnson	5–9	160	22	Madison, WI	Wisconsin
16	Mark Pavelich	5–7	160	21	Eveleth, MN	Minnesota-Duluth
15	Mark Wells	5–9	175	22	St. Clair Shores, MI	Bowling Green

LEFT WINGS

21	Mike Eruzione	5–10	185	25	Winthrop, MA	Boston University
7	Rob McClanahan	5–10	180	22	St. Paul, MN	Minnesota
25	Buzz Schneider	5–11	180	25	Babbitt, MN	Minnesota
27	Phil Verchota	6–2	195	23	Duluth, MN	Minnesota

RIGHT WINGS

11	Steve Christoff	6–1	180	22	Richfield, MN	Minnesota
28	John Harrington	5–10	180	22	Virginia, MN	Minnesota-Duluth
8	Dave Silk	5–11	190	22	Scituate, MA	Boston University
19	Eric Strobel	5–10	175	21	Rochester, MN	Minnesota

Coach: Herb Brooks
Assistant Coach: Craig Patrick
Captain: Mike Eruzione

U.S.A. RESULTS

Home Games in Capital Letters

U.S.A.	8	Holland Nationals	1(W)	U.S.A.	2	Canada	6(I
U.S.A.	11	Holland Nationals	4(W)	U.S.A.	3	Canada	4(I
U.S.A.	1	Reipas (Finland)	2(L)	U.S.A.	1	CANADA	2(I
U.S.A.	4	Saipa (Finland)	1(W)	U.S.A.	6	CINCINNATI	1(V
U.S.A.	6	Sapko (Finland)	0(W)	U.S.A.	6	Univ. of N.Dakota	1(V
U.S.A.	5	Karpat (Finland)	4(W)	U.S.A.	5	OKLAHOMA CITY	3(V
U.S.A.	5	Lukko (Finland)	3(W)	U.S.A.	6	Yale	1(V
U.S.A.	1	Jokerit (Finland)	4(L)	U.S.A.	0	Adirondack	1(I
U.S.A.	3	Norway Nationals	3(T)	U.S.A.	4	Sweden	2(V
U.S.A.	9	Norway Nationals	0(W)	U.S.A.	3	Canada	1(V
U.S.A.	2	MINN NORTH STARS	4(L)	U.S.A.	3	Czechoslovakia	0(V
U.S.A.	1	St. Louis Blues	9(L)	U.S.A.	5	Russia	3(V
U.S.A.	1	Atlanta Flames	6(L)	U.S.A.	4	Gorki Torpedo	2(V
U.S.A.	4	Washington Caps	5(L)	U.S.A.	5	Gorki Torpedo	1(V
U.S.A.	4	Maine Mariners	2(W)	U.S.A.	10	GORKI TORPEDO	3(V
U.S.A.	7	Canada	2(W)	U.S.A.	2	Indianapolis	2(T
U.S.A.	6	CANADA	0(W)	U.S.A.	2	Gorki Torpedo	3(L
U.S.A.	7	Salt Lake City	5(W)	U.S.A.	4	Oklahoma City	3(V
U.S.A.	10	Colorado College	1(W)	U.S.A.	5	Tulsa	2(V
U.S.A.	4	UMD (in Eveleth)	0(W)	U.S.A.	5	Houston	3(V
U.S.A.	8	U OF MINNESOTA	2(W)	U.S.A.	7	Tulsa	4(V
U.S.A.	1	Indianapolis	0(W)	U.S.A.	6	U of WISCONSIN	2(V
U.S.A.	15	Flint Generals	0(W)	U.S.A.	3	Ft. Worth	4(L
U.S.A.	5	BIRMINGHAM	2(W)	U.S.A.	4	Dallas	3(V
U.S.A.	3	Houston	4(L)	U.S.A.	4	IHL ALL-STARS	4(T
U.S.A.	6	Birmingham	4(W)	U.S.A.	4	U of Wisconsin	2(V
U.S.A.	5	Harvard	0(W)	U.S.A.	3	Ft. Worth	5(L
U.S.A.	9	RPI	3(W)	U.S.A.	10	DALLAS	6(V
U.S.A.	3	Cincinnati	2(W)	U.S.A.	10	Warroad Lakers	0(V
U.S.A.	6	SALT LAKE CITY	4(W)	U.S.A.	3	U.S.S.R.	10(L
U.S.A.	6	Canada	7(L)			(at Madison Square Garden)	

Pre-Olympic Record: 42-16-3

GOALTENDERS' STATISTICS

PRE-OLYMPIC GAMES

Goaltenders	G.P.	MIN.	G.A.	W-L-T	G.A.A.
Jim Craig	41	2371	95	30-8-1	2.40
Steve Janaszak	17	894	47	9-5-1	3.15
Bruce Horsch	9	410	25	3-3-1	3.66
TOTAL	67	3675	167	42-16-3	2.73

OLYMPIC GAMES

						Total Saves	Save Percent
Jim Craig	7	420	15	6-0-1	2.14	183	.924

PRE-OLYMPIC AND OLYMPIC GAMES

Jim Craig	48	2791	110	36-8-2	2.36

OLYMPIC GAMES

	Scoring by Periods 1 2 3	Shots on Goal	Final Score	
United States vs.	0 1 1	29	2	(T)
Sweden	1 0 1	36	2	
United States vs.	2 2 3	27	7	(W)
Czechoslovakia	2 0 1	31	3	
United States vs.	0 3 2	43	5	(W)
Norway	1 0 0	22	1	
United States vs.	2 2 3	51	7	(W)
Rumania	0 1 1	21	2	
United States vs.	0 2 2	32	4	(W)
Germany	2 0 0	26	2	
United States vs.	2 0 2	16	4	(W)
Soviet Union	2 1 0	39	3	
United States vs.	0 1 3	29	4	(W)
Finland	1 1 0	23	2	

Olympic Record: 6-0-1
Final Overall Score Record: 48-16-4

INDIVIDUAL STATISTICS (Pre-Olympic & Olympic Games)

Player	GP	G	A	TP	PIM
Mark Johnson	60	38	54	92	31
Rob McClanahan	63	34	36	70	38
Steve Christoff	64	37	27	64	30
Neal Broten	62	27	31	58	32
Mark Pavelich	60	16	36	52	14
Dave Silk	56	12	36	48	32
Mike Eruzione	50	21	25	46	22
Phil Verchota	61	19	24	43	56
Buzz Schneider	62	27	15	42	48
Eric Strobel	56	15	26	41	24
Dave Christian	66	10	28	38	30
John Harrington	58	14	23	37	16
Jack O'Callahan	56	7	30	37	85
Mike Ramsey	63	11	24	35	63
Bill Baker	60	5	25	30	74
Ralph Cox	31	13	13	26	27
Ken Morrow	63	5	20	25	12
Bob Suter	38	7	11	18	67
Jack Hughes	49	3	15	18	62
Mark Wells	28	9	7	16	2
Les Auge	29	0	14	14	14
Gary Ross	12	1	6	7	4
Dave Delich	13	4	2	6	4
Tim Harrer	4	1	3	4	0
Jim Craig	48	0	3	3	28
Steve Janaszak	17	0	1	1	0
Bench					8
Totals	68	336	535	871	823

INDIVIDUAL STATISTICS, OLYMPIC GAMES

	Games	G	A	Pts	PIM
Mark Johnson	7	5	6	11	6
Rob McClanahan	7	5	3	8	2
Buzz Schneider	7	5	3	8	4
Dave Christian	7	0	8	8	6
Mark Pavelich	7	1	6	7	2
Mike Eruzione	7	3	2	5	2
Phil Verchota	7	3	2	5	8
Dave Silk	7	2	3	5	0
John Harrington	7	0	5	5	2
Neal Broten	7	2	1	3	2
Steve Christoff	7	2	1	3	6
Mark Wells	7	2	1	3	0
Ken Morrow	7	1	2	3	6
Eric Strobel	7	1	2	3	2
Mike Ramsey	7	0	2	2	8
Bill Baker	7	1	0	1	4
Jack O'Callahan	6	0	1	1	2
Jim Craig	7	0	0	0	2
Bob Suter	7	0	0	0	6
TEAM	7	33	48	81	70

BIBLIOGRAPHY

Anderson, Chester G., ed. *Growing Up in Minnesota*. Minneapolis: University of Minnesota Press, 1976.

Brink, Carol. *The Twin Cities*. New York: Macmillan, 1961.

Current, Richard Nelson. *Wisconsin: A History*. New York: Norton, 1977.

Dryden, Ken, with Mulvoy, Mark. *Face-off at the Summit*. Boston: Little, Brown.

Eskenazi, Gerald. *The Fastest Sport*. Chicago: Follett, 1974.

Farrington, S. Kip. *Skates, Sticks and Men*. New York: David McKay, 1972.

Lass, William E. *Minnesota: A History*. New York: Norton, 1977.

Ludwig, Jack. *The Great Hockey Thaw*. Garden City, N.Y.: Doubleday, 1974.

Sinden, Harry. *Hockey Showdown*. Toronto: Doubleday, 1972.